BRITANNICUS

Jean Racine

Robert David MacDonald

OBERON BOOKS
LONDON

First published in 1998 by Oberon Books Ltd.
(incorporating Absolute Classics)
521 Caledonian Road, London N7 9RH
Tel: 0171 607 3637 / Fax: 0171 607 3629

e-mail: oberon.books@btinternet.com

British Library Cataloguing-in-Publication-Data
A catalogue record for this book is available from the British
Library.

ISBN: 1 84002 083 0

Cover design: Andrzej Klimowski

Typography: Richard Doust

Printed in Great Britain by Antony Rowe Ltd., Reading.

INTRODUCTION

Nicholas Dromgoole

That particular form of theatre called tragedy has long been regarded as a high point of French culture in the seventeenth century; and Racine has equally been regarded as the pinnacle, the unassailable, incomparable peak of French tragedy. It is true, this is very much a French assessment. Racine, like some of the best French wine, does not travel well. It is not so much that he is difficult to translate, although most poetry loses an intangible something in translation. Racine is after all a favourite author in A-level French for British students. His language is simple, and he uses a relatively small vocabulary. American academics have established, with beaver-like industry and that insatiable American demand for numbers and facts, that Shakespeare uses a dramatic vocabulary of 21,000 words, the King James Bible uses 6,500 words while Racine manages brilliantly with what must seem in comparison a poverty stricken, mere 600 words. Not being American, I have not worked out how many words Robert David MacDonald uses to translate Racine into English, but my guess is that he uses more than Racine. He is faithful to his author, but English makes more words available, with all the subtleties, echoes and associations that they create. MacDonald's sure judgement should satisfy even the harshest critic. He keeps Racine's alexandrine hexameter, but can be cavalier about the French rule of the mid-line caesura; justly so, since this depends on the equal stress of French syllables, where English verse and ordinary speech has less certainty and a much more inexplicable variety. Racine is well-served in this translation, and non-French speakers are brought as close as possible to what Racine intended his characters to say.

Yet even so, there tends to be a great gulf fixed between French culture and the rest of the world over Racine. The French quote him frequently, his plays still hold the French stage, he remains very much a part of their mental baggage. Elsewhere his influence remains slight. Compare and contrast, an examination question might say, the influence of Shakespeare on Russian or German literature with the influence of Racine. There is no contest. Compare and contrast the influence of Shakespeare on French literature with the influence of Racine on English literature. Again there is no contest. Yet for the French, Racine is one of the undoubted glories of their literary heritage. He is part of what makes the French special and different. The closer we get to Racine, the closer perhaps we shall get to what it actually feels like to be French.

That would sound better if Racine had been a nicer man, as well as a giant of French theatre. Sadly literature is studded with examples of great writers who were less admirable in their private live than in their works. Racine survives because of what he wrote, not as a result of what he did or did not do in private life. His play *Britannicus* is about life at court, the court of a despot with absolute power; and a nagging doubt intrudes. Did he have entirely to imagine what that kind of life would be like, or did he have some practical experience? In his play the despot is the young Nero – on his way to becoming one the most despicable tyrants of history. Racine lived in the age of Louis XIV, the most able and effective monarch France ever had, an administrative genius, but with all the ruthless *Realpolitik* of Machiavelli's Prince too. With due respect to Taine's "the race, the social context, the particular moment in time", *Britannicus* and its author need to be seen as the product of a key moment in history and perhaps Racine should be seen as an individual, a person on his own right before any approach to the play.

He was a bourgeois in the seventeenth century. That meant a great deal. This was an age when nobody in France (in England they were busily beheading Charles I) questioned the divine right of kings. God, after all, had ordained things the way they were. To question the system was to question God, and as that awful affair at Loudon was to show, hideous medieval punishments still awaited anyone blasphemous enough, foolish enough to question God. Just as the king ruled by virtue of birth and primogeniture, so did the nobility, the aristocrats who felt themselves equally as God-given as the king. Power and money in the seventeenth century were slowly but increasingly passing to a growing class, the bourgeoisie, the middle-class, and as well as a *noblesse de sang*, a nobility by right of birth, there also grew up a *noblesse de robe*, a nobility dependant on office at court. Molière's father had just such an office – upholsterer to the king – and intended to pass it on to his son, but Molière was obsessed with the theatre and could not have cared less about an office at court. He threw all such chances away and devoted his life to forming and running a theatre company, acting leading roles and writing plays for himself and his company to perform.

From an early age Racine had no father nor mother. Born in 1639 he was orphaned while still an infant, and was brought up on the charity of others. His relatives were Jansenists, an extreme sect of the Catholic church, and he was educated at Port Royal, the abbey which was the spiritual centre of the sect, and given a wide-ranging and altogether excellent education, including a thorough knowledge of ancient Greek that was unusual for the period. A further two years at the Jansenist college at Beauvais gave Racine a network of contacts within aristocratic circles. The Duc de Luynes had as his chief steward a cousin of Racine's, and the Duke encouraged Racine who was already showing his gifts as a poet. To read the list of aristocrats to whom he dedicated his ten successful plays is to realise how assiduously Racine took advantage of the network of contacts opening before him. The King frowned on Jansenism, so the Duc de Luynes did too and Jean Racine followed their lead. Already by 1660 he was working on a play of which we know nothing. In Paris he became a friend of the free-thinking hedonist La Fontaine (of the Fables) and of Molière, who put on Racine's first surviving play *The Thebaïd* (1664) which was a success. He wrote another play entitled *Alexander the Great* in 1665 which Molière also staged, and by then Racine was in more than Molière's theatre as a playwright, he was in the bed of one of Molière's leading ladies, Mlle du Parc, as her lover. He then showed a more calculating aspect of his nature. He owed Molière much. Molière had encouraged him, shared his expertise and a wide knowledge of the theatre, put on his first and second play, been tolerant of the affair with du Parc. But the rival theatre of the Bourgogne was anxious to score off Molière wherever possible, and was certainly considered better at tragedy than Molière's players. As soon as it was successful Racine took *Alexander the Great* away from Molière and gave it to the Bourgogne company. Worse still, Mlle du Parc went with it. Molière was mortified, never forgave Racine, and cordially loathed him from then onwards. Ill fortune awaited Mlle du Parc.

Firstly, how could Racine do it? Perhaps it is important to remember his network of aristocratic acquaintances. Actors and actresses were then considered the lowest of the low. The church condemned all theatre, excommunicated all actors and would only bury them in sacred ground if they had repented of their sins on their deathbed and received absolution. Otherwise, even in a cemetery, the self-respecting souls of the corpses around them would be insulted and outraged by their very presence. In writing plays, Racine clearly had to be involved in the theatre, but equally clearly he never felt *of* the theatre. He despised the very creatures on whom he depended for his successes. No doubt he found the theatre an exciting place (how could he write so well for it otherwise?), and no doubt equally exciting were the beds he shared with some of its actresses. But he never dreamed of marrying one of them as Molière did. They were just actresses. The theatre was just the theatre. Men of quality visited both but only for brief pleasure, brief affairs. Real life was a much more serious matter.

Secondly, there was the infamous, almost unbelievable, scandal of La Voisin. The worst of this was kept secret from Racine's contemporaries, but even the little they knew outraged the whole of French society. La Voisin was a horrifying fraud. She was a midwife, the wife of a jeweller, who practised fortune-telling. She sold love potions. She dabbled in black magic and sorcery generally. For those clients who needed it, she sold poisons. For those who were desperate, she would, with an unfrocked priest Guibourg, hold a black mass which included the killing and sacrifice of a newborn child. Here her profession as a midwife gave her access to a suitable supply of the infants required. Worse still she was not alone, but one of a ring of similar fortune tellers and accomplices in the black arts. Learning about her is like lifting the lid off this pompous, self-important, outwardly religious and responsible aristocratic world, and seeing what actually went on in terms of greed, lust and the selfish self-obsession of the rich.

La Reynie, *lieutenant de police*, had been alerted to the prevalence of poisoning by the recent but earlier scandal of the Marquise de Brinvilliers, who had poisoned her father because he sent her lover to the Bastille. She was in the habit of making charitable visits to a hospital, and she made sure the poison worked by testing it first on patients there who duly died as did her father. She then poisoned her two brothers to get all of her father's estate. Evidence against her emerged on the death of her lover, and she was arrested, tried and executed in 1676. Two years later La Reynie started investigating La Voisin and soon discovered an alarmingly widespread ring of accomplices. A carefully chosen court was set up to speed the legal system and more and more came to light. Thirty-six were found guilty and executed, five sent to the galleys, twenty-three banished, but as the investigation proceeded increasing numbers of high-ranking aristocrats were seen to be involved and the whole legal apparatus faltered. The King's mistress from 1668-1680, Madame de Montespan, who had born the King no less than seven children, had been a client of La Voisin since 1666, had administered various potions to the King himself, and had taken part in no less than three black masses with the consequent sacrifice of three infants. When her attractions faded, hell having no fury like a woman scorned, she had planned to poison both the new mistress and the King, and was only prevented from doing so by the investigation. This was too much. The King destroyed the police report (although the notes for it have survived) and the court was closed with its findings kept secret, although very much alive in rumour and gossip. Amidst these frightening events in high places, one fact went almost unnoticed. La Voisin remembered that she had provided the poison that Racine used in 1668 to murder his mistress Mlle du Parc. A warrant for his arrest was drawn up, but the court was dissolved before it could be put into effect.

Remarkably little is known about Racine's private life from 1664 to 1667. His sons, to protect their father's reputation, destroyed anything that showed him a less than satisfactory light. The fact they seem to have destroyed all his correspondence would imply there was a good deal to hide. There is a hint in a contemporary verse, that his current mistress left him for another before he wrote his last play for the professional theatre, *Phèdre,* whose heroine has long angst-ridden speeches luxuriating in the pangs of rejection. What is known is that after writing ten successful plays from 1664 to 1667, he stopped writing for the professional theatre. He became reconciled with the deeply religious Jansenist circle that had originally nurtured him. He married for money, a marriage where, in his son Louis' words "Love was absent." Abruptly, the style and circumstances of his life changed. Cynics might notice that the La Voisin affair had an equally traumatic effect on Louis XIV and the court. The King, shocked at the revelations both of what had and might have happened, became more pious, and his court became more outwardly respectable. He still had a mistress, Madame de Maintenon, but she was herself both pious and a positive pillar of respectability. With the support of Madame de Maintenon's sister (how adept Racine was at knowing the right people at the right time) Racine was appointed jointly with Boileau to the enviable post of Historiographer to the King, moving up from his bourgeois origins to a desirable position among the *noblesse de robe.* It became his duty to be in personal attendance on the King and record the history the King was of course busily making.

There has been much speculation as to why Racine suddenly stopped writing for the theatre in mid-career when he was surrounded by success, admired by the public, admired by the learned and the intelligentsia, and admired by the King. Much of the speculation seems to miss the main point. As a courtier in regular attendance on the King himself, he could hardly be seen to be associating with the riff-raff of the theatre. More importantly, he did not stop writing. The creative problems of recording instant history, surrounded by the exciting events occurring at the centre of the most powerful and influential nation in Europe, must have proved a challenge indeed. Sadly, what he wrote as historiographer has not survived, and it remains a particular irony that the work of possibly one of its best historians was obliterated by history itself.

After twelve years, he was summoned back to drama at the request of Madame de Maintenon, to write a play, *Esther* (1689) for the girl pupils of a boarding school. Although only performed in private for the court, this was such a *succès d'estime* that he wrote another for them, *Athaliah,* in 1691. Both plays rank among his best achievements, but the Jansenists and other bigots did not approve of drama, even in private performance by a respectable girls' school, and such was their outcry, he wrote no more plays. He died in 1699, able to look back on sixty years of steady advancement, including twelve plays already accepted in his lifetime as masterpieces, a court post that was the envy of many true aristocrats, a prosperous marriage blessed with children, many mistresses much admired in their day, successful early forays into the corrupt world of sensuality and eroticism, the odd murder that went unpunished and the undying resentment of one of the nicest true men of the theatre. After Racine's death the adulation of French posterity has continued to grow steadily.

Before looking in detail at his fifth successful play *Britannicus,* armed and forewarned by this knowledge of Racine the man, it becomes possible to consider what qualities made Racine's plays so pre-eminent. Like all artists, he belongs to

Taine's "the race, the social context, the particular moment in time", but what keeps his work alive is his ability to transcend Taine's categories with a much more universal appeal. Great tragedy in drama is a rare phenomenon. Five centuries before the birth of Christ, the Athenian Greeks achieved it, and it is no accident that Racine, exceptionally among his contemporaries, had a thorough grounding in ancient Greek, including the tragedies of Aeschylus, Sophocles, and Euripides. For the ancient Greeks, vividly aware of the glory, the excitement, the pleasure of life, tragedy lay in the all too evident fact that life, with all its joys, must inevitably give way to annihilation and death and that even as the proud man enjoyed all the gifts and potentialities of life, an inexorable fate he could not hope to control could grind him down to nothingness and dust.

With the very dubious exception of Seneca in Roman theatre, tragedy did not achieve very much in European theatre until the Elizabethans in England and Lope de Vega in Spain. Medieval drama, propaganda for Christianity, showed the bad being punished and the good being rewarded, with absolution and the forgiveness of sins always lurking, like some *deus ex machina,* to descend from the clouds and offer the prospect of a happier ending. The Renaissance, among other developments a rebirth of interest in the ancient Greeks and Romans, set up new tensions in European drama, contrasting the classical world's emphasis on the possibilities of life here and now, with a still fervently accepted Christian belief that this life was a mere vale of tears, a preparation for the afterlife to come. It is this tension which makes Marlowe's *Faust* so effective as tragedy. His audience was dazzled by the possibilities of making the most of the here and now, bringing back Helen of Troy from the dead ("Was this the face that launched a thousand ships?") – and yet believed just as implicitly in the devils that emerged from the pit of hell to drag a screaming Faust down to everlasting fire. Great individuals brought low by misfortunes they cannot avoid and cannot control were still the stuff of tragedy, but there was an added turn of the screw in Renaissance tragedy: its heroes made a choice, a very medieval kind of choice, grabbing at what they want in the heat of the moment and what their conscience tells them is right, and then their very choices set in train the circumstances that bring them down.

Racine's audience was essentially no different from Shakespeare's or Lope de Vega's. They were deeply Christian. And yet they were aware, none of them more so than Racine himself, steeped as he was in Greek literature, aware of all the excitement, the sheer fun and the temptations of life in the here and now.

Racine's Jansenist background gave him an even bleaker view of life than most of his contemporaries. For Jansenists, man was not only born in sin, but was basically corrupt. Without God's grace to bolster the rather pathetic human longing for virtue and to stiffen the weak and wavering human will, the corruption of the flesh and the temptations of the world would triumph. Song and dance and theatre were all part of the world's insidious corruption. They trampled virtue and overcame the weak will. Racine returned to his Jansenist beliefs. In writing tragedies, he was in a sense like a man taking a beautiful woman to bed, wallowing in the pleasure of erotic, but secretly despising himself and her for succumbing to temptation at all, for doing what he felt to be wrong, besmearing virtue and surrendering the will.

(Incidentally, does this get any closer to understanding how it was possible for him to poison Mlle du Parc? Was she despised for leading him astray in the first place, for being so clearly corrupt and in the wrong, an actress on stage, a pretty one at that, a constant temptation to men to fall from grace. Was he merely putting an end to a squalid life gone terribly wrong? Was he God's chosen instrument? There is the making of another Racine tragedy in these very circumstances.)

It is this Jansenist background, with its bleak view of mankind as being essentially corrupt, which probably gave an edge to Racine's tragedies. When he wrote for the professional theatre, he had rejected the religious beliefs in which he was raised. The very fact of writing plays for the theatre at all makes that clear. He brings no panaceas. No *deus ex machina* descends from the clouds to save his characters, there is no last minute resolution of the problems in his plays. They regard corrupt, weak-willed, self-seeking human beings with an all-seeing, but not a forgiving eye. And they leave their audience profoundly troubled at what that all-seeing eye reveals.

What makes his plays special, is his ability to show what is going on in the mind of his characters. The audience has a clear idea what each character is thinking and feeling. The audience knows more than the characters on stage, they know what the other characters are thinking and feeling. Yet as each character speaks and reveals their motivation, sometimes the very mainspring of their existence, the audience can both share in that particular viewpoint and at the same time perceive where each individual is making a wrong choice, making a faulty judgement. The audience can do this because they know more, much more than the character on stage. As a result the audience often comes close to playing God in a Racine play, seeing all, understanding all and judging all. Perhaps this is the essence of Racine's tragedy, because the audience is a God who may be all-knowing, but a God who cannot intervene, and can only be appalled at the inevitability of the tragedy, as the characters intermesh and inter-relate with each other.

Characters in his plays are not petty. They are grandly mythological or historical personages. They are also intelligent. They speak in a language that is simple and direct, great poetry, a major ornament of French literature, but easily understandable and always remarkably apt for each speaker and each situation. Above all, the plays are marvellously theatrical. They move with pace and vigour, even if remarkably little actually happens on stage. It is not the action, so much as the reaction of the characters to the action and to each other, that fascinates his audience.

He accepted, seemingly with ease, the restrictions that current critical writings demanded from seventeenth-century playwrights. The dramatic unities: everything happening in one place; everything happening within twenty-four hours; and every action having some relevance to every other action, all part of the same story. An audience watching a Racine play does not feel that this obedience to the unities is a restriction at all, it seems simply how this play happens to be.

Some of his attitudes and assumptions have dated. The insistence on rank and aristocratic privilege now look snobbish. Phèdre can contemplate lust with her son-in-law – but it would, as has been pointed out, be quite beneath her dignity to make similar advances to a mere stable boy.

The way each protagonist in the drama sets about a rational analysis of their own motives and psyche generally, added to an equally rational attempt to analyse the motives of everybody around them, has come to seem very French. Characters in French fiction and drama have been doing much the same ever since. Yet to say that Racine is quintessentially French is to say more than just this. His characters clothe themselves and the world around them in a poetic language that is almost alienatingly rhetorical. This is not just fine-sounding language where a spade is never a spade but is always 'an instrument of toil' or something equally wrapped up, almost smothered in a grandly ornate language that seems far from everyday speech. It is rather that the characters are always 'putting on a show', making a theatrical event out of every exchange, never just leaving the room, always making a grand exit. Even when they are on their own, they seem to be a shade too self-regarding, always adjusting the impression they are making in some mirror seemingly permanently perched in front of them. They are always 'on view'. No doubt Britannicus urinates and defecates like the rest of mankind, but it is almost impossible to imagine his doing it. That would be hidden away in a closet, offstage and well out of sight. Racine's characters could never even break wind in public. They are much too grand for that.

This too is what we mean by being French, partly why Racine so permeates French thinking and is so greatly revered by his countrymen. Is there any other European nation quite so fond of striking public attitudes, dressing everything up in rhetoric, and finding it difficult to say in plain words exactly what they really think and mean? Perhaps because he so poetically represents the best of this element in the French character, Racine fails to travel well to other languages and other nations. It is not so much TS Eliot's "I gotta use words when I talk to you", because after all Racine does not deploy a large vocabulary. Nor does he deliberately hide his meanings from his audience. It is just that his characters seem to be constantly admiring themselves in different mirrors at the same time. The Hall of Mirrors in Versailles is aptly named. In Versailles Racine the courtier often sat with other courtiers, admiring performances of Racine the dramatist. There is something in French culture that sometimes makes it difficult to tell the difference between them.

Occasionally a modern audience longs for someone in a Racine play actually to do something, to be less dignified, less always on their best behaviour, if only a scratch in an intimate place, a spitting, a farting. There is nothing lavatorial in Racine's plays. But these are impious thoughts. Racine's world must be accepted on its own terms if we are to relive the frightening excitements he offers us.

Courtiers spend much of their time currying favour. Enough has been said of Racine's character to make it clear that he was essentially a courtier, good at making friends and influencing people, well practised at currying favour. In Paris, the theatre, like so much else, revolved in Racine's time around the tastes, the preferences, the attitudes of Louis XIV. He was the fount of most honours, posts and privileges. Only with the King's support could Molière survive the open hostility of the church over *Tartuffe*. One of the keys to understanding Racine's plays is to grasp that they were written, not just to massage Louis' ego, that would have been too obvious; rather they set out views and ideas with which the assiduous courtier, Racine, must desperately have hoped the King would find himself agreeing. We know that *Britannicus* had at least one direct effect on the King. Before this play, Louis had been accustomed to take a leading role in court performances. He enjoyed and prided himself on his dancing skills. Such is the sycophancy that surrounds a monarch, we shall never really know for sure just how good he actually was. After *Britannicus*, with its explicit references to Nero appearing in performances before his court, Louis never appeared on stage again. It is reasonable to assume from this that the King took the play seriously. Racine in his second preface to *Britannicus* refers to the hostility that greeted its first performance, 'but the critics gradually disappeared. The play remained.' What silenced this very vocal hostility? Partly no doubt the sheer intellectual quality of the play. But the approval of the King must have been just as important. Racine the courtier appears to have struck the right note. To ask what it was that the King found so much to his liking in *Britannicus,* is to go to the very heart of the play.

Yet it would be wrong to undervalue the sheer impact of *Britannicus* as exciting drama. Thomas Gray that admirable intellect, poet and literary dilettante, creator of the famous *Elegy in a Country Churchyard*, saw a performance of *Britannicus* in Paris in the 1760s and was so carried away that he set about writing a play on the same lines in English. He gave up after two hundred lines, a fascinating fragment and vivid testimony to the power of the drama decades after Racine's death.

The play is essentially about politics – not the politics of a democratic system, but the politics seething within the court of an all-powerful ruler, circumstances in their way just as applicable to Louis XIV as to the subject matter Racine chose, the young Emperor Nero in ancient Rome. This could have been very dangerous territory indeed for Racine. Like all ambitious courtiers, he had to take risks to achieve his ends. His previous play *The Litigants* had been a comedy. (Racine? A comedy?) Surprise, surprise, it proved to be exactly along the line of the very reforms the King was introducing into the legal system, and won the positive support of the monarch. As we have seen, so did *Britannicus.* So what was it that won such royal favour?

On the surface there could be no comparison. The play shows us the young Nero in the early years of his reign, not the despicable tyrant he later became. But everyone in Racine's educated audience, well-versed in Tacitus and the Latin classics, knew all about Nero. Racine did not have to labour the point. Clearly he had chosen a ruler, an absolute ruler, who was in no sense like Louis. Parallels were therefore prohibited from the start. And yet, and yet... The play is as much about Agrippina as anybody. Britannicus is the son of the Emperor Claudius and Messalina. Claudius then married Agrippina who already had a son, Nero, by her previous marriage. By a series of wily crimes she ensured that Britannicus, the rightful heir, did not succeed as emperor on the death of Claudius, but her son Nero did instead. Limited by the convention of the dramatic unities to a period of twenty-four hours for his play, Racine shows us a crisis reaching breaking point. Agrippina has been in effect all-powerful and running the empire for the first two years of Nero's reign. She has not done well, and the people are discontented. Nero is about to take control into his own hands. As the play opens Agrippina is seeking an audience with her son, but the door to his apartments remains firmly closed. She is falling from power. As the play proceeds it becomes clear that although she has formerly been a brilliant tactician she is losing her grip. The audience can understand why. All her plots and strategies have been designed to put Nero on the throne. Now her protégé, her own son, is turning against her, everything she has worked so hard for suddenly becomes unreal. She is fighting from the deck of a sinking ship. Yet the long list of crimes she has committed already ensures she does not get much sympathy from Racine's audience. That sympathy goes to Britannicus, the rightful heir to the throne, who is virtuous, admirable, a true hero. Nero falls for Junia, whom Britannicus loves, and forces her to lie to Britannicus and tell him she no longer loves him while Nero secretly listens and enjoys the situation. Nero decides to poison Britannicus, his rival to the throne as well as his rival in love, and is at first dissuaded from doing so by Burrus, an advisor who represents conventional wisdom, and then persuaded by Narcissus, a much more realistic advisor. Britannicus is duly poisoned. Junia seeks refuge as a vestal virgin (the nearest Roman equivalent for a seventeenth-century convent) and Narcissus is torn to pieces by a resentful mob. Agrippina, in an impassioned prophetic speech, foresees the long catalogue of crimes awaiting Nero that will end in his final suicide. The stage is set for Nero to become the tyrant of history and for the final curtain.

At one level, although the love of Britannicus is doomed and Britannicus dies, the audience is comfortably aware that justice is done. Agrippina has been swept aside into impotence. Narcissus has been torn to pieces. In the fullness of time Nero will commit suicide. Evil has engineered its just deserts. And what has all this to do with Louis XIV? As the King watched the play, what chords were struck? What was Racine the courtier saying? Britannicus may be virtuous and a hero, but he has also been outmanoeuvred. His heroic virtues chimed in with the feudal, chivalric attitudes of the aristocrats whose passionate convictions had so bedevilled France in the civil wars of the Fronde. Both Louis and Racine had read their Machiavelli and knew that a ruler must be decisive and unscrupulous if necessary, that reasons of state could overrule private morality. Even in the nineteenth century Cavour could say "If we did for ourselves what we do for our country, what villains we should be!" In disposing of Britannicus, Nero is being a realistic ruler, snuffing out a potential rival, safeguarding his throne. In dealing with Agrippina, are there not parallels in the way Louis had to deal with his powerful but corrupt minister of finance, Fouquet. Having lied and cheated Louis, Fouquet spent the rest of his life in impotent imprisonment in the Bastille. Far from simply being a straightforward contest between good and evil, *Britannicus* is more about the necessary evils a ruler has to commit to grasp and hold on to power. Did Louis possibly feel as he watched the play, that here at last was a playwright who glimpsed what the art of ruling, *Realpolitik*, was all about?

Louis XIV has long since turned to dust in a distant grave. Over three hundred years separate us from Racine's seventeenth century. Yet can anybody maintain that the subtext of this play, the tensions between public and private morality, the difficult choices that face any government, have lost their relevance? The Nazi persecution of the Jews, the death camps, the Jewish persecution of the Palestinians, ethnic cleansing, the behaviour of the Serbs, Islamic fundamentalism, the IRA, are there not still discernible gaps between public attitudes and private agendas, official morality and reasons of state? Louis probably sat fascinated as these characters from another age analysed their own and their opponents' motives, estimated their own chances, summed up the opposition, desperate to perceive where advantage lay. Despite itself a modern audience is still caught up in the same excitement and enjoys the privilege that every Racine audience always enjoyed, that of knowing more than the characters on stage, taking the larger view, watching as in Gray's words,

> "Alas regardless of their doom,
> The little victims play!"

In Racine's ultimately bleak world everybody is a victim and everybody is doomed. In the end he seems to have returned to his Jansenist beliefs in the grace of a God that could dissolve the sins of the world. That saving grace is hard to discern in *Britannicus*. There is no happy ending, only a tragic acceptance of what being human means.

Nicholas Dromgoole
1998

Britannicus was first performed at the Albery Theatre, London, on 29th October 1998, with the following cast:

ALBINA, Barbara Jefford

AGRIPPINA, Diana Rigg

BURRUS, David Bradley

BRITANNICUS, Kevin McKidd

NARCISSUS, Julian Glover

NERO, Toby Stephens

JUNIA, Joanna Roth

GUARDS, John Fairfoul and Colin Haigh

Director, Jonathan Kent

Designer, Maria Björnson

Lighting, Mark Henderson

Music, Jonathan Dove

Sound, John A Leonard

This new version of *Britannicus* was commissioned by the Almeida Theatre with the assistance of a French Theatre Season Award.

Characters

NERO
emperor of Rome, son of Agrippina

BRITANNICUS
son of the late emperor Claudius

AGRIPPINA
mother of Nero,
widow of Domitius Enobarbus,
and widow, by a second marriage,
of the emperor Claudius

JUNIA
lover of Britannicus

BURRUS
tutor to Nero

NARCISSUS
tutor to Britannicus

ALBINA
confidante to Agrippina

GUARDS

The action takes place in Rome, in a room in Nero's palace.

ACT ONE

Scene 1

ALBINA:
  What! While Nero lies asleep, dead to all cares,
  Can it be right that you wait here until he stirs?
  Must the Emperor's own mother, unescorted and alone,
  Keep watch at his door, entirely on her own?
  My lady, please withdraw; return to your apartment.

AGRIPPINA:
  No! Albina, no, I cannot. Not even for a moment.
  I shall wait for him here. The cares he leaves behind
  With me are quite enough to occupy my mind;
  All that I had foreseen, has now come to pass.
  Nero has come out against Britannicus:
  Headstrong, he shakes off all restraint; now his idea
  Is not to court the people's love, but rule by fear.
  Britannicus troubles him, Albina, – and each day
  I am made to feel I am a hindrance in his way.

ALBINA:
  What? You who gave him life? Where was he till the hour,
  You raised him from so low to the Imperial power?
  Dispossessing Claudius's son, Britannicus,
  To give the crown to your son, Nero Domitius;
  Everything speaks in favour of his mother, Agrippina.
  He owes you all his love...

AGRIPPINA:
                              Owed is not paid, Albina.
  If honourable, he will do all duty tells him to:
  If not, then everything will speak against me, I know.

ALBINA:
  If not? Lady! His behaviour all seems ruled
  And marked by a sense of duty, in a soul well-schooled.

23

In the whole last three years, what of his words and deeds
Have not presaged for Rome, the emperor she needs?
Under his sceptre, for two years, Rome has learned
How life might be, if the age of the Consuls had returned.
He rules Rome like a father. Nero, young and bold,
Shows all the virtues which Augustus showed, when old.

AGRIPPINA:

No, my own self-interest shall not make me unjust:
Where Augustus stopped, Nero starts, as he must.
Fear only that the future will destroy the past,
And where Augustus started, Nero will end at the last.
Disguise is useless; I can see it in his face,
The bloody-mindedness of the Domitian race;
The pride he draws from them, is mingled in him with
The ferocity of the Neroes – that was mine to give.
Tyrants always begin in quiet auspicious ways –
How Rome adored Caligula, in his early days!
Then, as madness overtook his feigned humanity,
The city's cruellest nightmare became reality.
And yet, what's it to me, if Nero, after all,
Dies as a model of goodness and virtue overall?
Have I thus far exalted, and elevated him,
Only to serve the peoples' and the Senate's whim?
Well! If he wants it, let him be his country's father;
Just let him not forget, I am the Emperor's mother.
Meanwhile what name are we to call, how best accuse
This outrage which, the dawn reveals, none can excuse?
He knows, since their affection can scarcely be ignored,
Junia is the one whom Britannicus adores;
And Nero, known to be so virtuous, in spite
Of this, had her abducted in the dead of night.
Is he moved by hate, or love? What does he hope to gain?
Or is it simply pleasure at inflicting pain?
Or may he not be moved perhaps by the spiteful thought
To punish them, because I lent them my support?

ALBINA:

You, their support, my lady?

AGRIPPINA:

                                    Albina, let it go:
It was I procured their downfall – yes, I know.
The legacy Britannicus held by blood, I mean the throne,
He saw himself thrown down from – by me alone.
Nero takes all. But to preserve some amity
Between the two of them, is a task that falls to me.
The rule holds for Britannicus, and some day he
Will have to keep a balance between my son and me.

ALBINA:

Such strategy!

AGRIPPINA:

                        I need a port out of the storm.
Nero must accept this balance as a norm.

ALBINA:

So many needless measures, and all against a son!

AGRIPPINA:

If he will not fear me, then I must fear him – soon.

ALBINA:

The fears you feel may be both groundless and unjust.
If Nero is undutiful towards you, then at least
The change in him is not remarked by us in Rome.
These things are secrets still, between you and your son.
He has refused all titles the city has conferred
On him, unless the honours are with his mother shared.
His generous love keeps nothing for himself alone;
Your name in Rome's no less respected than his own.
Can any further proof be needed of his gratitude?

AGRIPPINA:

A little less respect, and a more filial attitude.
Albina, all these honours can only rouse my gall;
Watching my glory grow, I see my credit fall.
No, no, the time is long gone now, when Nero thought
To transmit the admiring wishes of the court;

When Nero would rely on me to rule the land
When the Senate would assemble, here, at my command.
I would be present, though concealed behind a screen:
I became that body's soul, all-powerful but unseen.
Not yet intoxicated with the imperial power,
Nero was of the city's temper still unsure;
Then came that dismal day, still graven on my mind,
When Nero, drunk on his own glory, almost as if struck
blind,
That day that embassies from many kings had come
To acknowledge in him the sovereignty of Rome...
I do not know what ill advice caused my disgrace –
But as I approached the throne, to take my usual place –
Beside my son, as soon as Nero looked at me,
He made his displeasure plain in his face for all to see...
I felt the premonition of some grim event;
The ungrateful boy, disguising the insult that he meant,
Rose, ran to me, embraced me, adroitly making sure
I could not reach the throne I had been making for.
Since then, the power of Agrippina has been waning.
And rapidly. The merest trace remaining
Is all that's left to me. Now people come as suitors
To lobby Burrus, and Seneca, his tutors.

ALBINA:

These thoughts, these dark suspicions that are filling you,
Why do you cultivate this venom? It is killing you!
At least make clear to Nero what your position is.

AGRIPPINA:

Caesar no longer sees me without witnesses.
In public, by appointment, I have his condescension;
His answers, even silences, dictated by convention:
Two ever-present guardians, his masters and my own,
Make sure he does not speak one word they've not set down.
But I'll pursue him faster than he can fly from me.
I must make and take advantage of his uncertainty.
What is that noise? Let us go in, and find

Out what we can. Burrus! Leaving already? What's behind
All this?

Scene 2

BURRUS:

My lady, in the Emperor's name I come
To explain an order which may have caused you alarm.
It is, however, merely the dictate of policy,
Which Caesar wished to be conveyed to you, through me.

AGRIPPINA:

He will convey it better, since he wishes; let me in.

BURRUS:

Caesar for the moment has no wish to be seen.
But let me just go back, perhaps I can entreat...

AGRIPPINA:

No, no, I would not wish to disturb his royal retreat.
Perhaps we could set by our usual reticence,
Try to exchange our views without undue pretence.

BURRUS:

Burrus has always felt a detestation of lies.

AGRIPPINA:

How long do you mean to keep the Emperor from my eyes?
Must I, to get a glimpse of him, break down the door?
Is this what I decided to raise your fortunes for?
To have you put a barrier between me and my son?
Do you not dare to leave him a moment on his own?
Are you in competition with Seneca, to see
Who can erase me quicker, out of his memory?
Did I trust him to you, so you could make of him
An ingrate, while you ruled the Empire in his name?
Certainly the more I think of it, the less
I can believe you thought that I would acquiesce!
I could have let you rot, along with your ambition,
In some provincial legion, *such* an enviable condition!

I, who could take my place, on the throne of my ancestors,
Daughter, mother, sister, and wife of your past masters.
Who do you think you are? Do you think my vote
Has made him emperor – to have all of you at my throat?
Nero is not a child – now it is time he reigned.
That he should fear you still – how long do you intend?
Can he see nothing, then – unless it's through your eyes?
For conduct has he not his ancestors as guides?
Augustus and Tiberius? Now that he is a man,
Let him copy Germanicus, my father – if he can.
Among such heroes I'd not dare assume a place:
Nevertheless there are some virtues I can trace
For him. I can instruct him what degree of trust
And distance he should keep from his subjects – should,
and must!

BURRUS:

My duty at this time was merely to excuse
A single one of Caesar's acts, but since you choose
To make me guarantee his whole life's future course,
(Even if not to excuse his latest show of force)
I shall reply, my lady, with all a soldier's candour,
Without the camouflage of court intrigue and slander.
You gave his youth into my care, I admit it;
Nor for a single moment shall I dare forget it.
But did I swear an oath to you I would betray
Him, making him a ruler fit only to obey?
Lady, I account to you no more – that task is done;
He is the master of the world – no more your son.
I account only to the Roman people, and
They know I hold their health or ruin in my hand.
Look! If you wished him to be reared in ignorance
Were Seneca and I the only choice – by chance?
Were exile and the Army the only spots where tutors
Could be found? Why drive away those empty, flattering
neuters?
If it was slaves you wanted, a thousand from the court
Of Claudius had come forward, where only two were sought,

All eager for the honour; and he would have been spoiled,
Allowed to grow to old age as a perpetual child?
Why complain, lady, you are revered as it is.
Romans swear by your name at least as much as his.
It is true the Emperor no longer comes each day
To pay you court, nor kneels down there to lay
The Empire at your feet. But should he? Should his
                                        recognition
Of you be shown in lowering himself to that position?
If Nero always showed such meek humility
A cardboard Caesar would be all he could claim to be.
His justification, if I may be frank, is Rome.
Subject to powerful interests as she had become,
Bearing their yoke till now, enforced into submission,
Rome dates her freedom from the Emperor's accession.
Further, virtue herself has once more taken root.
The Empire is no longer some bloody tyrant's loot.
Their magistrates are those the people now appoint;
Caesar names the leaders whom the soldiers want.
Why should not Caesar then believe us? If his crown
By our advice accrues both power and renown?
If, in the prosperous reign this promises to be,
Caesar can be all-powerful, Rome can be always free.
The Emperor does not need our advice to sway him,
I seek no longer to instruct him, but obey him.
His ancestors may be his models, even so
He needs to be himself to prosper and to grow.
How happy if his virtues, linked in a powerful chain,
Could bring back every year, the first years of his reign...

AGRIPPINA:

So, with no confidence in the future, what you say
Is that you think, without you, Nero will go astray?
You think his training shows such manifest completeness?
(And you have to his character so eloquently witnessed)
Then tell me why this boy, so admirably instructed,
Turns ravisher, and orders Junia abducted?

Does he mean this outrage to insult my family?
To insult the ancestral blood, which flows in her and me?
Of what does he accuse her? By what oversight
Has she become a dangerous criminal overnight?
Brought up in modesty, in any normal circumstance
She would not have given the Emperor a second glance.
She might even have thought it a happy stroke of freedom,
A virtuous deed of his, if she had never seen him.

BURRUS:

She is suspected of no crime; neither has Caesar
Condemned her – yet. Here's nothing to displease her–
She's in the palace of her forefathers, but she,
As the last surviving princess of Augustus' family,
Has, you are aware, rights of inheritance,
That make whoever weds her a potential rebel prince.
The blood of Caesar may not ally itself to those
Whom Caesar has not yet approved; I must suppose
That you yourself would see it as the most rank injustice,
To wed, against his wish, the grandchild of Augustus.

AGRIPPINA:

I understand you. Nero informs me, by your voice,
Britannicus should not build his hopes upon my choice.
In vain, in his unhappiness, to give him courage,
I comforted his love with dreams of longed-for marriage.
Now, to humiliate me, Nero means to show
That Agrippina's promises way outrun her power.
Rome is convinced – too much so – of my favour. He
must want
To disabuse them of it by giving me this affront.
He wants to terrorise the whole world, so they learn
The difference between the Emperor and my son.
And he can do it. But I still dare warn him, too,
To strengthen his control before staging such a coup
And, in reducing me to this extremity,
Forcing me to use my weak authority,
His own will be exposed, and, in the final count,
He may miscalculate my power, by no small amount.

BURRUS:

Why, lady, must you always question his respect?
Can he not take a single step you don't suspect?
Will the least remark that is retailed to you
Encourage you to split the Empire into two?
Must you both always fear what the other intends?
Must your embraces always conclude with arguments?
Leave off this grim, censorious care, to play another,
And better part; that of the conciliating mother.
Ignore these minor coldnesses, though they may have
                                  annoyed you
It simply gives the court the signal to avoid you.

AGRIPPINA:

Who would throng round me now, to beg for Agrippina's
Favour, when I'm accused of criminal procedures?
When, in my downfall, he will not see me any more?
When Burrus seems determined to keep me from his door?

BURRUS:

Lady, I must be silent. You are displeased; somehow
My candour has betrayed me more than I should allow.
Hurt pride admits no justice, no argument. All those it
Does not perceive as friends, it believes oppose it.
Here is Britannicus. I shall give up my place
To let you sympathise with him in his sad case –
And recognise such errors as may have resulted
From the loving care of those the Emperor least consulted.

Scene 3

AGRIPPINA:

Prince! Where are you going? What reckless fears are these
That drive you blindly on – towards your enemies?
What are you looking for?

BRITANNICUS:

                      What am I looking for?
Lady, all I have is lost, all I was working for.

Junia has been dragged away to this palace by
A horde of brutal soldiers, borne off shamefully...
What horror must the tender-spirited girl have felt
At this new outrage, this new blow Fortune has dealt!
She has been stolen from me. A cruel, harsh decree
Will separate two hearts now linked by misery.
Perhaps they do not want us mingling our despair
To give each other strength to help us bear our cares.

AGRIPPINA:

Enough. I feel your wrongs; understand your dejection;
My anger had been heard long before your objections.
But I make no pretence that impotence and rage
Will settle scores between us. My word is still engaged.
No, I shall not explain. If you still wish to hear
Me, come to Pallas' chambers – you will find me there.

Scene 4

BRITANNICUS:

Narcissus, am I to believe her? Should I be
Ready to let her arbitrate between her son and me?
What should I do? She is the woman who was the ruin
Of Claudius – marrying her was his, and my undoing.
If you have told the truth, it was she, by her own hand,
That hastened on his death, too slow for what she planned.

NARCISSUS:

No matter. She, like you, feels she has been outraged.
She wants to give you Junia, she said – her word's engaged.
Combine your grievances: unite your interests.
The palace echoes uselessly to your regrets.
If you are only known here for complaining, supplicating,
Not as a vengeful angel, you'll spend a long time waiting.

BRITANNICUS:

You know quite well, Narcissus, that I have no mind
To tolerate this slavery for any length of time.

I am stunned by my fall, but be in no doubt,
I'll not give up the crown for which Fate marks me out.
But I am still alone. My father's friends are strangers
To me, frozen by my misfortune and its dangers:
My very age, or lack of it, now keeps from me
Even those whose hearts retain their loyalty.
After this year's experience, I think that I can state
I have acquired some slight awareness of my fate.
Nothing but venal, purchased friends I see around me;
Painstaking doggers of my footsteps, they surround me.
Expressly cast by Nero in their shameful role,
They traffic with him for the secrets of my soul.
However it is, Narcissus, I am betrayed each day;
He foresees all my plans, hears every word I say.
He knows the inmost workings of my heart. Like you.
Narcissus, what do you think?

NARCISSUS:

If that were ever true...
Then you should take more care, in whom you would
confide;
Don't broadcast your inmost secrets far and wide.

BRITANNICUS:

I know, Narcissus, that is true. But such mistrust
Is the hard lesson which a generous heart learns last.
It can be long deceived. But I believe you, in the end,
Or rather, take a vow to believe no other friend.
My father, I recall, once said to me that you
Alone of all his counsellors, would continue true.
The constant watch that you have kept on my behaviour
In a treacherous world of snares, has been my only saviour.
Now go, and find out, if you can, if this last news
Has roused the mettle of the friends that we thought ours.
Observe their looks, their words, fathom their thought;
Calculate if I can expect their loyal support.
Inquire, but with discretion, in the palace here,
How Nero guards the Princess, above all, with what care.

Find out if she's recovered yet, discover where
They're keeping her, and if I'm allowed to speak to her.
And I shall seek out Pallas, my father's counsellor too,
Go to his rooms, and find the Emperor's mother, whom
I mean to stir, to move, pursue to gain my ends
To engage her in my cause, more than even she intends.

ACT TWO

Scene 1

NERO:

No, Burrus, no! Despite her unmaternal acts
She is still my mother. So – I shall ignore the facts.
But I'll not ignore her insolent adviser – Pallas,
Nor suffer the constant drip of overweening malice
He feeds her daily. He is poisoning my mother,
And every day makes efforts to infect my brother,
Britannicus. He is all they listen to – you'll find them
At his apartments now, with the doors bolted behind them.
I've had enough. I've said they should be kept apart.
That is my final word. Enough! He must depart...
It is a simple order. Let the end of the day
Find him no longer in my city, my court, my way.
Go – this command affects the well-being of the entire
Nation. Narcissus, here! Guards, you may retire.

Scene 2

NARCISSUS:

Thank God, my lord, with Junia safely in your hands,
The rest of Rome in future will hang on your commands.
Your enemies, frustrated in their hopes, without defence,
Are gone to Pallas, mourning their total impotence.
But what's the matter? You seem distracted and unnerved,
More even than Britannicus. Why should you be disturbed?
All smiles upon the fortunes that you are master of.

NERO:

Narcissus, all is lost! Nero is in love.

NARCISSUS:

You?

NERO:

It only took a moment – the instant that I saw her,
I worshipped Junia. I loved – no, more, adored her.

NARCISSUS:
>You love her?

NERO:
>>>Drawn along by curiosity,
>Last night I watched them bring her here, I watched as she
>Raised her sad eyes to heaven, eyes that shone with tears,
>Radiant amid the tumult, the torches and the jeers,
>Beautiful, unadorned, in the dishevelled dress
>Of one who's dragged from sleep to painful wakefulness.
>I don't know if it was the unaccustomed violence,
>The sudden shouts, the shadows, then the frightening silence,
>The brutal looks of her abductors, taken with
>Her disarray, combined with all the rest to give
>An added, helpless beauty to her – but I was made weak
>By the sight, I tried to talk to her – I could not speak,
>I could not stir. Struck dumb, astonished, I stood by,
>Let her go to her chamber undisturbed, while I
>Went to my own, and there, torn by self-doubt
>And longing, tried in vain to blot her image out.
>It would not leave me. I thought I spoke to her, but no...
>I even loved those tears that I had caused to flow.
>Sometimes, too late now, I would beg her to forgive me;
>I wept, I even threatened, to force her to believe me.
>Rehearsing all the sleepless night what I might say,
>Enveloped in my love, I waited for the day.
>Perhaps I was mistaken. Do I exaggerate?
>Her beauty – was it just a trick of flattering light?
>What do you think, Narcissus?

NARCISSUS:
>>>But how could anyone
>So beautiful remain concealed from you so long?

NERO:
>All too easily done, Narcissus: either grief
>At her brother's death (arranged by me as she believes)
>Or else that heart, too proud, too wilful, too austere,
>Hid from me the sight of her beauty in full flower.

Shut in by shadows, nursing her grief, her one obsession,
She did not even suspect her justified reputation.
And it's this constant virtue, at court so out of fashion,
That lends a sharpened edge to my new passion.
Admit, Narcissus, there is not, in all of Rome
A woman who, if I offered love, would not succumb;
Only the modest Junia, alone in all this place,
Seems to regard such honours as if they spelt disgrace.
She flies from me. Does she not even deign to observe
If Caesar loves at all, or if he merits love.
Tell me – Britannicus – does he love her?

NARCISSUS:

                                Yes.

Need you ask, my lord?

NERO:

                       So young still. Can he guess
His nature – does he not know yet? Some beauty acts
                                like poison!

NARCISSUS:

Love can be impatient with the slower tread of reason.
Love her he does, though; schooled already by her
                              attractions
He knows the taste of tears, shed from his deep affections.
He knows how to obey each beating of her heart.
Who knows? Perhaps already he has learned persuasion's art.

NERO:

What? Do you think already he has some claim on her?

NARCISSUS:

That I can't say, my lord, but tell you, on my honour,
I have observed him sometimes, escaping from this place,
Resentment raging in him – written on his face,
Tired of the court's avoiding him and the pretence,
Tired, too, of your great power, and his subservience,
Wavering between open revolt and fear,
He goes to visit Junia – then returns, his features clear.

NERO:

> So much the worse for him, for knowing how to please her.
> He would do better to incur her anger. Caesar
> Will not submit to jealousy, not without some revenge.

NARCISSUS:

> My lord, what is the reason for this sudden change?
> Junia may have shown him pity in his woes:
> The tears that he has shed are the only tears she knows.
> But now she will acquire a wider field of view,
> Once her eyes are exposed to the splendour that is you,
> Monarchs, bare-headed, unnoticed in the crowd – as is
> Her lover too – before you, declare their loyalties.
> When in such glory you approach her, let her see
> How you, with sighs, concede her the palm of victory,
> You need be in no doubt, you shall be master of
> A heart already won – you may command her love.

NERO:

> Nor need I doubt how many troubles will ensue
> And criticism in its wake...

NARCISSUS:

> But what inhibits you?

NERO:

> Them – Agrippina, Burrus – yes. My wife Octavia,
> The whole of Rome, three years of virtuous behaviour.
> Octavia's constancy has wearied me for years;
> Her dog-like loyalty, reproaches, endless tears.
> I should be happy if an opportune divorce
> Would take away this yoke, imposed on me by force.
> Heaven itself seems tired of hearing her complain –
> For four years without ceasing she's implored the gods
> in vain.
> They show no sign of hearing the prayers she has been
> offering,
> Our marriage-bed still lacks the slightest sign of offspring
> The Empire needs an heir, before it is too late.

NARCISSUS:

> Then cast her off, my lord, why do you hesitate?
> Your heart, the Empire, everything condemns Octavia.
> Augustus, your great forebear, was in love with Livia –
> It took twofold divorce to unite them – you owe the nation
> The Empire, too, to that convenient separation.
> Tiberius, his son-in-law, while Augustus was alive,
> Cast off Augustus's daughter, given him as a wife.
> Only you, so far, repress your true desires.
> Divorce, both pure and simple, is all that it requires.

NERO:

> And what of the implacable, unyielding Agrippina?
> To my uneasy lover's eye, it is as if I'd seen her
> Bringing Octavia to me, and, with eyes like burning brands,
> Insisting on the sanctity of a knot tied by her hands;
> Not only that, she will to complete my heart's distress,
> Read me a lecture on my wicked ungratefulness.
> Can I endure the humiliation of such an interview?

NARCISSUS:

> My lord, you are your own master, and, of course, hers too.
> Will you be shivering always beneath her tutelage?
> You've reigned for her too long. Reign for yourself now
> > – live!
> Are you afraid? If so, it is not her you fear:
> More the insolent Pallas, whom you've now exiled from
> > here,
> To whose audacity she gave protection and assistance.

NERO:

> Oh, yes, I reign, if I can make her keep her distance.
> I hear what you advise, I approve, I agree, I'm filled
> With absolute resolve to counteract her will,
> But – for a moment let me lay my secrets bare –
> The minute some ill-fortune has led me back to her,
> Either because I daren't defy the authority
> Which she has for so long exercised over me,

Or because I remember the many benefits
I have from her – everything in me submits.
My strong resolve is rendered totally ineffective;
Beside her genius, mine cannot remain objective.
It is to free myself from this subservience
That I avoid her, sometimes causing her offence.
From time to time, I even purposely arouse her
Just to make her avoid me, to upset her composure.
But I am keeping you. Go, or Britannicus
Will charge you with some form of untrustworthiness.

NARCISSUS:

No, no, he has blind faith in me; he even believes
It is by his command I see you – to retrieve
The slightest hint that can concern him, and to find
Out, through me, the secret workings of your mind.
Above all, he's impatient that my subtlest acumen
Will arrange for him to see his true love once again.

NERO:

Yes, I agree! He'll see her now – you hesitate
To spread good news?

NARCISSUS:

                Sir – keep them separate.

NERO:

I have my reasons, you your orders. Never fear.
The privilege of seeing her will cost him dear.
Meanwhile, though, boast to him, your brilliant strategy
Has been a signal triumph, deceiving even me,
And, without knowledge or consent of mine, he will see her.
The door! It's her! Go! Find your master. Bring him here.

Scene 3

NERO:

Lady, you seem perturbed. Your face betrays your thought.
Do you read in my eyes, some future ill-report?

JUNIA:

> My lord, I cannot hide from you, I was mistaken.
> It was not the Emperor, but the Empress I was seeking.

NERO:

> Oh yes! I know. I feel a stab of jealousy
> That she should be the object of such intimacy.

JUNIA:

> Jealousy, my lord?

NERO:

> You think, within these walls,
> Octavia's is the only heart you have in thrall?

JUNIA:

> Who else should I solicit, since I am refused
> Knowledge of a crime of which I am accused?
> Since you are punishing me, you if anyone
> Should tell me, and I beg you to, what wrong I've done.

NERO:

> What? You think your offence so trivial, so slight?
> Keeping yourself concealed for so long from my sight?
> All those charms too! Since heaven was kind enough to
> confer them,
> Did you accept those gifts, simply to re-inter them?
> Why did you exclude me from such glory till today?
> Why cruelly confine me to my court – locked away?
> And shall Britannicus watch your beauty, far away
> From here and me, your Emperor, blossom day by day?
> It's even said that you, without objection, freely
> Allow, encourage him to pay his addresses. Surely
> This just cannot have happened, not without my leave –
> That you should have given him hope – that I cannot
> believe.
> Nor do I think I should have had to learn by rumour's
> voice,
> You had consented to love, even you'd made your choice.

JUNIA:

> I admit there may have been occasions, when he'd sigh
> To give a weight to his desires – I'll not deny.
> But he has never, never turned his back on me,
> The last surviving ruin of a once-great family.
> Perhaps he may recall, in a happier time, that he
> Was chosen by his father to pay his address to me.
> He loves me: he obeyed the Emperor his father,
> And, I dare add, obeys, you, my lord, and your mother,
> Since her desires and yours so merge and intertwine.

NERO:

> My mother has her plans, lady, and I have mine.
> Let us speak no further of Claudius or my mother:
> My own choice will condition my conduct, not some other's.
> It is for me alone to answer for you, and
> You will therefore receive a husband at my hand.

JUNIA:

> My lord, do you imagine, by any other marriage,
> My forefathers, the Caesars, would somehow be disparaged?

NERO:

> No, Lady, for the husband whom I have in mind
> Is one whose ancestors could honourably be combined
> With yours. You may accept him entirely without shame.

JUNIA:

> Who is he then?

NERO:

> Myself.

JUNIA:

> You?

NERO:

> If a greater name
> Than mine should spring to mind, I'd gladly offer you
> The choice, but to confess the truth, I have run through

The names of all the families of the Empire, city, court,
To find a worthy candidate, but the more I sought
The more I knew there was no other to select.
Caesar alone could be the candidate elect.
I could not honestly entrust you to other hands
Than those to which Rome entrusted power over all her
lands.
Look back now to that time that you yourself just mentioned,
When Claudius made clear that it was his intention
To marry you to his son. But at the time, he meant
Britannicus, one day, to take the reins of government.
Destiny has spoken. It is not your business to defy it,
But to range yourself with the Empire, and stand by it.
The great gift that Fate has given me is empty if a part
Of that great gift does not comprise your loving heart –
If my incessant cares cannot find peace and calm,
My ceaseless vigils not find comfort in your arms.
And do not see Octavia as an impediment;
Rome, as well as I myself, gives her consent
To my divorce, and eagerly as I, unties
A knot which heaven does not wish to recognise.
Lady, reflect, give earnest consideration to
My choice, worthy of one who idolises you.
Worthy of your beauty, so long concealed from view,
And worthy of the wide world which you owe it to.

JUNIA:
My lord, I stand amazed, and with good reason. I
Have seen myself, all in the course of a single day,
Kidnapped and dragged like a criminal to this place,
And when I stand before you, fearful, face to face,
When, terror-stricken, I can scarce trust in my own
Innocence, you offer me Octavia's throne.
I have to tell you, neither such rank indignity,
Nor such excessive honour, are merited by me.
And can you, Caesar, wish me, who was made to see
As a mere child, the extinction of all my family,
Who nursed my grief alone, in blank obscurity,

Making my virtue conform to my state of misery,
Do you wish me to pass at once, from this dark night,
To a position where I'm exposed to a blaze of light,
Whose brightness, even from a distance, only spells distress,
And ask me further to usurp another woman's place?

NERO:

Have I not said already, I will have a divorce?
Less terror or less modesty would seem your wisest course.
Do not accuse my choice of being blind. Let me
Answer to you for yourself. You need only agree.
Be mindful of the ancestors you come from, and prefer
The real, enduring glory which Caesar can confer –
And means to – to the dubious glory of refusing,
A course that can lead only to repentance and confusion.

JUNIA:

The heavens see, my lord, through to my inmost thoughts.
I do not cheat myself with silly dreams. Be assured,
I know the measure of your magnanimity.
But the more this offer casts splendour over me,
The more it shames me, shows me in the unwelcome light
Of having robbed another, of what is hers by right.

NERO:

You take her interest, lady, far too much to heart:
Your friendship goes to infinite lengths to take her part.
Let's not deceive ourselves, forget the mystery.
It is Octavia's brother touches you more than she.
It is Britannicus...

JUNIA:

He's touched my heart. I will not hide it.
Nor have I ever had a mind to have denied it.
I should not say all this. I should be more discreet.
But what my heart has spoken, my lips always repeat.
The art of counterfeit, at such distance from the court,
Is one I never felt I would need to be taught.
I love Britannicus. We were to have been married.

The Empire was to have to come to him. When that
miscarried,
Those same misfortunes that cost him a nation's throne,
The loss of all his titles, of everything he owned,
His court sent into exile, banished by his ruin,
All these were ties that bound me closer to him.
Everything for you is as you wish: your days
Flow past you, spent in pleasure, serene in every way,
The Empire is a never-ending fount, and though
Some trouble may occur to interrupt the flow,
The whole, wide world, that holds your happiness to be
Paramount, will rush to erase the memory.
Britannicus is alone. I am the only one who's there
To care about his torments, and to show I care.
His pleasures are confined to his and my few tears,
Which sometimes help him to forget his cares and fears.

NERO:
Those pleasures and those tears, are what I most begrudge:
Any but he would die for them, were I their judge.
In his case I pronounce a sentence less severe.
Lady, in a little, he will be with you here.

JUNIA:
Ah, my lord, your kindness already calms my fear.

NERO:
It would be easy for me to forbid him entry here.
But, lady, I have every wish to avoid the danger
He might involve himself in, from resentment or from anger.
I do not wish to cause his death. Better that he
Should hear his sentence from someone he loves, not me.
If you value his future days, send him away from you,
Without his thinking I am jealous. What you must do
Is take on the burden of his exile, and make sure
He understands, by speech or silence, or by your
Coldness, at least, towards him, that he'll have to bear
His tears, his wishes, and his hopes of love elsewhere.

JUNIA:

> How could I pronounce, so cruel a decree?
> How many thousand times have I sworn the contrary?
> And even if I could, my eyes would soon betray me,
> And, even if I were dumb, forbid him to obey me.

NERO:

> I shall be hidden nearby. I shall be watching. So...
> Bury your love deep down. I warn you, there'll be no
> Secret signs or languages which can be kept
> From me, no silent looks I shall not intercept.
> If you think you can console him, with a gesture or a sigh,
> His doom will be irrevocable – he shall die.

JUNIA:

> If I may beg one wish, a single favour for
> Myself, then grant me I may never see him more.

Scene 4

NARCISSUS:

> My lord, Britannicus has asked to be received
> By the Princess. He is coming.

NERO:

> Let him!

JUNIA:

> My lord!

NERO:

> I'll leave.

> His future destiny now has rather less to do
> With me. Remember, when you see him, I'll see you.

Scene 5

JUNIA:

> Ah, dear Narcissus! Run to meet your master. Greet him
> From me, and say... too late! He's coming! I must meet him.

Scene 6

BRITANNICUS:

Junia, what grace of heaven now leads me back to you?
To whose good graces do we this precious interview?
But even in this joy I feel a sorrow. Can
I really hope to see you freely once again?
Or must I, by a thousand stratagems, find some way
To steal the joy I formerly could count on every day?
What did they do to you? Your tears, your very presence...
How could they not disarm their cruel insolence?
Where was I then? What jealous demon could refuse
The honour of a death, before your watching eyes?
In all the terror, by which you must have been possessed,
Was there no secret, silent prayer that you addressed
To me? Did your heart not cry "If only he were here!"
You know I would have died to answer your despair?
Nothing to say? No greeting? Just this iciness?
Is this your only comfort for my unhappiness?
Speak to me. We're alone. The enemy we fear
Has been deceived. He is now occupied elsewhere.
We are free, for a time, to take advantage of his absence.

JUNIA:

There is no place here that is quite free of his presence.
Nero is never far from here; do you not realise
The very walls have ears, and what is worse, have eyes.

BRITANNICUS:

Since when are you so timorous, your resolve so unsteady?
Have you let your love be disciplined already?
Where is the heart that swore a thousand times to me,
It would not fail to move even Nero's jealousy?
But try to banish from your mind your groundless fears.
I still have many loyal allies, it appears,
Support is growing for my cause – and besides
The Emperor's mother has come out now on our side.
Rome itself is appalled by his behaviour. Reports...

JUNIA:

> That is not true. Your words belie your real thoughts!
> You yourself have confessed to me many times that Rome
> Speaks with one voice, agreeing in their praise of him.
> And you have always paid a generous homage to
> His acts. I know your grief was speaking then, not you.

BRITANNICUS:

> Whatever it was, I admit, I truly am amazed;
> I did not come to see you, expecting to hear him praised.
> I came to bring you comfort in your fear and torment –
> Do you realise how hard it was to find a moment? –
> And now that moment, bought so dear, has to be spent
> In paying the enemy who frustrates me compliments?
> What can have made you, in a single day, become
> So changeable? Has the love you swore learned to be dumb?
> What is this? Are you even afraid to meet my eye?
> Does Nero somehow please you? Are you tired of me?
> If I thought that, I would... in heaven's name, speak out!
> Tell me, what is this reticence all about?
> Say something! Do you think of me any more?

JUNIA:

> The Emperor could come at any moment. Please withdraw.

BRITANNICUS:

> Narcissus, after this, who can I ever trust?

Scene 7

NERO:

> Lady...

JUNIA:

> No, my lord, no more now. I did it. Just
> Be pleased I obeyed your orders. Now, if you will allow
> The tears, that he must not be witness of, to flow...

Scene 8

NERO:

Well now, Narcissus, you see the degree of violence
Of love between them, obvious even in her silence.
She loves my rival. It's a fact. She makes it clear –
But I'll find consolation in his ultimate despair,
And picturing what must be the present condition of
His grief, since that moment's doubt was cast upon their
love.
I'll follow her. And meanwhile let me see my rival
Tortured with new doubts and suspicions, almost past
survival.

NARCISSUS:

Once more Fortune beckons. Do I have a choice?
Who am I to resist the promptings of her voice?
If she'll confirm the favour she has already shown,
We'll bring the wretched to their ends, to gain our own.

~

ACT THREE

Scene 1

BURRUS:
Pallas has gone, my lord.

NERO:
                How did my mother take
The blow to her authority?

BURRUS:
                Make no mistake;
The blow struck home. It hurt. You need be in no doubt. It
Will not be long before the whole world learns about it.
Her rage, my lord, has long been threatening to explode.
Let's hope a few vain threats will end the episode.

NERO:
What? Is she plotting something? Tell me, yes or no?

BURRUS:
Your mother was, and is, a formidable foe.
The city and the Army revere her ancestors;
Her father's still remembered as the great Germanicus.
You know her ambition well enough; she knows her
                        power,
But there is something else that makes me fear her more:
It is that you yourself add fuel to feed her anger,
You hand her a weapon to use against you – that's the
                        danger.

NERO:
I, Burrus?

BURRUS:
           Yes. This love that everyone can see
Obsesses you.

NERO:

I know – it is past remedy.
I blame myself much more than you do, be assured.
I must love her. I've no choice.

BURRUS:

You think you must, my lord.
You are content with faint resistance – self-deception! –
You're gripped by a malaise, weak at its inception.
But if you would resolve to pay the debt you owe
To duty, not to treat with your – and duty's – foe;
If you would just recall the youthful, soaring spirits
Of your early years, if you would call to mind the merits
Of your ill-rewarded wife, Octavia, whose chaste
And faithful love for you will outlast your distaste;
If, above all, you will keep Junia at a distance
For a few days; if you can do that without assistance,
You'll win. However strong the love that holds you fast,
No love, unless we wish it to, can ever last.

NERO:

Burrus, I would believe you, if, in the alarms
Of war, I should sustain the fame of Roman arms,
Or if, more calmly, in the Senate, should I see
Myself constrained to vote on the nation's destiny,
It's then on your experience that I would place reliance.
Love, though, I have to tell you, is quite another science.
I'd be reluctant to oblige you, to that extent
To lower yourself so far out of your element.
Goodbye. I suffer too much anguish away from her.

BURRUS:

Nero at last finds, and betrays his true character.
That savagery I thought that I could tame in him
Shakes off the feeble bonds that I had laid on him.
Into what byways, what excesses will he run?
In such a dangerous crisis, which way shall I turn?
But wait! If Agrippina's maternal instinct may
Be revived once again... it's her! Coming this way.

Scene 2

AGRIPPINA:

Well, now, was I so wrong, then, Burrus, in my suspicions?
I must say you've been teaching some valuable lessons!
Pallas is exiled. His only crime, that one can tell,
Was to make your master Emperor. And you know very well
Without his guiding hand, never would Claudius
Have made my son his heir, over Britannicus.
What else? Oh, yes, of course, Octavia has a rival.
Faithful marriage, it seems, is an archaic survival.
Such a success for a tutor, picked out especially
To keep temptation at bay, and curb his youthful fantasy!
You are like all the rest, encouraging him to
Despise his mother and forget his wife.

BURRUS:

                                        Not true!
Your accusation is, as ever, somewhat premature;
Nothing the Emperor's done is past excuse or cure.
Blame Pallas's exile on his pride and insolence,
Which have for some time now cried out for punishment.
The rest is... a misfortune. But not beyond repair.
Means may be found to comfort the sad Octavia.
Be gentler though. Be calm. Such a fierce maternal onslaught
Is not the way to persuade him to come back to his consort.
With goads and taunts one does not tame a savage beast.

AGRIPPINA:

Your poor attempts to muzzle me have not the least
Effect. I know that silence only merits scorn,
And I have worked too hard for that. With Pallas gone,
Don't think all my support went with him – not at all.
Heaven has left me quite enough to avenge my fall.
Britannicus is just beginning to resent
Crimes, in which I was implicated, and now repent.
I shall present him to the people, and excite
Their pity for the wrong that's done him. They'll put right
The injustice. I'll make the case. Here, on one side you'll see,

Demanding back the loyalty sworn to his family,
The son, if not the heir, of an emperor – Claudius;
Supported by me, the daughter of great Germanicus.
And, on the other, Nero, son of Caius Domitius,
Supported by Seneca, and you, his guardian, Burrus,
Both of you recalled from exile – and by me;
Now both involved in criminal complicity.
I intend to make public all of our common crimes,
I shall tell all the various paths by which I climbed
With Nero. I shall render his power, and yours, both odious,
Admitting to all the rumours and reports, however hideous;
I'll circulate confessions – of exiles, murders even,
Poisonings...

BURRUS:

        Lady, think – will anyone believe them?
They will see through you, feel their trust has been abused
By the spiteful stratagem of a witness self-accused.
I was the first to work for your designs. It was I
Who made the Army swear an oath of loyalty
To Nero. I do not regret my earlier zeal – but rather
Support the idea that a son succeeds his father.
Claudius adopted Nero as his son, and by the sequel
Showed his intention that his son and yours be equal.
Rome was free to choose. So chose. Without injustice.
As when they chose Tiberius, adopted by Augustus.
Your son's power today is so securely founded,
You'd be hard put to shake it, even should you be so minded.
And if I still have any influence with him,
His goodness will soon make you forget your present
                          scheme.
I have begun this task. Now I shall see it through.

Scene 3

ALBINA:

My lady, this is madness. What are you trying to do?
You think the Emperor can remain in ignorance for long?

AGRIPPINA:
Then let him come to me himself.

ALBINA:
Lady, be strong.
Conceal your anger: be the Emperor's loving mother,
And in the interests of Octavia and her brother,
Do not reveal too much, or give up your repose
Of mind. Leave Caesar the control of whom he loves.

AGRIPPINA:
What? Can't you see how he is humiliating me?
I am the one who has the rival now, not she.
If I do not soon break this wretched, fatal chain,
My place is lost, and I shall count for nothing once again.
So far, Octavia, honoured in name alone, was thought
To exercise no power, and was, therefore, ignored.
I used to be the one. My generous dispensation
Of favours – honours – guaranteed the courtiers' adoration.
And now there is this girl. She gives Nero "new life",
She arrogates the powers of a mistress and a wife.
The majesty of the Caesars, the fruit of all my cares,
Are sacrificed – for what? A single glance of hers.
I'm stunned. Already they ignore me and avoid me.
I cannot bear the thought, nor keep my rage inside me.
So, even if Heaven gives me scant hope of my survival
At my son's thankless hands, I... Now here is his rival.

Scene 4

BRITANNICUS:
Our common enemies are not invincible,
And our misfortunes find hearts that are not insensible
To our plight. But now we must not lose valuable time
The former reticence of our friends, both yours and mine,
Is fired by righteous anger at these iniquities.
They came to see Narcissus – told him of their unease.
Nero is not yet in full possession of

The girl who took my sister's place, and took my love.
If you still feel the wrong that has been done to her,
We can still rouse the sense of duty in the adulterer.
Half of the Senate is behind us, as we speak,
Sylla, Plautus, Piso...

AGRIPPINA:

                The aristocratic clique?
All the three foremost heads of the nobility...

BRITANNICUS:

You're unconvinced, you're wavering, I can see.
Your anger is irresolute, only half on fire;
You fear to gain the very ends that you desire.
But you are safe, you've made my downfall too complete.
You won't see any friend of mine come forward to compete
On my behalf. I have no friends. Far-sightedly you saw
To their estrangement, or seduction, long ago.

AGRIPPINA:

All these suspicions! Place a little less reliance
On them. Our common safety depends on our alliance.
My word is given. That's enough. Despite your enemies,
I shall not go back on any of my sworn promises.
Nero is guilty. He tries to escape, but I pursue
Him: in the end he knows that he must listen to
His mother. I shall use both gentleness and force
Alternately – or else... I shall support your sister's cause,
Broadcasting her distress, fostering Rome's fear of me,
And winning all their hearts to her great injury.
I shall lay siege to Nero from all sides. If I might
Advise you, stay away from him – keep out of sight.

Scene 5

BRITANNICUS:

Did you tell me the truth, Narcissus. Or were they just
False hopes? If they were, then who can I ever trust?

NARCISSUS:
> It was the truth, but, sir, this is not the place
> To talk about these things: perhaps we should retrace
> Our steps outside. What is it you are waiting for?

BRITANNICUS:
> Oh, God!

NARCISSUS:
>   What is it, sir?

BRITANNICUS:
>   If I could just, by your
> Ingenuity, see once again...

NARCISSUS:
>   Whom?

BRITANNICUS:
>   I may be blind,
> But I'd await my fate much easier in my mind.

NARCISSUS:
> After all I've said, can you still believe she's loyal?

BRITANNICUS:
> No, Narcissus, no, she is a criminal
> Deserving all my anger, but I cannot stop the thought
> That I do not believe that as strongly as I ought.
> Bewildered, obstinate, my heart excuses her,
> Justifies her behaviour – idolises her.
> I should so much prefer to drown my disbelief:
> A calculated hatred might even give some relief.
> How could so great a heart – as far as one could see –
> Brought up opposed to a court so steeped in treachery,
> Give up so much glory, committing, from the first,
> Betrayal unheard-of, even at that court at its worst?

NARCISSUS:
> Who knows if the wretched girl did not plan, from the start,
> A calculated conquest of the Emperor's heart?

She knew her beauty could not be hid for long: a thought
That prompted her to flee, in order to be caught?
To make her conquest harder? In consequence excite
The Emperor to subdue her yet unconquered pride?

BRITANNICUS:
I cannot see her then?

NARCISSUS:
                  Triumphant in defeat, she's
Hearing her royal lover's amorous entreaties.

BRITANNICUS:
Then let us go, Narcissus. Oh, God! It is her!

NARCISSUS: (*Aside.*)
This news must be at once brought to the Emperor.

Scene 6

JUNIA:
My lord, please go. He is possessed. It's like a fit
Of rage against you. My constancy occasioned it.
Nero is furious. I have stolen from his side.
His mother went to him – she keeps him occupied.
You must go, now. I love you, and I hope you may
Be satisfied to hear me justified one day.
Your voice, your face, are fixed here, in my heart and mind.
Nothing can blot them out.

BRITANNICUS:
                Oh, quite... I understand.
You want my flight to give you a reason to adduce
Desertion – that would serve as an ideal excuse.
No doubt, on seeing me, you feel a certain measure
Of shame – you have no more than an uneasy pleasure.
Ah, well, I'd better go...

JUNIA: My lord, you have imputed...

57

BRITANNICUS:

Perhaps a little more resistance would have suited
Better. I'm not surprised a commonplace affair
Should pick the winning side. It happens everywhere.
Nor that the Empire dazzled you, even if the price
To pay turned out to be my sister's sacrifice.
But that you would have been obsessed by it I doubted.
You'd so long seemed to me indifferent about it.
No, no, I admit it, my heart has now despaired:
For this one tragedy, I had not been prepared.
All manner of injustice has triumphed at my fall.
Heaven is allied with my enemies. Yet all
These horrors did not conquer me. One more was due –
It still remained for me – to be forgot by you.

JUNIA:

Another time, to make you regret your lack of trust,
I might refuse to listen – it would be only just.
But Nero threatens you; the danger's all too real.
I have other concerns than to torment you. Feel
Reassured, though, come now, you've nothing to complain
About. Nero was hidden – there! I had to feign
What I...

BRITANNICUS:
        Nero! ...

JUNIA:
                Witness of our whole interview.
His jealous eyes watched every move as I spoke to you,
Ready to catch the slightest look, the gesture that would
                    show
Our understanding. There was nothing he did not know.

BRITANNICUS:

Nero was listening to us? But even so... indeed...
You could have made a signal, tried not to mislead.
Couldn't your eyes have hinted at the author of my
                    anguish?

Must love be dumb, or does it only speak one language?
You could have spared me so much pain, with a single
look.

You should have...

JUNIA:

No! I should have taken the way I took.
To hold my tongue and save you. How often did I try
To speak the truth and tell you of my heart's agony?
How many sighs have I cut off, how often caught
Myself avoiding the very eyes I sought?
When with a single look, I could have brought you such
Comfort. But that one look would have cost us too much.
I was so frightened that my love might be betrayed,
I even came to hate the promises I'd made.
Unhappily for his, and our, good fortune, now
He's seen too far into our hearts for us to disavow
Our love. But hide yourself. When we meet again
I'll tell you everything you want to know, try to explain,
Along with countless secrets I long to tell you of.

BRITANNICUS:

This is too much. How can I understand your love,
Your goodness, kindness and my failing? Don't you see
All that you are preparing to throw away for me?
Here, at your feet, let me atone for my lack of trust.

JUNIA:

What are you doing? The Emperor's here! Get up! You must!

Scene 7

NERO:

Don't let me interrupt such charming ecstasies!
Your kindness must be prodigal to earn such thanks as these.
Lady, I surprise him *at* your feet, if not *on* his,
But he could show me just a little gratitude. This is
A place propitious to him. My aim in keeping you
Here is to facilitate just such a rendezvous.

BRITANNICUS:

My sorrow or my joy I shall lay at her feet
Whenever, in her kindness, she consents we meet.
As for this place, where you imprison her, I see
Nothing that is "propitious" – either to her or me.

NERO:

What you *should* see in this place, let it be said,
Is that I must be respected, and, furthermore, obeyed?

BRITANNICUS:

Nothing was said, during our common education,
That you should take the higher, I the inferior station:
Nor in the point of birth, could it infallibly
Be I that must obey *you*, you who'd challenge *me*.

NERO:

In that case, both our lives are crossed by Destiny;
At that time I obeyed. Now you must obey me.
If you've not learned to let yourself be guided...
Well, you're still young, and teachers can always be provided.

BRITANNICUS:

Who's to do that for me?

NERO:

The Empire – at its height.
And Rome.

BRITANNICUS:

And does Rome know you count among your
rights,
That of exploiting fully the cruelty of force,
The injustice of abduction – imprisonment – divorce?

NERO:

Rome is well-trained enough to turn its prying eyes
Away from things I wish it not to recognise.
Imitate such respect.

BRITANNICUS:

> What Rome thinks is well-known.

NERO:

But is not broadcast. Imitate such silence in your own.

BRITANNICUS:

Does Nero now throw off constraint and moderation?

NERO:

Nero begins to weary of this whole conversation.

BRITANNICUS:

The fortune of this reign, all Rome should bless sincerely.

NERO:

Fortune – misfortune? It's all one. Just let them fear me.

BRITANNICUS:

If I know Junia at all, that pitiless view
Is hardly going to lead to her admiring you.

NERO:

I may not have the trick of earning her approval,
But I can guarantee a rival's swift removal.

BRITANNICUS:

Whatever dangers lie in wait to torture me,
All that I truly fear is her hostility.

NERO:

Well, pray for it; that's the best advice I have for you.

BRITANNICUS:

To bring her happiness is all I ever want to do.

NERO:

But she has promised you, *that* you will always bring her.

BRITANNICUS:

At least I do not spy on her, and everything her
Mind conceives of me, I beg her to speak out;
Nor do I hide myself, to force her to be mute.

NERO:
> I understand you. Guards!

JUNIA:
> My lord, he is your brother!
> What are you doing? Maybe he is a jealous lover,
> But when misfortune in this way dogs his unlucky heels,
> Can you begrudge a glimpse of how good fortune feels?
> Let me bring you together, unite your hearts in love:
> Conceal myself from you, and, at the same time, remove
> Myself from him. Please allow me to do as I intend,
> To join the Vestal Virgins' order, and so end
> This feud between you both. Leave my wretched love
> To be a problem only for the gods above.

NERO:
> A sudden, strange decision, nearly without precedents.
> Guards, reconduct the lady to her residence.
> Confine Britannicus to where his sister's quarters are.

BRITANNICUS:
> Is this how Caesar sees emotion? As a war?

JUNIA:
> We'll bow before the storm: don't cross him any more.

NERO:
> Guards, you have your orders. What are you waiting for?

Scene 8

BURRUS:
> God! What is this?

NERO: (*Not seeing BURRUS.*)
> Their love's become twice as strong-
> minded.
> I recognise the helping hand that lies behind it.
> Agrippina only had one cause to seek me out...
> Those wearisome, long speeches... fooling me throughout,

And playing this malicious, hateful trick on me.
Do you know if my mother is still here? Go and see –
If she is still in the palace, she is to be confined.
Withdraw her guard and see that she is given mine.

BURRUS:

What? My lord, without a hearing? Your own mother?

NERO:

I know, you are hatching some devious plot or other.
For the last few days I've watched you, trying to restrict me
In every move – my censor, ready to contradict me.
You answer for her to me. If you refuse, I tell
You, others will answer both for her, and you as well.

~

ACT FOUR

Scene 1

BURRUS:
>Lady, you'll have both time and leave to plead your case.
>Caesar himself consents to receive you in this place,
>Where you may feel he causes you to be confined.
>Perhaps a friendly talk is what he has in mind.
>However it is, if I dare make an observation,
>It might be wiser not to offer provocation.
>Rather open your arms to him, extend a motherly hand.
>It is not him you attack, it is yourself you defend.
>The court, as you must see, looks toward him alone;
>He may be your creation, of course he is your son,
>But he's your Emperor as well. The power that you
>Conferred on him, we all of us are subject to,
>Yourself included, and, according to his mood,
>Threatening or loving, we all must follow suit.
>In seeking your support, they seek that of your son...
>Here is the Emperor coming now.

AGRIPPINA:
>   Leave us alone.

Scene 2

AGRIPPINA: (*Sitting.*)
>Nero, come over here, sit down and take your place.
>They summon me to clear myself with you, here, face
>   to face.
>Though what I am accused of, I, of course, have no notion,
>But of those crimes I did commit, I owe some explanation.
>You rule. But I'd remind you just how wide a gulf
>There was, at birth, between the Empire and yourself.
>My forebears' rights and claims could offer a guarantee
>Of nothing – things would have stayed so – but for me.

64

The moment Britannicus's mother was condemned,
Battle was joined for the prize of Claudius's hand,
You think I coveted his bed? My one desire
Was to ascend the throne, so as to raise you higher.
I enlisted the help of Pallas – yes, I swallowed my pride;
Night after night I lay, the Emperor at my side,
Fondled in his arms, and nourishing the love
That I, his niece, had fought to be so certain of.
But we were joined in blood, and the age-old taboo
Of incest barred the way to marriage for the two
Of us. He dared not wed Germanicus's daughter,
His niece. But the Senate was seduced, and brought a
Milder law into force, Claudius to my bed,
And all Rome to my feet – however, it must be said,
The honours they bestowed were not for you, but me:
I had you brought into the bosom of his family –
And more than that. Tying us closer still, I gave you
In marriage, to his only daughter, to Octavia.
But that was not enough. Could I, or anyone,
Think Claudius would prefer his son-in-law to his son?
Once more I went for help to Pallas. By his persuasion
Claudius adopted you. To celebrate the occasion,
He named you Nero, planned to share supreme authority,
Though you were still a few years short of your majority.
That was the moment everyone recalled my past...
Unmasked my plan. But I was steady. I held fast.
Murmurings were heard; the Emperor's friends could all
Begin to sense Britannicus's coming fall.
I made them promises, bought off most of them,
And exile spared me from most of the worst of them.
Claudius, tired out with endless complaints from me,
Dismissed from his son all those whose constancy
And loyalty had too long been given to him alone,
And might still beat a pathway for him to the throne.
And I did more. I chose from my own retinue
Those whom I wished his education entrusted to.
While, on the other hand, for you I took good care

To pick out tutors whom Rome would certainly revere.
Deaf to intrigue, I listened only to reputation,
Brought Seneca back from exile, Burrus from his station
In the army. Both of them have since... but never mind,
Rome was much impressed with their virtues – at the time.
Meanwhile, I handed out largesse, in your name, in amounts
Sufficient to exhaust the imperial accounts.
Circuses, honours, gifts, by whose seductive charm we
Could win the people's hearts, and more than that, the Army.
By now the Emperor's health had rapidly declined.
Claudius' eyes had long been closed, as had his mind.
They opened now. He saw his error. In his fear,
The glimmerings of pity for his own son appeared.
He hoped, too late, to reunite his allies, as a whole.
But his guard, his bed, his palace, were all in my control.
I let him fruitlessly consume himself in sighs,
Then made myself the mistress of his last energies.
Ostensibly to spare him grief, as he lay dying, I hid
From him all knowledge of the tears his son had shed.
He died. A thousand rumours blackened my reputation:
I kept all news of his death out of circulation,
While Burrus went in secret to the soldiers to demand
The garrison's renewal of allegiance to you, and
While you went to the camp, along with my desires,
The altars of all Rome smoked with sacrificial fires.
Following my false orders, the populace obeyed
With fervent prayers for the health of a prince already dead.
Only when your rule was ratified by the legions'
Approval, and their oath of absolute obedience,
Was Claudius shown to them; Rome learned of your
                                                  accession
And his death at the same time. There is the confession
I promised I would make you. Those are my crimes,
                                                  my lord,
Without omission or exception. My reward?
For six short months, with seeming gratitude, you appear
To enjoy the resultant fruits of so much tender care,

Now, tired of showing respect that irks you, like a sore,
You think you can affect not to know me any more.
Burrus and Seneca I saw, giving you welcome lessons
In rank ingratitude, poisoning you with suspicions,
So pleased to see their pupil outstrip their arguments.
I've watched you bestowing royal marks of confidence
On worthless flatterers, voluptuaries, rakes,
Pandering to your pleasures for their own selfish sakes.
And when I could no longer contain my indignation,
when I asked you at least for some proper explanation,
You gave me a reply of the most insulting sort.
(The ungrateful, when exposed, fall back on that resort.)
You know I promised Junia in marriage to your brother.
They both expressed delight at this choice of your
                                                                    mother.
And what do you do? You abduct her. Overnight
She is made the passive object of your obscene delight.
Octavia is forgotten, banned from your heart and head,
From where I took such pains to place her, in your bed.
Pallas, I hear, is exiled, Britannicus arrested,
And now, my freedom is attacked. Well, who was it
                                                                    suggested
Burrus be allowed to lay insolent hands on me?
And when you are convicted of so much perfidy,
When I require from you some adequate explanation,
I am the one who is summoned to plead in justification.

NERO:

I need not be reminded I owe my power to you;
So please don't give yourself the trouble that you do
Repeating it. Your kindness, lady, really could
Rely with perfect safety on my gratitude.
However, your incessant, violent accusations
Lead those who hear them to entertain suspicions
That you – and I dare say this now that we are alone –
Had only worked in *my* name, to secure your *own*.
"All those honours!" they'd say, "Surely a poor reward

for her help? What must he do to get her support?
This son she so condemns, just what was his offence?
Or did she only crown him to ensure obedience?
Is the imperial power in the hands of a trustee?"
Before, to have followed you would not have bothered me.
I would have yielded up to you all my power, as you
Seemed, by your complaints, to be asking me to do.
But Rome, you know, requires a master not a mistress.
You must have heard the rumours, occasioned by my
                                                    weakness.
The Senate, daily, and the people, irritated
At hearing me repeating the orders you dictated,
Began to say that Claudius's legacy to me
Was not so much his power, as his servility.
You've seen the Army, bearing their standards in review;
With what ill grace they have always lowered them to you.
Anyone else would listen to what the world was saying,
But, if you cannot rule, all you do is complain.
You join Britannicus, in league against me, and
Strengthen him by engaging him to Junia. While the hand
Of Pallas can be clearly seen, moving around behind
These plots; and when I try to regain some peace of mind,
I see you, a figure of hate, determined now to harm me,
Proposing to present my rival to the Army.
In the camps the rumour is already doing the rounds.

AGRIPPINA:

What? Me? Wished to make him Emperor? Is that what
                                                    you've found?
Why would I do that? What would be the purpose of it?
What honours would I find at his court? And what profit?
If, in your court, I find such minimal respect,
Where my enemies feel free to dog my every step,
If they abuse, unpunished, the Emperor's own mother,
What could I ever hope for at the court of another?
I'd be accused not merely of impotent stratagems,
Of plots and counter-plots, of stifled, still-born schemes,

But of crimes, committed in your name, and in your sight.
They would soon find grounds for convicting me outright.
I know you now. Moreover, I see through all of your
Devices. You're an ingrate, and you always were.
Even as a child, my care, love and protection
Only evoked from you displays of false affection.
Nothing could touch you, and the hardness of your heart
Should have cut short all loving kindness on my part.
God, how unhappy you make me! How can all my
                                        affection,
My care, my struggle for you, lead only to rejection?
I have only one son. Heavens, when have I ever sworn
An oath for anyone else's sake, since you were born?
Remorse, fear, danger – nothing has ever held me back.
I overcame your contempt of me. There was no lack
Of prophesies, even then, foretelling doom. I've done
All that I could. You rule. Enough for any one.
But now my freedom is curtailed. And, unimpeded,
You may curtail my life. Then do so, if you need it.
Be careful, though, that the people, angered at my death,
Do not take back from you, what cost my every breath.

NERO:

Well, then? Your orders! What principles must I practise?

AGRIPPINA:

First punish the audacity of my vile detractors:
Let Junia have the husband to whom she is engaged:
Let Britannicus's anger be assuaged:
Let them both have their liberty: let Pallas stay:
Let me have audience with you at any hour of the day:
Let Burrus, who is, as usual, listening at the door,
Learn not to come between son and mother any more.

NERO:

Lady, I wish my gratitude in future to be such
As to engrave your power on Rome's heart. Let this touch
Of coldness that has come between yourself and me,

69

Evaporate in the warmth of common sympathy.
What Pallas may have done, or not done, I'll ignore,
Make my peace with Britannicus – and more!
As for that love that caused this split and mutual fury,
We shall submit to you. You shall be judge – and jury.
Go now, convey this happy message to my brother.
Guards! Carry out the orders of my mother.

Scene 3

BURRUS:

My lord, does this embrace mean peace, then? Such a treaty
Promises a future union of love and duty.
You yourself know if I was ever in opposition
To her – or tried to prise you away from her affection.
Or if I have deserved her unjust anger now.

NERO:

I was suspicious of you – I am ashamed to avow.
I thought you were in league with her. But now I see
Her enmity, my trust in you returns to me.
Her victory is premature. Since she won't let me hate him,
I shall embrace my rival – until I suffocate him.

BURRUS:

My lord?

NERO:

It is too much. Only his utter fall
Can now deliver me from her rage, once and for all.
While he is still alive, I'm only half a man:
She enrages me by always harping on his name.
I shall not let her ambition or her wickedness
Give him a second chance to try and usurp my place.

BURRUS:

She will mourn for Britannicus, that much is sure.

NERO:

After this evening, I'll not fear him any more.

BURRUS:

But what possesses you to harbour this design?

NERO:

Glory, safety, life and love – all of it: mine!

BURRUS:

No, my lord, whatever you may say or do,
This wicked plot could never have been conceived by you.

NERO:

Burrus!

BURRUS:

This is not you – this is some other!
How could you entertain such thoughts without a shudder?
Think of the blood-guilt you will have to overcome.
Is Nero tired of ruling in the hearts of Rome?
What will Rome say? What is going on in your mind?

NERO:

Prisoner of my former glory? That now lies behind.
I'd have before my eyes, the love that, in one short day,
Chance gave, and I, shamefully, let Chance take away.
Slave to the general good, against my own desires,
An emperor who grants whose wishes – mine or theirs?

BURRUS:

And what of public happiness, my lord? Surely it's
A comfort for you, as one of the many benefits
You may bestow. Then choose. As Emperor you could
Still continue virtuous, continue so for good.
Your path's mapped out. You need be stopped by nothing
                                                    further:
All you need do is march from one virtue to another.
But listen to your flatterers, and in a little time,
You'll need to run from crime to ever-greater crime,
Sustain your harshness with progressively harsher guilt,
Washing your bloody hands in blood more freshly spilt.
Britannicus's death would rouse the zeal of those

Friends of his, all too eager to support his cause;
And these avengers would find other, new defenders,
Who, when they too were dead, would find their own
                                                avengers.
You will have lit a fire that cannot be put out.
Though feared by all the world, you'll live in fear and doubt,
Oppressing, punishing always, yet fearful to expose
Yourself to subjects whom you must now regard as foes.
Your happy early years of care and diligence –
Do they make you now regret your innocence?
Recall the happiness that marked them out, as they
Flowed calmly, peacefully, idyllically by.
What joy to think, to say as soon as you had thought it,
"Everywhere, at this moment, I am blessed and loved
                                                and courted.
Nowhere do people shudder when they hear my name;
Whatever their sorrows, heaven does not once hear me
                                                blamed.
In hatred and hostility they do not fly
Away from me. Their hearts leap up as I go by."
Those were your pleasures. Now, what a change, dear God!
You used to show regard, for those of the humblest blood.
I can recall a day, when the Senate urged you to
Sign the death-warrant of some felon. You
Resisted their demands, and their severity,
Even accusing yourself of harbouring cruelty,
Mourning the harsh necessities of your imperial might,
You said "I wish that I had never learned to write."
No! Either you reassure me of your confirmed belief
In me, or else my death must spare me further grief.
I'd rather not survive your glory – than look back
On the commission of a deed, blacker than black.

He throws himself on his knees.

Here I am, my lord, if you will not relent,
Then have them pierce a heart that will not consent:
Summon the men who prompted you, that vicious band,

So they may try on me their still unsteady hands.
I see my tears have moved my Emperor's heart. Your virtue
Now fears their frenzy; but let that fear alert you
To lose no time, name these monsters of infamy and vice,
Who dared to offer you this murderous advice.
Send for your brother. Embrace him and forget...

NERO:

You
Cannot ask me to do that.

BURRUS:

My lord, he does not hate you.
He is betrayed, my lord, I know he is innocent.
I answer to you, both for him and his obedience.
At least just see him – grant him an interview.

NERO:

Ask him to my apartments. Have him wait there – with you.

Scene 4

NARCISSUS:

My lord, I've seen to everything. Some deaths are just. A
Poison is prepared. The famous – infamous! – Locusta
Has, in her care for me, outdone herself. She caused
A prisoner to die right there in front of me: my lord,
Cold steel could not cut off a life as rapidly
As this new venom, with which she's entrusted me.

NERO:

Thank you, Narcissus. I am grateful to you for
Your care, but do not wish you to pursue this any more.

NARCISSUS:

What? Has your hatred of Britannicus cooled? Does this
Prevent...

NERO:

Narcissus, yes. We have declared an armistice.

NARCISSUS:

Far be it from me to try to dissuade you here, my lord,
But he was just now your prisoner. Can you afford
To let that injury fester, as it surely will?
There are no secrets Time will not – some time – reveal.
He will find out he was to have been given – by my hand –
A poison which had been prepared – by your command.
May heaven turn him away from such a wicked scheme
As doing to you what you do not dare do to him.

NERO:

His heart is answered for. I'll control mine as well.

NARCISSUS:

And is his marriage to Junia to set the seal?
My lord, do you mean to say you'll sacrifice that too?

NERO:

None of your concern. However it seems to you,
I do not count him as an enemy any more.

NARCISSUS:

A fact that Agrippina has counted on, I'm sure.
She has regained control. From now, you will be swayed
By her...

NERO:

What's that? What do you mean? What has she said?

NARCISSUS:

She boasted of it publicly enough.

NERO:

Of what?

NARCISSUS:

That all she had to do was see you, and you forgot
Your rage; your sound and fury, all your threats of violence,
Would sink into a meek and decorous silence.
She always said you'd be the first to sue for peace,
Happy to have her kindness grant you your release.

NERO:

    Well, what am I to do? Narcissus, counsel me!
    I long to punish her for her mean audacity,
    And to make sure her triumph, unbridled, indiscreet,
    Should be succeeded by a lifetime of regret.
    But what of the world's reaction? What will that be?
    Am I to follow in the steps of tyranny?
    And have Rome cancel all my honourable acts,
    Leaving the one name "Poisoner!" to fit the facts?
    They would see my revenge as fratricide, at best.

NARCISSUS:

    Will you be led by everything Rome may suggest?
    Do you imagine they would hold their tongues
                         forever?
    Is it for you to listen to their chatter? Never!
    Will you lose track of your own desires? And must
    You be the only Roman whom you dare not trust?
    My lord, you do not know the Romans. In their speeches
    They are much more reserved. Experience teaches
    Fastidiousness will undermine your rule. They'll see
    That they are feared, and think that they deserve to be.
    With such long years of servitude, stretching out behind
                         them,
    They slavishly kiss the hands, and love the chains that
                         bind them.
    One sees them all the time, desperate to please.
    Tiberius was worn out by their servilities.
    I myself, often, when my power was at its height,
    Tested out their patience, but never tired it out.
    You fear a poisoning may tarnish your name in time to
                         come?
    Have the brother killed, and drop the sister. Rome,
    A city of smoking altars, even if neither one
    Is guilty, will find crimes for them to have done.
    The anniversaries of their births will soon be calculated
    As liable to be especially ill-fated.

NERO:

>Let me repeat, there is no way I can continue:
>I promised Burrus. He made me give in. You
>Would not have me break my word to him again,
>To give him arms against me, or reason to complain.

NARCISSUS:

>Burrus says what he thinks, but does not think all he says:
>His shrewdness shores up his prestige in many ways:
>All of the rest are moved by love of power alone.
>They'd see your show of strength as weakening their own.
>But you'd be rid of them, my lord, you would be free,
>And those proud masters would, as we do, bow the knee.
>Can you be ignorant of what they dare to say?
>"Nero is not born to rule, nor fit to, anyway.
>He says nothing, does nothing, except as he is bid.
>Burrus controls his heart, and Seneca his head.
>His greatest, yes, his only talent is to work as
>A professional chariot racer in the circus.
>Competing for unworthy trophies, he'll perform,
>Making a spectacle of himself to all of Rome,
>Exhibiting himself, reciting on the stage,
>Singing songs he wishes to become all the rage,
>While henchmen circulate, just before the interval,
>Ensuring the applause is no less than fanatical."
>Can they not hold their tongues? Can we not force them to?

NERO:

>Narcissus, come with me. We'll see what we must do.

~

ACT FIVE

Scene 1

BRITANNICUS:
> Yes, Nero, it is he – whoever would have thought? –
> That he would ever wait to welcome me at court?
> The young men in his suite will certainly be there:
> He wants a celebration – vine leaves in the hair! –
> To ratify, to set the seal on the validity
> Of the oaths and the embraces he has sworn to me.
> And he relinquishes his love, source of so much
> Hatred. Now he makes you my sovereign and my judge.
> Though I am still denied my proper rank, and he
> Flaunts himself in the spoils he stole, in front of me,
> Since he has given up his love, and seems to yield
> The prize, and leave me here, the master of the field,
> My heart, deep down, seems to forgive him. I confess
> To having no regret at leaving him the rest.
> What? Not to have to part from you? What? Can I
> Look at you without fear at last? Look at those eyes
> That terror could not shake? that sighs have left unmoved?
> That Empire and Emperor have sacrificed to me, my love?
> What is it now? What sudden pang, what new fright
> Holds your joy at bay, while I live in delight?
> What are you frightened of?

JUNIA:
>   I do not even know.
> But I'm afraid.

BRITANNICUS:
>   Do you love me?

JUNIA:
>   Oh, God! You know I do.

BRITANNICUS:
> Nero no longer stands between us, never fear.

JUNIA:

But how can you be really sure he is sincere?

BRITANNICUS:

Do you suspect him of a secret hatred after all?

JUNIA:

This afternoon he loved me, he swore to achieve your fall.
Now it is you he courts, me he avoids. It's strange
To think a moment's work can bring about such a change.

BRITANNICUS:

That moment's work is what Agrippina has achieved:
My downfall would mean hers as well – so she believed.
Thanks to the political skill that she has shown,
Our enemies fought for us, not just on their side, but our
own.
Burrus I trust – I even trust his master – and I reason
That, just like me, he is not capable of treason.

JUNIA:

You must not judge his nature by your own: you march
With your two different natures, along quite different paths.
One day is all I've known of Nero and the court,
But how far what is said there is from what is thought!
People are pleased to break their word. Heart and mouth
agree
So little. It's a foreign land for you and me.

BRITANNICUS:

Whether Nero's friendship is counterfeit or real,
If you fear him, it's possible he too may feel
Fear himself. He dare not risk my assassination;
Senate and people would condemn the provocation.
He has confessed remorse for his earlier injustice;
He was sincere in that, even to Narcissus.
If you had heard it from him, Princess, as I heard...

JUNIA:

But is Narcissus really a man who keeps his word?

BRITANNICUS:

You wish me not to trust him? But why, for Heaven's
sake?

JUNIA:

What can I say? My lord, it is your life's at stake.
I suspect everything. I fear that everyone can be
Corrupted. I fear Nero, and the dark star that follows me.
Haunted by a black presentiment, despite
Myself, it is with regret I let you leave my sight.
Oh God! Maybe this peace, for all it seems to fill you
With happiness, conceals a trap that's set to kill you.
If Nero, angered by our affection, should once more change
His mind about us, choosing tonight for his revenge.
If, even as I look at you, he has prepared a crime,
And even as I speak to you, is it for the last time?
Oh, God!

BRITANNICUS:

Don't cry! My love, does your heart's sympathy
Stretch in its infinite depth, so far and all for me?
What? On this same day, in this same place,
You refuse a throne and weep before my loving eyes?
Only you must, I beg you, dry those precious tears;
I shall be back at once, to drive away your fears.
To stay here longer would make me suspected of
Duplicity. I leave you now – heart full of love.
I go among the ecstatic young, who, being blind,
Know nothing of the beauty I carry in my mind.
Goodbye.

JUNIA:

Prince...

BRITANNICUS:

I must go. I cannot – must not stay.

JUNIA:

Wait here, at least until they summon you away.

Scene 2

AGRIPPINA:

> Prince, you must come at once! What is this delay?
> Nero's impatient, thinking you purposely stay away.
> The joy and pleasure of the guests he has invited
> Waits to explode at seeing you finally united.
> Their prayers are still unanswered: you must be their saviour.
> Go now! While, lady, you and I visit Octavia.

BRITANNICUS:

> Go. Junia, my dearest love, and, with a quiet mind
> Visit my sister, with whom I leave you safe behind.

> *To AGRIPPINA.*

> The first moment I can, in deepest thankfulness,
> I shall return to thank you for all your services.

Scene 3

AGRIPPINA:

> If I am not mistaken, there are tears in your eyes.
> What has upset you in these temporary goodbyes?
> What can possibly have happened to you to cast this cloud?
> You can't mistrust this peace, of which I am justly proud?

JUNIA:

> After the endless torments of this day, I find
> It normal to retain some torments in my mind.
> I still can scarcely understand the miracle;
> I'm still afraid your kindness will meet some obstacle.
> Changes of heart at court, I know, are common, where
> True love is never unaccompanied by fear.

AGRIPPINA:

> Enough! I've spoken. Everything has changed. And there
> Is no more room left for your suspicions here.
> I answer for Nero's vows, all given for my benefit –
> His pledges, sworn to me, were absolutely definite.
> If you had only seen him, there, embracing me,

Assuring for his promises a further guarantee;
The tenderness with which he came forward to embrace me.
When he said goodbye, his arms would not release me.
And how his loving kindness, written on his face
Took in each feature of my own, each in its proper place!
He came to me as a son, freely, to forget
His adult pride, relaxing on his mother's breast,
But then severity came back into his face,
He was once more the Emperor, seeking his mother's advice.
Majestic confidence was placed between my careful hands,
Those secrets upon which the nation's fate depends.
No, to his great glory, it has to be confessed,
His heart has not a grain of levelled wickedness.
It is our enemies who malign him, being loth
To admit his loving kindness extended to us both.
But in the end their power, in turn, is on the wane.
Rome will soon welcome Agrippina once again:
Already it hails the rumours of my return to favour.
Let us not wait for evening here, but go to Octavia,
And dedicate to her the last hours of a day
Whose outcome is as happy as its outset was grey.
What is that noise? Those cries?

JUNIA:
God! Save Britannicus!

Scene 4

AGRIPPINA:
Burrus, where are you going? Stop there! What is this...?

BURRUS:
It is the end. Britannicus is dying.

AGRIPPINA:

Dying?

BURRUS:
He is already dead.

JUNIA:

Oh, God!

AGRIPPINA:

Where are you going?

JUNIA:

I'll go to him. I must. If there is no relief
To bring him, I'll follow him. Or live in endless grief.

Scene 5

AGRIPPINA:

What has he done now, Burrus?

BURRUS:

I must go, leave here,
for good.

AGRIPPINA:

Did he not even shrink from shedding a brother's blood?

BURRUS:

The plan was subtler than that. The minute Nero saw
His brother enter, he got up, to meet him at the door.
He embraced him. There was silence. Suddenly, at a stroke,
A silver cup appeared in Caesar's hand. He spoke:
"To be assured this day may end under the best
Of auspices, all witness that my hand is the first
To pour the draught into this cup. This libation
Is a solemn earnest of our reconciliation!"
Britannicus then binds himself by a similar pledge.
Narcissus fills the goblet to the very edge.
Britannicus's lips had barely touched the brim...
No sword could more fatally have struck at him.
The light is instantly extinguished from his eyes;
He falls back in his chair; cold, motionless he lies.
Imagine for yourself the effect on all those there.
Half of them ran from the chamber, desperate with fear.

But those who had a better grasp of court affairs
Looked at Caesar's expression, before adjusting theirs
Accordingly. He sits there, on his chair, his gaze intent
Ahead of him, no vestige of astonishment.
"The sickness, which appears to cause you such alarm, is
One he has had from early childhood. It is harmless."
He said. Narcissus tried to affect some grief, although
He could not hide his triumph, for all his pious show.
For me, even should Caesar punish me for pride,
I ran out of the room, through the detested crowd,
Prostrated by the crime. Now I am going home
To mourn for Caesar, for Britannicus, for Rome.

AGRIPPINA:
Here he is. Understand – it was not at my instigation.

Scene 6

NERO:
God!

AGRIPPINA:
Nero! Stop! You owe some explanation.
Britannicus is dead. I know the cause – and who
The murderer is.

NERO:
Pray, who might that be?

AGRIPPINA:
You!

NERO:
Me? You harbour more suspicions than I could ever name.
No evil can occur, but I must take the blame
If I were minded to pay heed to all you say,
It would transpire that my hand put Claudius away.
His son was dear to you – his death may dash your hopes,
But why must I answer for Fate's arbitrary strokes?

AGRIPPINA:
  No, no, Britannicus was poisoned. It was you
  Ordered Narcissus to do what you wanted him to do.

NERO:
  Lady... who has been saying such things to you?

NARCISSUS:
  My lord, do not let suspicion upset you so.
  Britannicus, my lady, nourished a secret plan,
  Which would have caused you far more pardonable pain.
  Your kindness would have become a rod for your own
                                              back:
  Marrying Junia was, for him, a secondary act.
  He was deceiving you. His slighted pride would be
  Intent, at some future date, on reversing history.
  Whether, despite all this, Fate would have been kind
  To you, or whether Caesar had been put in mind
  Of plots against him, he relied on me to do
  What he required. Leave weeping to those enemies, who
  See this event as being the greatest of disasters,
  But you...

AGRIPPINA:
            Nero! Such colleagues are worthy of such masters!
  Go on then! Glorious deeds earn glorious renown;
  You did not take this step in order to back down.
  Your hand has started with the blood of your own brother,
  And I foresee its blows extending to your mother.
  You ache to free yourself from my yoke of obligation.
  In your heart of hearts, I read my condemnation.
  But do not think my death will bring you that release;
  Do not think, when I die, I shall leave you in peace.
  Terror will dog your steps like the Eumenides;
  You will try to placate them with new barbarities.
  Gorged with fresh blood each day to satisfy its need,
  Your blood-lust on itself must soon begin to feed.
  But, finally, your deeds will tire a weary Nemesis,

And she will add your own name to your victims' list,
So that, not glutted with their blood and mine alone,
You'll see yourself at last obliged to shed your own.
And your name will go down to future generations
Of tyrants to come, as the cruellest of condemnations.
There! That is all my heart bequeaths. A prophecy.
Very well, you may go now.

NERO:

Narcissus, come with me.

Scene 7

AGRIPPINA:

Oh, the irony! How unjust I was to be suspicious.
Burrus, I blamed you, listened only to Narcissus.
You must have seen the implacable, furious look that he
Turned on me just now. My son's last farewell to me.
It is the end. Now he will stop at nothing at all.
My death at his hands is foretold – the blow will fall –
On you as well, poor man, unless I'm very wrong.

BURRUS:

Lady, I have already lived a day too long.
I would have been so glad, if, with careless cruelty,
He could have tested this new frenzy, first, on me,
Rather than by this dreadful crime to aggravate
The ills that undermine the structure of the state.
It is not just the crime – I could believe that he
Could have murdered him in a fit of jealousy
But, no, it wasn't that. What led me to despair
Was that he watched him die, and did not turn a hair.
His eyes already have acquired the indifferent glaze
Of tyrants, utterly inured to crime since earliest days.
Let him end it, lady; since I no longer fear him,
An inconvenient servant who can no more endure him,
Far from wishing to see his anger turned aside,
My dearest wish would be the quickest death allowed.

Scene 8

ALBINA:
> Lady, my lord, the Emperor – we must make haste to
> > save him,
> To rescue Caesar from himself. He's frenzied, raving.
> Junia is torn eternally from his side.

BURRUS:
> What, is she dead?

AGRIPPINA:
> > What was it? Suicide?

ALBINA:
> The Emperor is condemned to an unending sorrow.
> She is not dead, she is – where Nero may not follow.
> When she escaped from here, she ran as if to go
> To see Octavia, but then she took a road
> That leads to nowhere. I watched her as she ran, distraught,
> Out of the palace gates. She soon found what she sought,
> The statue of Augustus. Falling down, she wept
> At the marble feet, her arms around him, prayed:" Accept
> My prayers, Prince; by this cold stone that I embrace,
> Protect, both now and henceforth, the last of all your race.
> Rome has just seen the murder of the only one
> Of all of us who worthily could have called himself your
> > son.
>
> They wished me to betray him after he had died.
> But I must keep faith with him. So I here decide
> To dedicate myself to that eternal god,
> Whose altar you now share, your virtue's just reward."
> Meanwhile the people, by the confusion worse confounded,
> Press on her from all sides, until she is surrounded
> By a multitude, that, moved by her tears, and pitying
> Her obvious distress, take her beneath their wing,
> And lead her to the temple, where they still maintain,
> As in ages past, the eternal Vestal flame.

Nero sees all of this, but does not dare to enter:
Narcissus, more intent to please, makes for the centre,
Approaching Junia, fearlessly, with utter lack
Of shame, begins, profanely, to try to force her back –
A blasphemy that falls victim to a hundred blows:
His sacrilegious blood incontinently flows,
Drenching Junia. Nero, barely comprehending
What he is looking at, abandons him to his bloody ending –
And goes back. All avoid him. Silent, grim,
Junia's name the only sound that comes from him.
His walk is aimless, he seems not to dare to raise
His eyes to heaven, with their distraught, unsteady gaze.
When night falls on his loneliness, people begin to fear
That circumstance might sharpen the agony of despair.
If any longer we refuse him our assistance,
His grief is such that he may show death no resistance.
Time presses. Hurry! The slightest anxiety for your son
Could make him kill himself.

AGRIPPINA:

                  And justice would be done.
Burrus, we shall go in. See this fit take its course
And see what changes may be wrought in him by remorse.
Perhaps his conduct may yet alter to fit the times.

BURRUS:
Would that this worst might be the last of all his crimes!

The End.

NEW ESSAYS ON THE EDUCATION OF HENRY ADAMS

The American Novel series provides students of American literature with introductory critical guides to great works of American
literature. Each volume begins with a substantial introduction by
a distinguished authority on the text, giving details of the work's
composition, publication history, and contemporary reception,
as well as a survey of the major critical trends and readings from
first publication to the present. This overview is followed by a
group of new essays, each specially commissioned from a leading
scholar in the field, which together constitute a forum of interpretative methods and prominent contemporary ideas on the
text. There are also helpful guides to further reading. Specifically
designed for undergraduates, the series will be a powerful re-
source for anyone engaged in the critical analysis of major American novels and other important texts. The introduction and four
original scholarly essays in this volume address the established
reputation of *The Education of Henry Adams* as a classic work
of American autobiography and canonical work of American
literature. Examining *The Education* in terms of early twentieth-
century American attitudes toward education, gender, U.S. foreign policy, and historiography, these essays add considerably to
our understanding of *The Education* as an expression of its time,
while helping to explain its continuing importance in ours.

*   The American Novel   *

GENERAL EDITOR
Emory Elliott, University of California, Riverside

Other books in the series:

New Essays on *The Education of Henry Adams*

Edited by

John Carlos Rowe

University of California, Irvine

CAMBRIDGE
UNIVERSITY PRESS

CAMBRIDGE UNIVERSITY PRESS
Cambridge, New York, Melbourne, Madrid, Cape Town, Singapore, São Paulo

Cambridge University Press
The Edinburgh Building, Cambridge CB2 8RU, UK

Published in the United States of America by Cambridge University Press, New York

www.cambridge.org
Information on this title: www.cambridge.org/9780521445511

© Cambridge University Press 1996

First published 1996

A catalogue record for this publication is available from the British Library

Library of Congress Cataloguing in Publication data
New essays on the education of Henry Adams / edited by John Carlos Rowe.
p.   cm. – (The American novel)
Includes bibliographical references (p.   ).
ISBN 0-521-44551-5. – ISBN 0-521-44573-6 (pbk.)
1. Adams, Henry, 1838–1918.   The education of Henry Adams.
2. Adams, Henry, 1838–1918.   3. Historians–United States–
Biography – History and criticism.   I. Rowe, John Carlos.
II. Series.
E175.5.A2N48   1996
973′.07202—dc20   95-21110
CIP

ISBN 978-0-521-44551-1 hardback
ISBN 978-0-521-44573-3 paperback

Transferred to digital printing 2008

Contents

v

Contents

Series Editor's Preface

In literary criticism the last twenty-five years have been particularly fruitful. Since the rise of the New Criticism in the 1950s, which focused attention of critics and readers upon the text itself – apart from history, biography, and society – there has emerged a wide variety of critical methods which have brought to literary works a rich diversity of perspectives: social, historical, political, psychological, economic, ideological, and philosophical. While attention to the text itself, as taught by the New Critics, remains at the core of contemporary interpretation, the widely shared assumption that works of art generate many different kinds of interpretation has opened up possibilities for new readings and new meanings.

Before this critical revolution, many American novels had come to be taken for granted by earlier generations of readers as having an established set of recognized interpretations. There was a sense among many students that the canon was established and that the larger thematic and interpretative issues had been decided. The task of the new reader was to examine the ways in which elements such as structure, style, and imagery contributed to each novel's acknowledged purpose. But recent criticism has brought these old assumptions into question and has thereby generated a wide variety of original, and often quite surprising, interpretations of the classics, as well as of rediscovered novels such as Kate Chopin's *The Awakening*, which has only recently entered the canon of works that scholars and critics study and that teachers assign their students.

The aim of The American Novel Series is to provide students

of American literature and culture with introductory critical guides to American novels now widely read and studied. Each volume is devoted to a single novel and begins with an introduction by the volume editor, a distinguished authority on the text. The introduction presents details of the novel's composition, publication history, and contemporary reception, as well as a survey of the major critical trends and readings from first publication to the present. This overview is followed by four or five original essays, specifically commissioned from senior scholars of established reputation and from outstanding younger critics. Each essay presents a distinct point of view, and together they constitute a forum of interpretative methods and of the best contemporary ideas on each text.

It is our hope that these volumes will convey the vitality of current critical work in American literature, generate new insights and excitement for students of the American novel, and inspire new respect for and new perspectives upon these major literary texts.

Emory Elliott
University of California, Riverside

1

Introduction

JOHN CARLOS ROWE

Think now
History has many cunning passages, contrived corridors
And issues, deceives with whispering ambitions,
Guides us by vanities.
      – T. S. Eliot, "Gerontion" (1919)

I.

THROUGHOUT his adult life, Henry Adams was always writing a book, so it is quite probable that his private publication of *Mont-Saint-Michel and Chartres* in 1905 is one way to date the beginnings of his next book-length project, *The Education of Henry Adams*, privately published in 1907.[1] Of course, the precise "origins" of Adams's *Education* are far more difficult to determine, as they usually are for works of comparable influence and complexity. In his biography of Adams, Ernest Samuels "dates" Adams's first plans for *The Education* in a variety of ways, including "the anniversary of Henry's wedding day in June 1904," with its reminder of his wife, Marian's, suicide in 1885, and Adams's reading of his friend Henry James's *William Wetmore Story and His Friends* (published in 1903), with its evocation of their New England generation and its fatal innocence of what history would bring.[2] As he wrote James on November 18, 1903: "So you have written not Story's life, but your own and mine, – pure autobiography, – the more keen for what is beneath, implied, intelligible only to me, and half a dozen other people still living. . . ."[3]

Adams's mood of reminiscence, sometimes maudlin or excessively self-critical in the years 1903–1905, mixed with yet other, practical concerns Adams felt about putting the historical record in order regarding the significant lives of his powerful friends and relatives. From 1900 on, Adams's close friend and Washington neighbor, John Hay, had been in ill health made worse by the demands of his office as Theodore Roosevelt's Secretary of State. A year and a half before John Hay died in July of 1905, Adams wrote his friend from Paris in a jovial yet prophetic vein: "Please read Harry James's Life of Story! Also Morley's Gladstone! And reflect – wretched man! – that now you have knowingly forced yourself to be biographised! You cannot escape the biographer" (*Letters*, V, 526). Yet, it may well have been to "escape" becoming Hay's biographer that Adams wrote *The Education*, anticipating Hay's death and trying to find an alternative to what he described in that letter as the biographer's tendency to stick "pins" into historical figures, propped in their "cages," in the vain effort for them to "keep the lively attitude of nature" (*Letters*, V, 526).

In the aftermath of Hay's death, Adams would use *The Education* explicitly as his excuse for refusing the task of "biographising" his friend that Hay's widow and Adams's friends insisted he take on. As it turned out, Adams avoided the dreaded task only by agreeing to serve as "a kind of sub-editor" to Mrs. Hay's "artless" project of publishing *Letters of John Hay and Extracts from Diary*, which Ernest Samuels judges "one of the oddest memorials ever printed" (*Major Phase*, 397).[4] Typically ironic as Adams's claim was to have written *The Education* " 'wholly due to piety on account of my father and John Hay (the rest being thrown in for mass),' " it nonetheless has a measure of truth in terms of what scholars have judged the pragmatic reasons for writing an "autobiography" so elusive and ironic (*Major Phase*, 397). Adams's *Education* reveals as it protects, explains as it mystifies, "confesses" as it represses some of the most significant personal and historical records of American modernity.

In the summer of 1905, following Hay's death during the final negotiations of the Portsmouth Treaty (settling the Russo-Japanese War of 1904–1905), Adams was writing at what Samuels speculates "must have been furious speed" (*Major Phase*, 329). When he returned to Washington for the winter that year,

Adams must have had a substantial part of the manuscript completed, because he made "preliminary arrangements for printing it with Furst and Company, the same firm which had done the *Chartres*" (330). Even so, Adams passed another summer in Paris before returning to Washington in November 1906 with the "main part of the *Education*, if not all of it, . . . in proof" (332). This was the very time when Adams was most pressed by Mrs. John Hay to help with her memorial work to her husband, and Adams found and used the excuse of work on the proofs of *The Education*.

Perhaps with the negative example of Mrs. Hay's editing of her husband's letters and diaries in mind, Adams planned to send what he called "proof sheets" of *The Education* "to friends who were mentioned in the text, asking them to let him know if they objected to anything said of them" and requesting that they do so by returning the text "with offending passages stricken out as might be called for" (*Letters*, VI, 39). This was a ruse of sorts, because Furst and Company had printed one hundred beautiful copies unlikely to be "marked" by friends in the manner requested; indeed, only three copies are known to have been returned to Adams. Had he really wanted to elicit candid comments and encourage such collaborative "proofing" from his friends, he might have circulated copies of the printer's proofs he was reading in December 1906. Instead, the elegantly printed "proofs" came complete with a "Preface" dated "February 16, 1907," Adams's sixty-ninth birthday. Samuels explains that Adams could not have written this Preface on his birthday, so that this too was a symbolic touch likely to convince first readers that the text was indeed quite finished (*Major Phase*, 332).

The usual story of *The Education*'s private circulation is that Adams was under almost constant pressure to publish a work declared by President Theodore Roosevelt (who received the "first" formally distributed copy) a "masterpiece," but that Adams insisted on keeping the work exclusively in private circulation until his death. Nine years after he privately printed and distributed it, Adams wrote Senator Henry Cabot Lodge, President of the Massachusetts Historical Society, "requesting that the book be published on behalf of the Society." Accompanying that letter was "a sealed packet containing a corrected copy of the 1907 private printing and an 'Editor's Preface,' which Adams himself composed but to which he affixed in a shaking hand the initials 'H. C. L.,' with the puzzled but indulgent acquiescence of Lodge."[5]

The first public edition was published in 1918 by Houghton Mifflin and Co., with "Lodge's" "Editor's Preface" and Adams's original "Preface," dated February 16, 1907. Insistent that *The Education* be published without the subtitle "An Autobiography," Adams was foiled by posthumous editors, since the 1918 edition carries that subtitle. Ernest and Jayne Samuels would restore the intended title in their scholarly edition of 1973, reminding modern readers that Adams planned to subtitle the work, "a Study of Twentieth-Century Multiplicity," to emphasize its connection with the companion text, *Mont-Saint-Michel and Chartres:* "a Study of Thirteenth-Century Unity," both of which subtitles are mentioned in the "Editor's Preface" to the 1918 edition (*EHA,* xxvii).

Adams had ended his *Chartres* with the long chapter on "St. Thomas Aquinas," which was the part over which Adams had "worried" the most. St. Thomas both explained and thus hastened the transformation of Catholic religious authority in the Latin Middle Ages; what was a cultural "unity" for Adams under the authority of the Virgin Mary (the Cult of Mariolatry) was already multiplied in the rationalism of the Scholastics from Albertus Magnus to St. Thomas. In short, St. Thomas was a figure worthy of "biography" not for the sake of his "personality," but by virtue of the historical transformation his work and life happened to identify and clarify. It has often been thought that Henry Adams is the modern equivalent of St. Thomas, and there is, of course, much to support this view. Adams would have been pleased, indeed, to have been taken for a latter-day St. Thomas, figuring out the "secrets" of modern Science and History with the same enthusiasm and intelligence as St. Thomas had theorized God's ways in the intricacies of scriptural hermeneutics.

The parallelism is both too neat and too exclusive, however, to tell the entire story of *The Education* as proper "companion text" to *Chartres*. St. Thomas is unthinkable without the Virgin, and I think that "Henry Adams," at least as this name figures in

The Education, is unthinkable without John Hay. The medieval Virgin points to the unknowable Godhead of the Catholic Church; the modern Secretary of State points to the equally unfathomable Authority of the nation-state. St. Thomas ushers in modern "multiplicity" in his efforts to rationalize what the Virgin symbolically represents; Henry Adams carries that multiplicity a step further by attempting to "explain" and render "intelligible" the political authority that John Hay came to embody.

In the end, Adams did, then, write the "biography" of Hay that he tried so desperately to avoid, even as he did avoid "biographising" his friend, the statesman. He also wrote his "autobiography," despite his best efforts to keep such indulgence from the "title page" of a book he hoped would represent more than the mere vanity served by the many memoirs published by his powerful contemporaries.

II.

Henry Adams's *Education* has exasperated generations of readers and still maintained its classic status, even though we know today that the "classic" must undergo several transformations by different generations of readers to warrant the title. Books that exasperate and perplex readers often survive because there is some elusive pleasure in the hardship they provoke. Joyce's *Ulysses* and *Finnegans Wake,* Faulkner's *Absalom, Absalom!,* Eliot's *Waste Land* have *vexed* several generations of readers still tantalized by the promise of understanding their secret meanings, whether these be located in the inner workings of the literary mechanism or in some metaphysical message tapped, as it were, between their lines. Even in the Moderns' immediate predecessor and friend to Adams, Henry James, the impatience of the reader is often tolerable in hopes of the unraveling either of a plot or its modern equivalent, a character's intricate psyche, in the course of a story still readable amid the distractions of the difficult, modern style.

Yet, Adams gives the reader little such satisfaction in *The Education,* even as he forces us to endure in condensed form the tormenting bafflement before the modern age that he himself experiences throughout the sixty-seven years of admittedly failed education. *The Education* is not "difficult" to read in the same sense that the great modernist literary works are, even if it is justifiably celebrated for its stylistic originality. The "difficulty" of *The Education* is not so much the complexity of Adams's style, philosophy, or even his own life (complex as that surely was, given his ancestry); it is first and foremost the difficulty of *history*, especially as we understand this history in terms of the great powers – England, France, Germany, Spain, and increasingly the United States – working out our dismal inheritance for the rest of the twentieth century. It is history that baffles and torments us in *The Education*, not Adams's rhetorical flights or his philosophical speculations.

The great literary moderns I mentioned above all attempted to compete with history, often even claiming to *replace* history with some sort of literary or aesthetic genealogy. Adams never claims to compete with history in *The Education*, even though I think there are subtle ways in which he does participate in the redesign of history from an American vantage, as I argue in my contribution to this collection of essays. Yet, the reader's impression is still carefully constructed by Adams to be that of the autobiographical figure, "Henry Adams," as always subjected to historical forces both more powerful and complex than any he can muster as mere intellectual. The baffling multitude of historical characters, significant events, and political currents has generally been the first obstacle to the reader's involvement in this narrative. Ernest and Jayne Samuels's wonderfully annotated edition of *The Education* was not published until 1973; it still amazes me that readers helped turn a book of such difficult historical references into a classic in the several reading generations separating its private publication in 1907 and scholarly publication in 1973. Yet, in the sixty-six intervening years, the *Education* continued to exert significant influence on intellectuals, literati, and political leaders, as Brook Thomas points out in his contribution to this volume.

It is by now conventional to explain the success of *The Education* as a consequence of Henry Adams's distinguished legacy – great-grandson of John Adams, grandson of John Quincy Adams, son of Charles Francis Adams, Free Soil Party vice-presidential candidate in 1848 and Ambassador to Great Britain during the Civil War. Certainly, Adams's autobiography owes its historical complexity and its interest for readers in part to the access it gives us to the Adamses' family power, not only in American but also in emerging global politics from the eighteenth to twentieth centuries. If it is the promise of the "inside story" of the first American "ruling" family – our "first royalty," as the Adamses were sometimes called – that attracts us to *The Education*, then it is one repeatedly broken by a narrator who insists upon the family's steady loss of power and confirms it by virtually erasing from the narrative any traces of real, flesh and blood "Adamses," including "Henry Adams" himself.

Ernest Samuels suggests in his biography that one of Adams's motivations for writing *The Education* grew out of discussions Henry had with his brothers, Charles Francis, Jr., and Brooks, concerning "the disposition of the family papers" (*Major Phase*, 316). Samuels reasonably concludes that such decisions put Henry into a "retrospective mood," especially since he was concerned at this time (1903–1904) with deciding the "relative success of the leaders of his generation" (Samuels, 316). Yet, the three brothers decided to restrict access to their father's papers for the next half century, and *The Education* seems more to contribute to that privacy of the family's interests and secrets than to the public judgment of the Adamses' *achievements* that Samuels argues might have been one of Adams's aims in writing *The Education*.

Adams opens his Preface by quoting Rousseau's *Confessions*, both to draw on a great autobiographical pretext and to distinguish his own work from such romantic expressivism. When it comes to revelations about the Adams family, Henry is just as circumspect as he is with regard to confessing any of his "least agreeable details." The other autobiographical classic invoked in Adams's Preface is Benjamin Franklin's *Autobiography*, decidedly less "revealing" and more mythically "controlled" than Rousseau's *Confessions*, and it is the former that informs Adams's own attitude toward the representation of his ancestors in his own autobiography. The "inside story" of the Adamses is no more

7

given in *The Education* than Franklin tells us the "truth" of his early days as a printer's apprentice in Philadelphia. Rousseau confesses to libidinous passions, masturbation, petty theft, childishness; the Adamses confess to failing to bring a treaty around, loss of a national political contest, "failure" to be as meretricious as the new age demanded.

The inside story of the Adamses is by no means what *The Education* gives us, and it doesn't even promise the sniff of scandal to lure us further into the labyrinth of modern history so relentlessly reconstructed by Adams, complete with dates and names. What compels us to read this book without the customary pleasures of story, identification, secret meanings (literary, personal, historical) must be our imaginary projection of the "Henry Adams" of *The Education* as the special "product" of this history between 1838 and 1905 that we can begin to call "the American," especially insofar as just this history marks the beginning of the "American Epoch." For the person of Henry Adams – short, thin, sardonic, ironic, Socratic, slyly supercilious – the normal reader would have to prefer Gore Vidal's generous portrait of Henry Adams in *Empire,* the third novel in Vidal's historical series. To be sure, previous generations of readers did not have *Empire* available, as they did not have more recent accounts of the problems with alcoholism and insanity in the Adams family, but these "inside" accounts are not at all what readers have wanted – and would have necessarily found elsewhere, had Adams not written it – in *The Education.* Readers have wanted the "American Self."

Insofar as the "Henry Adams" that combines both historical fact and imaginative projection appeals to several generations of readers, "he" satisfies such readers by offering them a character for that abstraction, the American Self. Even without the help of historical commentary, without literary plot, or the titillations of "inside knowledge," the reader still finds "Adams" acting out various expectations of what from 1918 to 1973 belong identifiably with that mythology and ideology. The four essays in this collection all address at various points just what was once meant by this American Self and how Adams's *Education* belongs to its cultural tradition. I shall try here, then, only to sketch a few of its most recognizable features before turning to the interesting problem facing today's reader, who may well be fully conscious that such an American Self no longer governs so singularly our experiences of the many cultures and literatures shaping the multicultural United States.

Shortly after Ernest and Jayne Samuels's scholarly edition of *The Education* was published in 1973, Sacvan Bercovitch published two important books, *The Puritan Origins of the American Self* (1975) and *The American Jeremiad* (1978).[6] As most readers recognize, they are complementary works that theorize and then interpret the ways Puritan immigrants and their heirs transformed the religious jeremiad from "an immemorial mode of lament over the corrupt ways of the world" into the fundamental genre in cultural symbology that interrelated political and moral, social and religious concerns.[7] At the heart of the American Jeremiad is the concatenation of cultural criticism and utopianism in the sheer exhortative voice of the great Puritan Divines from the Mathers to Jonathan Edwards. It was this powerful voice, full as it must have been of the contradictory pulls of conscience and higher consciousness, present corruption and future redemption, that informs the American Individualism so convincingly constructed by those secular Divines, the American Transcendentalists, especially Emerson, Thoreau, and Whitman.

The voice of the jeremiad depends crucially upon its power and authority, originally derived quite self-evidently from the Church and later by the Transcendentalists more problematically drawn, sometimes even teased from Nature, History, or the "visionary company" of artists. Yet, there is another sense in which the jeremiad depends crucially upon the *vulnerability* of its speaker – the "frailty" that the Puritan Divine could claim as part of his mortality and his dependence on God's grace. For the romantic heirs of this tradition, it was a certain "negative capability," a refusal to "know" the true and the good, even as the latter shaped indispensably the rage against social corruptions at the center of the jeremiad. A crucial, central bewilderment, like that of the child or the noble innocent faced with evil (Melville's Billy

Budd, for example), is necessary for the speaker and then author of this American Jeremiad to achieve a certain mythic identity as a "Self."

This "American Self" is a decided revision of the traditionally "self-reliant American" we also identify with many of the authors I have mentioned from Cotton Mather to Henry Adams in the so-called "Puritan Origins of American Culture" that dominated American Studies from Perry Miller to Sacvan Bercovitch. "Self-reliance" is qualified in this account with a certain "self-doubt" and even "self-criticism" urging what Bercovitch considers the necessary cultural "revolution" that will carry democracy into its next epoch. If Bercovitch is right that this "American Jeremiad" is at the heart of cultural and thus literary expression in America, then he has also explained quite effectively why Adams's *Education,* despite its demonstrable "unliterary" qualities, remains a crucial text in American literature and culture.

At the end of *The American Jeremiad,* Bercovitch includes Adams's *Education* among American literary works traditionally associated with the mid-nineteenth-century American cultural unity to which F. O. Matthiessen gave a name in his 1941 study, *American Renaissance.* Bercovitch dubs *The Education* an "anti-jeremiad," respecting Adams's apocalyptic modern tone and mood, but Bercovitch certainly considers *The Education* a kind of capstone to the cultural tradition he has interpreted so well in these two important books: "The distinctive quality of the *Education* is that it reverses all the effects of the jeremiad while retaining intact the jeremiad's figural-symbolic outlook. Adams is not a Victorian sage calling halt to a rampant industrial capitalism. He is a prophet reading the fate of humanity, and the universe at large, in the tragic course of American history." Even so, Bercovitch argues, the old utopianism survives even in this anti-jeremiad: "It is true that he never allows the reader to lose sight of the old faith, and that his condemnation of the dynamo, accordingly, gains much of its substance from the counterforce of the national symbol. America is represented, for example, in the figure of his grandfather, the remote, majestic incarnation of 'moral principle' . . ." (195).[8] At the end of *The Education,* Secretary of State John Hay, Adams's lifelong friend, will take the place of John Adams as the great-grandson's modern "incarnation of moral principle," but neither typifies adequately the "American Self" I have described by way of Bercovitch's American Jeremiad. Both the second President and the most recent (and successful) Secretary of State are far too authoritative, too full of "moral principle," to satisfy what the cultural rhetoric of the jeremiad requires to be uttered and then heard (or read).

Henry Adams "himself" is that somewhat less "majestic" but for all that more compelling "character," who has typified for so many readers that American Self. He is capable of claiming an authentic descent from power – political, moral, cultural, even economic; indeed, never has there been a family as powerful and influential in these areas in U.S. history as the Adams family. Yet, Henry Adams is also capable of claiming powerlessness, marginalization, even victimization by the forces of history and, often enough, the corruptions or abuses of that history, despite its democratic aims. It is that uncanny combination of powerful agency and a sense of disempowerment that has often prompted the very best of our American Jeremiads from Cotton Mather's *Magnalia Christi Americana* to Dr. Martin Luther King's "I Have a Dream," from Emerson's "Emancipation in the British West Indies" to Toni Morrison's *Beloved*, from Thoreau's "Civil Disobedience" to the American Indian Movement's resistance at Wounded Knee.

Already in *The Education*, Adams suspects that the particular "manikin" on which he has contrived to drape the clothing of the American Self is no longer adequate to the demands of complex individualism represented by the different cultures and interests hinted in my preceding list of literary and cultural consequences. In the second chapter of *The Education*, "Boston (1848–1854)," Adams reflects on how little has changed between 1776 and 1848, at least if you were an Adams: "Between him and his patriot grandfather at the same age, the conditions had changed little. The year 1848 was like enough to the year 1776 to make a fair parallel. The parallel, as concerned bias of education, was complete when, a few months after the death of John Quincy Adams, a convention of antislavery delegates met at Buffalo to organize a new party and named candidates for the general election in November: for President, Martin Van Buren; for Vice-President, Charles Francis Adams" (*EHA*, 25). But what the rest of *The Education* records is how very much will change between 1848 and 1905, in large part the consequence of the eventual success of that work of Abolition to which those unsuccessful Free Soilers had contributed in 1848. Indeed, the New England white liberal in the postbellum era could no longer "represent" the American Self as Emerson and John Quincy Adams had done in the antebellum period.

In the third chapter, "Washington (1850–1854)," the adolescent Adams can identify with the African-American's suffering under slavery: "Slavery struck him in the face; it was a nightmare; a horror; a crime; the sum of all wickedness! Contact made it only more repulsive. He wanted to escape, like the negroes, to free soil. Slave States were dirty, unkempt, poverty-stricken, ignorant, vicious!" (*EHA*, 44). So eager is the young Adams to identify with African-Americans that he rhetorically casts himself among "the negro babies and their mothers with bandanas," even as he inadvertently reproduces ethnocentric clichés about African-American "indolence" by sentimentalizing "the freedom, openness, swagger, of nature and man" with which he wishes to identify (*EHA*, 45).[9]

Throughout *The Education*, Adams struggles to "represent" either culturally or politically the "interests" of other Americans, either different by virtue of class, gender, race, or region. This is the "civic virtue" of the eighteenth-century, representative man from whom Adams is philosophically as well as genetically descended. But it is no longer a possibility in the emerging multicultural society of postbellum America, especially as America began to play an ever more powerful role in global politics as the nineteenth century wore toward the modern age. Just as *The Education* represents the capstone of a great tradition from Mather to Adams and Henry James of the "idea" of an American Self – at once complex and yet singular, a model to which different Americans might adapt and aspire, *The Education* also marks the end of that "representative" status either for the American thinker or literatus as well as for his ideas or works.

For in the end, Henry Adams fails to represent the African-

American either under or beyond slavery, just as he fails to represent "Woman" either under patriarchy or prior to its domination, just as he fails to represent the "interests" of the Cuban or Philippine insurgents in the Spanish-American War of 1898. These are the sorts of "failures" that Adams himself does not anticipate by way of his strategic rhetoric of failure, and for that reason they are the places to begin to read *The Education of Henry Adams* in the aftermath of the nation-building that the American Self served so well in early modern U.S. history. In that aftermath, we can understand better the breakdown of the "representative man" as the "type" of the "eighteenth century" values Adams mockingly but also quite seriously mourns in their passing throughout this work. But we can also begin to understand what other kinds of "representation" might be possible in the gaps left by the unsuccessful efforts of the American Self to be all things to all peoples within a diverse, vital, and always changing democracy.

III.

The essays collected in this volume can be introduced by way of just this effort to rethink the boundary separating *The Education* from its role in culminating the cultural and literary tradition of the American Self to its anticipation of the necessary divergences of cultural and literary representations in twentieth-century America. In sum, each of the following essays explores a different organizing principle of *The Education* in relation to the common concern with the changing paradigm of the "American Identity." Brook Thomas focuses on the changing ideal of "classical education" as it is worked out both in *The Education* and educational philosophies with which it is often associated. Martha Banta addresses changing cultural ideas of gender as they intersect with Adams's familiar sympathies with "feminine" consciousness and even his anticipations of twentieth-century performativity in the personal and social constructions of gendered identity. I deal with the emergence of the United States as a global power in the period Adams wrote *The Education* and his friend, John Hay, achieved international prominence as the architect of U.S. foreign policies. Howard Horwitz links the enterprises of modern "education" and history in *The Education* by interpreting the "manikin" in Adams's narrative as the figure of a new, modern subjectivity capable of "apprehending" new historical forces and thereby "saving" the Enlightenment project of historical progress.

In "The Education of an American Classic: The Survival of Failure," Brook Thomas offers contemporary readers a fascinating account of how *The Education* anticipates and informs twentieth-century changes in modern conceptions of the "literary classics." In so doing, Thomas explains why *The Education* has been so durable throughout the many such changes of this contentious century, even as he acknowledges the great difficulties imposed on the reader by *The Education*. Written as the old eighteenth-century ideal of "classical education" was dying out in the United States, *The Education* offers its own modern version of the rigorous training in classical languages and rhetoric that once identified the "education" of a "gentleman." Showing how *The Education* complements the aims of another contemporary "educational" project, Charles W. Eliot's fifty-volume *Harvard Classics*, the famous "five-foot shelf of books," which was begun in 1909, Thomas argues convincingly that one of the purposes served by both cultural works was the redefinition of "liberal knowledge." As Thomas points out, the different "topics" by which Eliot organized the *Harvard Classics* – History, Religion, Philosophy, Education, Science, Politics, Voyages and Travels, Criticism of Literature and the Fine Arts – are just the disciplines treated centrally in Adams's *Education,* celebrated by so many for its interdisciplinary qualities.

Following this transformation of the "classical education" from its neoclassical model to its modernization in the liberal arts' curriculum we have inherited, Thomas tracks the divergence of conservative and liberal political aims as he subtly elaborates "new" and "modern" theories of the "literary classic" to support such educational values. T. S. Eliot, Ezra Pound, Frank Kermode, and Hayden White offer aspects of a more traditional conception of the "modern classic" as that which will put us back in touch with enduring values obscured by the poor "translations" or sheer ignorance and forgetfulness of impatient moderns. To be sure, Adams's world-weariness, his fin-de-siècle temper, and his aloof irony all suggest something of this sort of tradition-bound theory of the "classic" *Education* (and education).

Even as he explains how and why *The Education* continued to influence and be referred to by these conservative moderns, Thomas wants to show its more liberal, even potentially *radical*, qualities as provoking the redefinition of "liberal education" and its "canonical" (or "classical") works. Unlike Charles Eliot's *Harvard Classics* or T. S. Eliot's *The Waste Land*, Henry Adams's *Education* points to the monuments of the past in terms of their historically significant *failure*. They are, of course, all "failures" – from the cultural to the political monuments, insofar as they have been respectively incapable of anticipating entirely the "history" they all attempted to interpret. This is the meaning of the "classic" for Thomas's Henry Adams: the struggle to move into the future, even as that gesture is bound to *situate* this effort in a particular time and place. It is this "future-oriented" quality in Adams's *Education* and thus its acceptance of its inevitable "failure" that is *liberating* and thus liberal, in ways that the nostalgia for the past in T. S. Eliot and Ezra Pound is decidedly not.

What Thomas inadvertently touches upon in this regard is just that divided quality of the American Self I adapted earlier from Bercovitch's sense of the speaker of the jeremiad – the figure full of righteous indignation derived from the authority of God or Truth, but qualified by his own sense of historical limitation, of a mortal proclivity for just what that speaker condemns in the present. This utopian dimension to the American Self takes a decidedly modern cast in Martha Banta's "Being a 'Begonia' in a Man's World," in which Adams's ambivalent attitudes toward conventional nineteenth-century gender roles are interpreted in the larger context of Anglo-American culture's struggles to restabilize the rapidly changing boundary between masculine and feminine at the end of the century.

Against the backdrop of the scandal of the Trial of Oscar Wilde and the recent English laws demonizing "homosexuality," *The Education* challenges its contemporary readers with a protagonist (or subject of education) apparently as unsuited to the "work" of a "man's world" as the characters in Wilde's own *Picture of Dorian Gray*. Like the James children, who were expected to "do nothing," but simply "to be," so the heirs of John Adams and John Quincy Adams and Charles Francis Adams, Sr., could indulge the cultural "work" their more famous ancestors admired as delightful luxuries. Banta shows how Adams's anxieties about what he "did" or, more commonly, did *not do* are shot through with the sort of feminization of his own identity that in other places he identifies in the sexist rhetoric of his times as characteristic of "female" inferiority.

Adams's much-celebrated "studies" of historically important women from the "archaic women-as-progenitors of the Family" in his Address to the Lowell Institute in 1876, "The Primitive Rights of Women," to his celebration of the medieval Virgin in *Mont-Saint-Michel and Chartres* and the "New Woman" of his own time are interpreted by Banta as primarily "opportunities" for Adams to appropriate the "feminine" in decidedly patriarchal ways. In this way, Adams defends against his own sense of inadequacy regarding the questionable "work" of Harvard Professors of History, dilettante writers, and "brilliant" conversationalists in the "salons" of power, such as Washington, D.C., in his own time. In the end, however, "woman" is both universalized and essentialized as surely as other "primitive peoples" are in Adams's writings; both such subjects of political and imaginary colonial projects are infantilized, exoticized, and thus subordinated to the masculine need to "improve" their conditions and "enlighten" their ways.

In *The Education*, however, there appears to be a difference in Adams's handling of his wife, Marian "Clover" Hooper's suicide in 1885. Of the inside stories kept decisively private to the point of downright secrecy, the omission of her suicide from Adams's own *Education* is read as tellingly significant in Banta's reassessment of Adams's relation to changing ideas of gender. Banta describes a "feminine sublimation" in the "charged gap between Chapters 20 and 21," where Clover's suicide belongs temporally, "by not-writing, not happening." In this significant textual moment, Banta argues that "the man who was already half-female prior to his wife's death is transformed into something very similar to her full being through his 'feminine sublimation' of her loss."

Nevertheless, the work of such textual facilitation is by no means the "feminization" of Adams's *Education*. If the "woman question" undoes Adams in his life and his *Education* in ways uncommon for most powerful men in patriarchal America in the early 1900s, then he is still divided between what he *fails* to understand in Clover's suicide and what he *insists* on interpreting and sublimating in his countless figures of "feminine power," grandest of which is the "Virgin" in Chapter 25, "The Dynamo and the Virgin (1900)." For Banta, Adams's contradictions regarding gender roles, both in his identification with both genders and his interpretation of specifically gendered subjects are more interesting for what they tell us of what happens to the American Self in the early modern period. No longer capable of containing "its" contradictions, that "Self" certainly splits and thus requires what Banta announces as the "need" for a "new universal history." Quoting Gerda Lerner in 1977, she answers Henry Adams's call in 1907 for an equally new "dynamic theory of history" by insisting on writing part of this "new universal history," which must be a "synthesis of traditional history and women's history."

The American Self that seeks to renew itself in response to social and historical failings often becomes an Imperial Self, which finds novelty in expansion and authority in the promise of Civilization. This is the demonic other of Bercovitch's myth that has a specific part to play in most of the cultural work of early modern America. I argue in "Henry Adams's *Education* in the Age of Imperialism" that Adams and Hay represent two "aspects" of a new and complex figure of the American Imperial Self as the United States began to assume leadership of global politics in the twentieth century. Avowedly an anti-imperialist among his contemporaries and in the specificity of such terms as "imperialist" and "anti-imperialist" in the 1890s, Adams often distanced himself from his friend, John Hay, especially as the latter became ever more associated with the "Atlantic System" of global domination. Whatever resistance Hay had given to President McKinley's "inadvertent imperialism," as it was sometimes called, Hay served under President Theodore Roosevelt in a manner decidedly neoimperialist. From his deft manipulation of the news to his skillful settlement of conflicts between other nations that resulted inevitably in an increase of U.S. power, Hay developed a foreign policy predicated on the control of "markets" and thus dependent on "spheres of influence" and trade and communication routes, rather than the command of physical territory, native labor, and natural resources.

The conventional scholarly wisdom is that Adams watched sadly as his more powerful friend was drawn into the clutches of the relentless American political machine. The aged Secretary to President Lincoln becomes, in this scenario, the puppet of a modern America outrunning its best eighteenth-century and democratic origins. But there is another story coded in *The Education*, one that seems confirmed by Adams's own composition of that work as an obligation both to his family's and his friend, Hay's, judgment by future generations. I argue that the philosophical and scientific speculations, the literary self-doubts and relativisms of *The Education* have as at least one purpose the mystification and disguise of his otherwise reasonably consistent commitment in these years to the neoimperialist foreign policies endorsed by John Hay.

If Adams's correspondence in the years leading from the Spanish-American War (1898) to the conclusion of the Russo-Japanese War (1905) is credible evidence of his personal convictions, Adams differed from Hay in details only. On the question of whether America should or should not seize the opportunity offered to it to become a world power, they both agreed that America should seize the day. The reasons to do so all seem to turn less on political pragmatism, the realpolitik necessitated by the new global instabilities occasioned by the realignments of the great imperial systems (including the breakdown of several, such as Spain's and England's), and more on the inherent superiority of those "Americans" that Hay and Adams recognized in their ancestors and, of course, in themselves.

In my account, this has something of the quality of a secret message coded in *The Education*, suggested more by what is not addressed centrally – the Spanish-American War and the Philippine revolution against the United States in the aftermath of that war – in a work otherwise filled with historical details requiring the precise annotations of scholars to remain readable today. This way of treating absences in *The Education*, somewhat like Banta's treatment of the silence regarding Clover Adams's suicide, may tend to exaggerate its own little drama and make too much out of its elusive evidence, but there it is a method of interpretation that, at the risk of cultural paranoia, nonetheless yields some surprising and provocative reflections about the literary purposes of *The Education*. Along with the purpose to disguise from public view the manipulation of the nation's foreign policies, there is also the construction of the American Self as increasingly a Corporate Self, composed as it is here of both "Henry Adams" and "John Hay," as well as an Imperial Self.

This problematic new version of the American Self, much in need of criticism and transformation, if not thorough deconstruction, is what Howard Horwitz addresses in the final essay of this collection, "*The Education* and the Salvation of History." Were Horwitz to focus his primary attention on the techniques of *The Education* in Adams's retheorization of history as a post-Enlightenment project, then we might conclude that Horwitz is really writing about saving historiography. But Horwitz is less interested in the mechanics and techniques of how to write modern history than he is with the rhetorical modes by which Adams places his "manikin" in a subject-position at once distinct from and yet uncannily resembling the bourgeois subject and its emancipatory narrative.

Jean-François Lyotard has argued that the "postmodern condition" begins with the recognition that the "grand narratives" of Enlightenment and emancipation are no longer possible.[10] Just where this leaves us in regard to the organization of events into something recognizable as history remains a still urgent problem. Horwitz shows how Adams writes a predominantly *literary* work – a fictional autobiography – that generates its own model of a subject-position capable of being educated by the new dynamic of forces characteristic of the new, complex, global politics. In effect, Adams ends up devising a kind of "fictional ego" – the "manikin" of education – capable of adapting to the acceleration and thus multiplication of different historical forces and, presumably, cultural influences. A sort of pluralistic self, appropriate to William James's conception of a "pluralistic" and thus "unfinished" universe, anticipates postmodern performative "subjects," not entirely dissimilar from those we discuss today in texts far more overtly complex and theoretically "sophisticated" than we find in *The Education* of 1907.

What Adams has saved by translating and transforming, then, is some idea of progress in a history that is no longer identical with the Enlightenment or emancipation of the History that stretches from the later Renaissance to the end of the nineteenth century, but it is nonetheless a history that Adams can still image as apprehensible to the modern subject-position as developing, evolving, *progressing,* even if all of these terms will have to be redefined along with the consciousness that has invented them. In Horwitz's argument, *The Education* has endured as a classic precisely because this "American Self," expanded now to become the "bourgeois self" of Western progressive history, has adapted, just as industrial capitalism made the "leap" from domestic production to international markets in the period of Adams's own lifetime.

Collections of essays on classic works often conclude by claiming that the very diversity of scholarly judgment testifies once again the enduring value of those works. The essays in this volume do not build a monument to an unquestioned classic; instead, they question the meaning of this "classic" status. In so doing, they may well allow *The Education of Henry Adams* to become readable for this generation of students. For it will take more than just annotations of historical events, persons, titles, and places for us to continue to "understand" the mind of Henry Adams that is expressed so extraordinarily in his *Education.* Something else is needed today, something that will mark the boundary dividing his conception of the American Self from the many different identities, cultures, and peoples that today are essential for a new American Jeremiad.

NOTES

1 Privately printed by the Washington, D.C., firm of Furst and Company in 1905, *Mont-Saint-Michel and Chartres* was published for the American Institute of Architects by Houghton Mifflin and Co. in 1913, during Adams's lifetime. *The Education*, also printed privately by Furst and Company, as described later in this introduction, was published for the Massachusetts Historical Society by Houghton Mifflin and Co. in 1918, with an "Editor's Preface" written by Henry Adams but signed by "H. C. L." (Senator Henry Cabot Lodge).

2 Ernest Samuels, *Henry Adams: The Major Phase* (Cambridge, Mass.: Harvard University Press, 1964), p. 318. Further references in the text as *Major Phase*.

3 *The Letters of Henry Adams*, eds. J. C. Levenson, Ernest Samuels, Charles Vandersee, and Viola Hopkins Winner, 6 vols. (Cambridge, Mass.: Harvard University Press, 1982 and 1988), vol. V (1899–1905), p. 524. Further references to this collection of Adams's *Letters* in the text as *Letters*, V, 524.

4 To solve the problem of her husband's private correspondence giving possible offence to the many public figures mentioned in his letters and diaries, Mrs. Hay adopted the simple but disastrous solution of reducing "all proper names to an initial and a dash and, by doing so, made the volumes almost unreadable" (*Letters, VI, 40*).

5 Henry Adams, *The Education of Henry Adams*, eds. Ernest Samuels and Jayne N. Samuels (Boston: Houghton Mifflin, 1973), p. xxi. Further references to the *Education of Henry Adams* are to this text, unless otherwise indicated, and are included in the text as: *EHA*.

6 Sacvan Bercovitch, *The Puritan Origins of the American Self* (New Haven, Conn.: Yale University Press, 1975) and *The American Jeremiad* (Madison: University of Wisconsin Press, 1978).

7 Bercovitch, *The Rites of Assent: Transformations in the Symbolic Construction of America* (New York: Routledge, 1993), p. 79.

8 *The American Jeremiad*, p. 195.

9 There is a rhetorical hint of a fantasy of miscegenation in this passage that I do not think has been previously commented upon. Recognizing in the African-American's "want of barriers, of pavements, of forms" as something "most boys" would be drawn to, Adams goes on to comment that it was an atmosphere that especially "soothed his Johnson blood." Referring in this way to his grandmother's line of descent, which he earlier had characterized

21

by "her vague effect of not belonging" to Boston "but to Washington or to Europe," Adams then portrays his grandmother as a constant foreigner, from the moment of her birth in London to the American merchant, Joshua Johnson, and Catherine Nuth, "of an English family in London" (*EHA*, 16). Early years of cultural and national displacement must have caused "her sense of nationality" to "have been confused," thus again explaining her possible rhetorical affiliation with the spirit of these African-Americans in Washington. It is an identification that is so rhetorically complex and deft as to make the actual "bond" tenuous indeed by the time we are finished identifying it, but Adams clearly wishes to find in his own "blood" something of that variance from Puritan coldness and rigor that he sentimentally projects onto the African-Americans of Washington, D.C., in the antebellum period.

10 Jean-François Lyotard, *The Postmodern Condition,* trans. Geoff Bennington and Brian Massumi, vol. 10, Theory and History of Literature (Minneapolis: University of Minnesota Press, 1984), p. 31.

2

The Education of an American Classic: The Survival of Failure

BROOK THOMAS

AIMED to "encourage participants to think for themselves about questions of enduring human significance," the Great Books Foundation includes *The Education of Henry Adams* in its fifth series of reading and discussion.[1] This honor would have surprised one of the most successful editors of a collection of "great books" in the United States, Harvard President Charles W. Eliot. The fifty volumes of Eliot's *The Harvard Classics* began publication in 1909. Two years earlier, Adams had privately circulated *The Education* to a highly select circle, including Eliot, Theodore Roosevelt, and Henry and William James. Eliot's response, Adams confided to Roosevelt, was the one he feared above all others. "Eliot's sentence will be damnation forever." Eliot did not even provide a sentence of blame. He returned his copy without a word. Later he was reported to comment, "An overrated man and a much overrated book."[2]

Eliot's response, however, has not consigned *The Education* to literary hell, even though Adams himself often seems to share his judgment by continually calling attention to the book's failure. Comparing his effort to St. Augustine's and Rousseau's, Adams wrote to Barrett Wendell, "I feel certain that their faults, as literary artists, are worse than mine. We have all three undertaken to do what cannot be successfully done – mix narrative and didactic purpose and style. The harm of the effort is not in winning the game but in playing it. We all enjoy the failure" (E 514). Critics have so enjoyed Adams's failure that, like the Great Books Foundation, they have turned it into an American classic. I want to explore reasons for the success of Adams's rhetoric of failure by linking the production of *The Education* to pedagogical concerns that led to the production of *The Harvard Classics* and examining *The Education* in terms of discussions of a classic by Frank Kermode, Hayden White, Eliot's distant cousin, T. S., and Ezra Pound. I will end with some speculative comments on what the didactic role that *The Education*'s implied sense of a classic has for us today as we heatedly debate the educational value of the classics.

* * * * *

Both *The Education of Henry Adams* and *The Harvard Classics* were shaped by the failure of a traditional classical education that Adams experienced while a student at Harvard and that President Eliot attempted to reform. But whereas for Eliot his collection of classics signaled a successful remedy to the shortcomings of a traditional education, for Adams *The Education* admits to no successful replacement for an admitted failure. Thus, the two imply different roles for the classics in twentieth-century education. Unlike *The Harvard Classics*, which claims to have successfully adjusted the traditional classical education to the twentieth century by an act of historical translation, *The Education* becomes a classic of failure by insisting on the failure of the classics.

The classical education that Henry Adams received at Harvard College from 1854 to 1858 fit the needs of eighteenth-century notions of republican virtue. Republicanism depended on a classical education to ensure virtue in government. Classically trained leaders were relied on to guarantee disinterested government. Appropriately, the early years of the republic saw a self-conscious evocation of the republican tradition of Greece and Rome in architecture, symbology, and political institutions. Most important was the stress placed on developing skills in public oratory and rhetoric through exposure to the classics. Such skills were necessary, it was felt, for the political health of the republic.

The Adams family was directly involved in republicanism's classicism. John Adams appealed to Roman history to argue that the proper virtue necessary for government developed in a few aristocratical families. No doubt he had his own family in mind. John Quincy Adams seems to have proved him right. The product of a classical education, he was appointed Boylston Professor of Rhetoric and Oratory at Harvard in 1806 and in 1810 published *Lectures on Rhetoric and Oratory,* which are indebted to Isocrates. Nonetheless, as Howard Mumford Jones notes, his presidential administration (1825–1829) "probably closed the era in which the classical past was a dynamic force in American public life" (NW 265). The "Age of Jackson" brought a very different mode of governance to American politics. Born in 1838, Henry Adams lived in a world in which various fields of force influenced politics, but, as far as he could see, a classical past was not the dominant one. His formal education, however, was not all that different in kind from his greatgrandfather's.

For John Adams a study of the classics gave the insight into human nature necessary for someone who hoped to govern both efficiently and virtuously. He marvels, "Has there ever been a nation who understood the human heart better than the Romans, or made a better use of the passion for consideration, congratulation, and distinction?" (NW 261). In contrast, Henry writes of Harvard, "Beyond two or three Greek plays, the student got nothing from the ancient languages" (E 60). Reserving praise for a course on "the Glacial Period and Palaeonthology," he concludes, "The entire work of four years could have been easily put into the work of any four months in after life" (E 60). Harvard's eighteenth-century education was simply inadequate for someone who would live in the twentieth century.

Adams was not alone in his complaints. Charles Eliot shared them and set out to do something. As Adams notes, "The fault he had found with Harvard College as an undergraduate must have been more or less just, for the college was making a great effort to meet these self-criticisms, and had elected President Eliot in 1869 to carry out its reforms" (E 300). Eliot's reforms, like *The Education,* were in part a response to the failure of a traditional classical education. Most important was the introduction of the elective system, which undermined the prescribed classical curriculum by allowing students to choose from various required courses. By 1887, after previously dropping required Latin and Greek for the freshman year, the faculty was convinced to drop the Greek entrance requirement. Summing up these reforms, the historian Samuel Eliot Morison (Harvard, Class of 1908) laments, "It is a hard saying, but Mr. Eliot, more than any other man, is responsible for the greatest educational crime of the century against American youth – depriving him of his classical heritage."[3]

Eliot would not have agreed. On the contrary, a year after Morison graduated, Eliot oversaw the publication of *The Harvard Classics,* which hoped to give *any* American access to the classical heritage so dear to Morison's heart. This publishing venture resulted from Eliot's public boast that "a five-foot shelf would hold books enough to give in the course of years a good substitute for a liberal education in youth to anyone who would read them with devotion, even if he could spare but fifteen minutes a day for reading" (HC 8). The publishing firm P. F. Collier & Son called Eliot's bluff, and the fifty-volume collection known as "Dr. Eliot's Five-Foot Shelf of Books" was born.

The Classics should be seen as related to Eliot's educational reforms. The traditional classical education might have failed to meet the needs of students, but to replace it with an elective system risked depriving them of a center to their education, what Morison calls a student's classical heritage. *The Harvard Classics* are Eliot's proof that this center has not been lost, even if Eliot's reforms seemed to undermine the need for a prescribed set of books to read.

The major argument against a curriculum that does not prescribe a set content of study is that it places so much faith in training the mind how to think that it deprives it of any content with which to think. Eliot is quite aware that his reforms stressed the training of ways of thinking. His goal was to develop a "liberal frame of mind or way of thinking" (HC 3). He does not, however, believe that proper education can proceed without content. In fact, *The Harvard Classics* is proof that he believes that acquaintance with a particular body of knowledge is crucial for the acquisition of the proper way of thinking. Thus, whereas Eliot was a leader in liberal reforms that stressed training a mind how to think rather than the content of its thought, his reforms assumed a specific relationship to a specific body of knowledge.

Because *The Classics* were not required in the Harvard curriculum, they may seem to be a mere supplement to the Harvard education, a substitute for those not able to attend that prestigious institution. But in fact Eliot's reforms rested on his belief in the existence of the tradition that he incarnated in *The Classics*. Eliot's reforms were possible only because the "discoveries, experiences, and reflections" (HC 3) of the classical tradition made possible the liberal way of thinking that his reforms promoted. Thus, on the one hand, *The Harvard Classics* was necessitated by Eliot's reforms to fill the gap created by the demise of a classical curriculum. On the other, the reforms were made possible by the prior existence of a classical tradition that *The Classics* merely record. This sense of the classical tradition leading to the present helps to explain why Eliot can be satisfied with classical texts that appear in translation rather than in their original language.

Eliot's use of translations would seem to be merely the logical consequence of his desire to give *The Classics* wide circulation. The aim of the collection made it "essential that the whole series should be in the English language" (HC 3). Recognizing that classical scholars would fault him for that decision, he admits that perfect translations are impossible, but adds, "translations can yield much genuine cultivation to the student who attends to the substance of the author's thought" (HC 4). Eliot, like the traditionalists, insists that the defining element of a classic is its substance, but he disagrees with them on our ability to translate that substance.

Traditional republicans located the height of classical virtue in the past. The present could return to that moment of virtue only by experiencing its cultural monuments directly. Only in the original language could someone experience the substance of classical thought. In contrast, Eliot's belief in progressive evolution implies the translatability of the classics' essential substance. Teleologically directed, what is crucial about our classical heritage records humanity's "intermittent and irregular progress from barbarism to civilization" (HC 3). What is not crucial is that which resists translation into the present. Thus, unlike other collections, *The Harvard Classics* does not try "to select the hundred or fifty best books in the world" (HC 3). Instead, its purpose is "to present so ample and characteristic a record of the stream of the world's thought that the observant reader's mind shall be enriched, refined, and fertilized by it" (HC 3). For Eliot knowledge of the *direction* that our classical heritage has taken is even more important than detailed knowledge of its content.

Given Eliot's teleology, his faith in translation makes perfect sense. For him our classical tradition has been created by a perpetual transmission of its substance from one generation to the next. Whereas for traditional republicans each generation needs to possess the classical heritage anew, Eliot's evolutionary model implies that the present, civilized generation is the product of the classical tradition's last translation through time.

For traditionalists, students needed to *acquire* the classical tradition by reading the classics in the original. For Eliot, such an acquisition is not necessary. Instead, "The best *acquisition* of a cultivated man is a liberal frame of mind or way of thinking" (HC 3, my emphasis). Nonetheless, *The Classics* aid the possession of this way of thinking, for "there must be added to that possession *acquaintance* with the prodigious store of recorded discoveries, experiences, and reflections which humanity in its intermittent and irregular progress from barbarism to civilization has *acquired* and laid up" (HC 3, my emphasis). Born into a civilization that has itself acquired the classical tradition, American students inherit it as their birthright. As products of the tradition that a liberal education acquaints them with, students don't even need special training to understand its substance. All that is necessary is that the tradition be made readily available to them and that they have the motivation to read it.

Thus Eliot proposes a self-help program of education. He selects works that "any intellectually ambitious American family might use to advantage, even if their early opportunities of education had been scanty" (HC 3). Possessing the qualities of a liberal mind *in potentia* because they have inherited the classical tradition, those willing to take the effort to acquaint themselves with that tradition will find their minds "enriched, refined, and fertilized by it" (HC 3), a process that in turn will give birth to a higher stage of civilization for the next generation.

Compared to the traditional view of education, Eliot's sounds extremely democratic. Rather than limit a successful education to the few who can possess the classical tradition through mastery of the classical languages, Eliot seems to make possession of a liberal state of mind available to everyone. But, in fact, his model turns out to be potentially exclusive. Members of cultures who are "outcasts from evolution,"[4] those who do not belong to that strain of humanity that has acquired the prodigious store of information recorded in *The Classics*, are not necessarily capable of acquiring the liberal frame of mind that Eliot prizes. Furthermore, whereas people hoping to acquire it need only an acquaintance with the classical tradition, the choice of the works that form the basis of a liberal education is not arbitrary.

Eliot has selected works that an American family might use to "advantage." Works that fall outside the stream of civilized thought are, by implication, less advantageous. Thus, the enrichment, refinement, and fertilization that Eliot's program promises most likely results when a particular group of students comes in contact with a particular body of knowledge. There is no guarantee that a liberal state of mind will result when people from the wrong culture acquaint themselves with works that he has selected or when people from "higher" cultures acquaint themselves with the wrong works. In this respect, the classical vision of the eighteenth century turns out to have a democratic potential that Eliot closes off. For traditionalists, possession of the classical tradition was limited, but it was available to anyone who could acquire it. By turning its possession into a matter of inheritance rather than acquisition, Eliot grants it to all members of a particular culture while excluding it from members of others.

Eliot's optimistic faith that he had found a democratic solution to the failure of traditional classical education is in obvious tension with the pessimism of Adams's *Education*. That tension manifested itself long before the appearance of either *The Harvard Classics* or *The Education*. One of Eliot's first moves toward reform after being elected president was to hire Adams to teach history at Harvard, an experience that Adams recalls in a chapter appropriately entitled "Failure (1871)." "In spite of President Eliot's reforms and his steady, generous, liberal support," Adams writes, "the system remained costly, clumsy and futile" (E 304). It is

29

unlikely that Adams would have regarded *The Harvard Classics* as a successful solution to the problems that he experienced while teaching. But before turning to differences between *The Classics* and *The Education*, I should point out important similarities.

The most obvious is their comprehensiveness. In his "Reader's Guide"· Eliot groups the content of the fifty volumes according to various topics: History, Religion and Philosophy, Education, Science, Politics, Voyages and Travels, Criticism of Literature and the Fine Arts. Each is treated in *The Education*. Especially important is the position that Eliot grants to "Education," a reminder that *The Classics*, like *The Education*, had a didactic purpose. Furthermore, like Adams, Eliot felt that stories of people's lives help fulfill his educational purposes. The first volume of *The Classics* includes, "The Autobiography of Benjamin Franklin," "The Journal of John Woolman," and "The Fruits of Solitude" by William Penn. Eliot also includes models that Adams mentions for his work, such as St. Augustine and Rousseau.

In turning to individual lives to combine narrative and didactic purpose both Adams and Eliot reveal their links to the eighteenth-century tradition of republican virtue that they end up rejecting.[5] Adams pleads that historians need to study mechanics and statistics, but he still presents history as the playing field of a few great men. The two visions are not necessarily incompatible. Just as some argue that literary classics are the best registers of the complexity of an age, so the figures that Adams treats become nodal points, an economic way of bringing together the lines of force constituting a particular historical moment. Similarly, Eliot uses the lives of great men to mark nodal points in the forward movement of civilization. But at this point their similarities end.

In the late nineteenth century people from Eliot's and Adams's circle, known as Mugwumps, provided a link between the republican tradition of the eighteenth century and the progressive movement of the early twentieth century. In an age of laissez-faire individualism, Mugwumps clung to the republicans' effort to subordinate individual interests to those of the community while stressing the value of self-sufficient individualism as the only basis for a healthy body politic. They also maintained the republicans' stress on education as the shaper of virtuous citizens. Nonetheless, they recognized that educational reform was needed to meet the needs of a changed society.

Eliot is a crucial figure in this movement because he felt that he found a way successfully to translate the founders' republican vision into the present. In contrast, Adams insists upon the failure of any such translation of republican ideals into the twentieth century. Part of the reason that *The Education* has been granted classical status is that the twentieth century has seemed to bear him out, especially his challenge to Eliot's faith in progressive evolution.

To be sure, early in his life Adams flirted with theories of evolution, especially those of Sir Charles Lyell, the British author of *Principles of Geology*. According to Lyell, history was an unbroken evolution taking place under uniform conditions. Because he insisted that human beings did not have a unique origin but evolved out of other species, Lyell was attacked by religious thinkers. In 1867 Lyell commissioned Adams to write an essay to ensure the proper reception of this "geological champion of Darwin" (E 225) in the United States. Adams's review was favorable, but he inserted a qualifying sentence: "The introduction [by Louis Agassiz] of this new geological agent seemed at first sight inconsistent with Sir Charles's argument, obliging him to allow that causes had in fact existed on the earth capable of producing more violent geological changes than would be possible in our own day" (E 227). Disrupting the flow of his essay, this sentence is crucial for an understanding of Adams's attacks on the evolutionary model in *The Education*.

Agassiz was the one professor who captured Adams's imagination while he was at Harvard. Challenging Lyell, Agassiz argued that evolution occurred in response to violent or catastrophic conditions, conditions that could only be explained by some outside force, which he attributed to the hand of God. Agassiz also denied that one species could evolve into another. "Species do not pass insensibly one into another, but . . . appear and disappear unexpectedly, without direct relation to their precursors" (quoted in C 95). Theologians supported Agassiz because he offered a model that reconciled religious thought with geological

31

knowledge. Adams, in contrast, saw in him a challenge to evolutionary thought that had become "the very best substitute for religion; a safe, conservative, practical, thoroughly Common-Law deity" (E 225).

Adams expresses his doubts about progressive evolution through the *Pteraspis*. A cousin to the sturgeon fish, *Pteraspis* was the first vertebrate known to man. For Lyell, *Pteraspis* illustrated his theory of uniformity over time. But not for Adams. If from the beginning of geological time, a species has existed virtually unchanged, how, he wondered, can we speak of evolution? How can evolution cope with something "older than evolution itself" (E 230)? The continuity of *Pteraspis* would seem to rule out the possibility of evolutionary continuity. Movement does not necessarily occur uniformly from one species to an evolutionary higher one or, to extend the analogy, from one era to the next. For Adams Agassiz's insistence on the uniqueness of types can account for *Pteraspis* while Lyell's evolutionary model cannot. *Pteraspis* has survived without fitting into the evolutionary current. As Adams insists, it seems "to have survived every moral improvement of society" (E 352). As far as the classics are concerned, *Pteraspis* is important because it resists the translatability that is essential to Charles Eliot's belief that they record civilized progress. That resistance is crucial for an understanding of how Adams's stress on failure distinguishes him from various twentieth-century defenders of the classics. We can start with Charles's distant cousin T. S. Eliot.

* * * * *

T. S., who experienced Charles's reforms firsthand while a student at Harvard, has, like Adams, gained fame for his challenge to evolutionary progress. For instance, *The Waste Land* would seem to undermine Charles Eliot's belief that the "stream of the world's thought" should persuade us of the "upward tendency of the human race" (HC 3). In Eliot's poem the stream has been disrupted, leaving a desertlike sense of fragmentation. Not surprisingly, therefore, the poet's notion of the classics is at odds with the university president's. Nonetheless, T. S. does agree with Charles that classics are not necessarily the greatest works. In "What is a Classic?" (1944) he argues that classical status depends upon a work's relation to history. But whereas for Charles a classic's value depends upon its ability to be translated into an evolutionary stream of thought leading to the present, for T. S. the supreme classic is *The Aeneid* because of its relation to Rome. Aeneas

is the symbol of Rome; and, as Aeneas is to Rome, so is ancient Rome to Europe. Thus Virgil acquires the centrality of the unique classic, he is at the centre of European civilization, in a position which no other poet can share or usurp. The Roman Empire and the Latin language were not any empire and any language, but an empire and a language with a unique destiny in relation to ourselves; and the poet in whom that Empire and that language came to consciousness and expression is a poet of unique destiny. (WC 128–9)

The unique position of Rome causes Eliot to restore Latin and Greek to an importance that Charles's move to the elective system threatened to destroy. "No modern language," he insists, "could aspire to the universality of Latin" (WC 130). And, thus, "No modern language can hope to produce a classic, in the sense in which I have called Virgil a classic" (WC 130). For T. S., unlike Charles, the classical standard set by Virgil is not translatable. But even if it is impossible to reach again, the health of Western civilization depends upon maintaining it. "It is sufficient that this standard should have been established once and for all; the task does not have to be done again. But the maintenance of the standard is the price of our freedom, the defence of freedom against chaos" (WC 130). Like eighteenth-century republicans, Eliot does not see civilization progressing from the past to the present, but locates a moment of classical virtue in the past, a moment whose significance lies in its power to serve as a model for the achievements of the present. Even so, his vision of civilization betrays surprising similarities with that of his cousin.

The Waste Land may challenge evolutionary narratives, but T. S. hasn't completely abandoned a belief in the flow of the main currents of Western civilization. Just as Charles claims that his classics chart the essential "stream of the world's thought"

33

(HC 3), so T. S. argues that "The blood-stream of European literature is Latin and Greek" (WC 130). *The Aeneid* takes on special status because it is through Virgil's poem that the Greek tradition flows into Latin so as to create, not "two systems of circulation, but one" (WC 130). Thus, whereas the younger Eliot did not share the elder's faith in progress, he still held on to a notion of a unified "mind of Europe." For instance, T. S.'s citation of Mallarmé in *The Four Quartets* implying that the poet's role is "To purify the dialect of the tribe"[6] takes on added resonance when juxtaposed to Charles's belief that his selection of poetry from Homer to Tennyson will provide a "vivid conception of the permanent, elemental sentiments and passions of mankind, and of the gradually developed ethical means of purifying those sentiments and controlling those passions" (HC 7). Furthermore, if *The Waste Land* is dominated by images of sterility, there remains an implied hope that an engagement with it, like an engagement with the classical tradition represented in Charles's collection, will lead to enrichment, refinement, and fertilization. It wouldn't be too much of an exaggeration to claim that one way of transforming *The Waste Land*'s fragments into a unified whole would be to fill in its gaps with knowledge gained from *The Classics*.

Of course the same might be said of *The Education*. Through allusion and citation, Eliot's *Classics* could be said to become a part of *The Education*, which is another way of saying that one of the best ways to understand *The Education* would be to establish an acquaintance with the knowledge amassed in Eliot's volumes. Nonetheless, Adams's relationship to the classical tradition is different from T. S. Eliot's. Whereas *The Waste Land* implies that it can be fertilized by a reader immersed in the stream of thought charted by the classics, *The Education* suggests that someone immersed in that stream will remain adrift, aimlessly floating or risking shipwreck, like Adams who "found himself launched on waters where he had never meant to sail, and floating along a stream which carried him far from his port" (E 203). *The Waste Land* holds open the promise that its fragments can be made whole by a consciousness that would bring the classical tradition within its textual field. But to bring the same context within the text of *The Education* is not to transform its rhetoric of failure into one of success. This is because that rhetoric is in part generated by a failure of the very tradition that forms its context.

Adams, like Eliot, describes the contemporary existence of that heritage as a field of waste. "History, like everything else, might be a field of scraps, like the refuse about a Staffordshire iron-furnace" (E 221). Adams, also like Eliot, posits a moment of unity in the past. Unlike Eliot, however, Adams does not feel that by establishing the proper relation to the classical past his wasteland imagery had the power of renewal. Nonetheless, he does draw our attention to the present existence of the scraps of history which, like *Pteraspis,* survive. The sheer weight of those survivals helps to explain why *The Education* resists a semiotic model of the classics put forth in different ways by Frank Kermode and Hayden White.

* * * * *

Kermode draws on T. S. Eliot to argue that the traditional notion of a classic depended upon a combined sense of typicality and exemplum. The exemplary force of a classic's typicality depended on its ability to represent a world whose interpreting system was not human-made but a "record of either God's deeds or of his prophecies" (C 98). To read a classic was to have access to the signature God had stamped upon nature or history. The substance of a text could remain exemplary over time because God's signature was unchanging. Such a view of the world received a severe challenge with the discovery of the "new world" in the Renaissance, a discovery that threatened to make change rather than stability a constant. The Enlightenment with its elaborate systems of classification was able to meet the challenge. But the discoveries of nineteenth-century geology made it virtually impossible to accept a world in which, "the types could be regarded as divine inscriptions, as part of a mystery both stable and divinely systematic" (C 98).

Charles Eliot responded to that challenge by adopting the evolutionary model and insisting that the classics are that body of texts that translates the spirit of civilization forward in time.

35

In contrast, Kermode turns to Agassiz and his revision of Lyell's evolutionary model to describe what he calls a "modern" version of the classic. According to Kermode, Agassiz offers a model that allows the classic to preserve typicality while accommodating to change. Agassiz's stress on the uniqueness of various species asserts the persistence of types. Types lose their status as examples, however, because they too are subject to substantive change, even complete disappearance. For Agassiz, in other words, typicality becomes a formal rather than substantive concept. The world may no longer be stable. The substance of a type may change over time, but formal types still guide the direction of change, change which is no longer channeled into one homogenous stream.

For Kermode, the author whose works most closely correspond to Agassiz's model is Hawthorne, an author familiar with Agassiz's thought. Hawthorne's works remain typical because of their form, not their substance. As a result, his works resist conclusive interpretations that appeal to substance for their validity. According to Kermode, Hawthorne's modern classics

cannot be, as the Bible had been, and Virgil too, a repository of certain unchanging truths. . . . This is why one cannot even try to read Hawthorne . . . as one is still urged to read Virgil. To say that the meaning of *The Scarlet Letter*, or of *The House of Seven Gables*, is the meaning Hawthorne meant, is pointless; his texts, with all their varying, fading voices, their controlled lapses into possible inauthenticity, are meant as invitations to co-production on the part of the reader. (C 113)

As Kermode's occasional references to Roland Barthes indicate, his description of a "modern classic" is indebted to semiotics. Indeed, it is very close to the semiotic model advocated by Hayden White. Like Kermode, White stresses a classic's formal rather than its substantive typicality. Such typicality allows an act of translation from the text's moment of production to its moment of reception. Rather than reveal a set meaning, a classic "reveals, indeed actively draws attention to, its own processes of meaning production and makes of those processes its own subject matter, its own 'context' " (CF 211). For White *The Education* is a perfect example. Turning into a strength the flaws that critics

36

have noted in Adams's efforts to unify various discourses, White argues that these "flaws" become "for the semiologically oriented commentator its very virtue as a 'document' of intellectual history. . . . It is precisely its 'flaws' that point us to what makes *The Education* a classic work, an example of self-conscious and self-celebrating creativity, poiesis" (CF 212).

White turns to semiotics to transform Adams's rhetoric of failure into a celebratory act of poeisis, but it seems to me that Adams's own insistence on his failures points to the inadequacy of White's model to account for the strange power of *The Education*. After all, as Adams makes clear, *The Education* does not so much call attention to the possibilities of meaning production as to its failure to produce a meaning. To be sure, given White's premises, that failure is an illusion. Adams may insist that he has failed to "mix narrative and didactic purpose and style" (E 514), but White implies that narrative inevitably moralizes.[7] What White neglects, however, are those *Pteraspis*-like elements of the text that resist our efforts to moralize, those elements that resist White's and Kermode's transformation of content into form.

To stress the untranslatability of such a content is not to deny the importance of form. As Adams insists, "The pen works for itself, and acts like a hand, modelling the plastic material over and over again to the form that suits it best. The form is never arbitrary, but is a sort of growth like crystallization, as any artist knows too well; for often the pencil or pen runs into side-paths and shapelessness, and loses its relations, stops or is bogged. Then it has to return on its trail, and recover, if it can, its lines of force" (E 389). The form is crucial, but, as Adams reminds us, his effort perfectly to merge form and content ends a failure. Those *Pteraspis*-like bits of content that resist his imposed lines of force play havoc with White's celebratory reading of *The Education*. In doing so they raise questions about how it and, perhaps, other classics are taught.

Traditional classical education stressed the content of the classics because they offered timeless monuments to emulate. Charles Eliot reformed classical education by stressing the development of a "liberal frame of mind or way of thinking" (HC 3) over the teaching of content. By using *The Education* to offer a

37

model of the classics in which their survivability comes from their transformation of content into form, White takes Eliot's reform one step further. He does so by offering a more complete apology for the classics than either Eliot or content-oriented educators. Many content-oriented critics insist on *The Education*'s greatness, but still admit its flaws. Eliot (who would not have considered *The Education* a classic), like White, defends a translation model, but admits that some elements of *his* classics are not translatable into the forward march of civilization. In contrast, White claims to offer a model that can "give an account of every element" (CF 196) of *The Education*. It is a classic because its formal typicality "makes it translatable as evidence of [a past age] that a reader in our age can comprehend" (CF 213).

White clearly has a different experience teaching *The Education* than I do. Rather than translating its every element into the present, most undergraduates are frustrated by the shear weight of its historical detail that resists their efforts at comprehension. That resistance helps to explain James N. Cox's lament that "*The Education of Henry Adams* remains a neglected book in American literature."[8] To be sure, a teacher can adopt the Eliotlike solution of admitting that it contains certain untranslatable elements and stressing instead those passages that students can "relate" to. But to do so is to ignore the challenge that Adams's rhetoric of failure poses to our sometimes complacent goals of liberal education. Charles Eliot saw that challenge clearly and linked it to Adams's elitist tendencies. As he wrote Grace Norton, "I should like to be saved from loss of faith in democracy as I grow old and foolish. I should be very sorry to wind up as the three Adamses did. I shall not unless I lose my mind" (HA 359).

The Education's resistance to liberal models raises the possibility that it fits an elitist, undemocratic model of the classics. That possibility is heightened by a link between Adams's sense of education and that of a famous poet who was diagnosed as losing his mind as a result of losing faith in democracy – Ezra Pound. Pound was fascinated by a story George Santayana told him in 1940. Visiting Adams late in his life, Santayana was confronted with, "So you are trying to teach philosophy at Harvard. . . . I once tried to teach history there, but it can't be done. It isn't really possible to teach anything." Pound passed this story on to T. S. Eliot, who passed it on to the English publisher Faber, who suggested a book by Santayana, Pound, and Eliot, to "save further generations from the horrors of past education." The aim of the volume, according to Pound, was to imagine the "Ideal University, or the Proper Curriculum, or how it would be possible to educate and/or (mostly or) civilize the university Stewddent and . . . how to kill off bureaucratism and professorality" (HA 452). The volume never appeared, but the plan for it indicates how easily Adams's rhetoric of failure lends itself to appropriation by the conservative tradition constructed by Pound. But a crucial difference exists between Pound's notion of a classic and that implied by *The Education.* To see what it is we need to turn to *The Education*'s image of Rome, the city within the Western tradition that has come to be the measure of a classic.

* * * * *

Adams's great grandfather evoked Rome as a standard of virtue for the new republic. Charles Eliot, following the *topos* of the Western course of empire, saw the United States fulfilling the promise of earlier civilizations such as Rome. A translation of the classics for him was not a falling away from an original fullness but a way of advancing the spirit of civilization forward in time. Confronting the disillusionment occasioned by the twentieth century, his distant cousin returns to Rome as a measure of present failings. For T. S., Rome embodied an impossible-to-achieve unity whose fullness evokes a standard to guard the modern world from anarchistic chaos. Seeming to share John Adams's vision, T. S. adopts an even more conservative position. Adams turned to republican Rome and virtue; T. S. to imperial Rome and order.

Like his grandfather and T. S. Eliot, Henry Adams grants Rome special status. "Rome was a bewildering complex of ideas, experiments, ambitions, energies; without her, the Western world was pointless and fragmentary; she gave heart and unity to it all" (E 93). So in Rome even Adams seems to locate a vision of unity. But his Rome is neither republican nor imperial, but medieval.

Adams's fascination with the Middle Ages is well known. Its label implies an era of transition, but its mystery for Adams is its *Pteraspis*-like resistance to evolutionary schemes. "The man who should solve the riddle of the Middle Ages and bring them into the line of evolution from past to present, would be a greater man than Lamarck or Linnaeus; but history had nowhere broken down so pitiably, or avowed itself so hopelessly bankrupt, as there. Since Gibbon, the spectacle was almost a scandal. History had lost even the sense of shame. For all serious purposes, it was less instructive than Walter Scott and Alexander Dumas" (E 301). The Middle Ages resist evolutionary schemes for Adams because there is no clear line of progress from them to the present. To make this point critics usually turn to *The Education's* companion piece, *Mont-Saint-Michel and Chartres: A Study of Thirteenth-Century Unity,* or to his description of the symbolic power of the Virgin in *The Education's* most famous chapter. I, however, want to stick with the image of Rome in *The Education,* because it best reveals Adams's model for the classics.

For Adams Rome, like the Middle Ages, defies evolution. "Rome could not be fitted into an orderly, middle-class, Bostonian, systematic scheme of evolution. No law of progress applied to it" (E 91). The reason why is revealed in Adams's description of his first trip to Rome made after failed efforts to receive education at Harvard and in Berlin.

The month of May, 1860, was divine. No doubt other young men, and occasionally young women, have passed the month of May in Rome since then, and conceive that the charm continues to exist. Possibly it does – in them – but in 1860 the lights and shadows were still medieval, and medieval Rome was alive; the shadows breathed and glowed, full of soft forms felt by the lost senses. No sandblast of science had yet skinned off the epidermis of history, thought, and feeling. The pictures were uncleaned, the churches unrestored, the ruins unexcavated. Medieval Rome was sorcery. (E 89–90)

This passage is one of the most lyrical in *The Education.* For Adams much of Rome's seductive power resulted from its mystery. "The mystery remained unsolved; the charm remained intact. Two great experiments of Western civilization had left there the chief monuments of their failure, and nothing proved that the city might not survive to express the failure of a third" (E 91). The link between Rome's mystery, its charm, and its monuments of failure deserves close attention.

The Rome that Adams visited was seductive because it was "actual" (E 91). Ironically, the actuality of its monuments was threatened by the sandblasts of science that tried to restore them. Rather than give them new life, these efforts at restoration consigned them to a museum past in which they were deprived of the very "epidermis of history, thought, and feeling" needed to keep them actual. It is the actuality of Rome's monuments of failure that accounts for its *Pteraspis*-like ability to resist evolutionary schemas, for like *Pteraspis* they are survivors from another age. They are, in other words, the best model we have for the sense of the classic implied by *The Education*.

The life that Rome's ancient monuments continued to breathe for Adams in 1860 reminds us of how close *The Education*'s implied sense of a classic is to that of Pound, who marveled at a classic's "eternal and irrepressible freshness" (ABC 14). The similarity between Adams and Pound is not surprising, given their common admiration of Agassiz. Indeed, Pound's most famous book on the nature of a classic begins with a lesson on how to read from Agassiz. As Robert Scholes has pointed out, Pound's attraction to Agassiz has a dark side, for it might help to explain his racism.[9] After all, Agassiz's theory of race and the persistence of types served to legitimate racist thought in nineteenth-century America. Very likely, part of Pound's attraction to Adams had to do with the Bostonian's own racism.[10] But as deplorable as these racist attitudes are and as close as the two come on the sense of a classic, differences exist between them.

Whereas both challenge variations of the translation model, they do so for different reasons. Translation is unnecessary for Pound because the classics have the power to speak directly to anyone who has the capacity to listen. To be sure, Pound urged us "To make it new." But that imperative was directed at the

41

production of new works, not the reading of those that offer "news that STAYS news" (ABC 29). Even so, Pound's sense of a direct encounter with a classic depends upon the very stripping away of a work's "epidermis of history, thought, and feeling" that makes an act of translation necessary in the first place. A work so curated demands translation because it is taken out of circulation in the present and forced to exist at an unbridgeable historical distance from us. Pound may insist that a classic has within itself the power to bridge that gap, but in doing so he denies it the epidermis that for Adams keeps monuments of the past alive.

Pound is radically anti-institutional. Because the classics survive in a realm outside the materiality of history, their survival is ensured. "There is one quality which unites all great and perdurable writers, you don't NEED schools and colleges to keep 'em alive. Put them out of the curriculum, lay them in the dust of libraries, and once in every so often a chance reader, unsubsidized and unbribed, will dig them up again, put them in the light again, without asking favors" (ABC 14). Pound saw his task as critic and poet to be such a reader. Possessing the antennae of the race, he granted himself the power to tune in to the mysterious realm inhabited by the classics so as to gather "from the air a live tradition."[11]

In contrast, Adams implies that the sorcery of Rome's monuments is linked to their survival within the materiality and contingency of history, which includes the institutions that keep them alive. Because their survival is linked to the material present, it is always at risk. The monuments that Adams experienced in Rome were alive. But they existed side by side with present buildings, part of a living, breathing city. If their existence within the interconnected network of the present grants them life, it also makes them vulnerable. Those in the present may find no more use for them and raze them to make room for new buildings. Or the present may decide to sandblast them and turn them into museum pieces that require acts of translation to keep them alive for the present. In contrast, Rome's monuments survive because they continue to maintain a function within present fields of force. That function is linked to their failure.

42

Adams's monuments are not the steppingstones on which the past transports itself into the present. Nor are they, as the classics are for Pound, self-contained success stories. To be sure, like *Pteraspis*, they survive because they do not fit into the evolutionary current that destroyed the civilizations that produced them. Nonetheless, they are reminders of failure, not records of success. The significance of that reminder for today's battles over the canon comes into focus if we compare Adams's description of Rome with Raymond Williams's of London.

* * * * *

According to Williams, H. G. Wells, came out of a meeting discussing social and political change, looked at London, and concluded "that this great towering city was a measure of the obstacle, of how much must be moved if there was to be any change." "Looking up at great buildings that are the centers of power," Williams knows this feeling, but, unlike Wells, he does not say, " 'There is your city, your great bourgeois monument, your towering structure of this still precarious civilization,' or I do not only say that; I say also 'This is what men have built, so often magnificently, and is not everything then possible?' "[12] Looking at Rome, Adams shares Williams's wonder, but he does not see Rome's monuments as the "centers of power." This difference may seem to result from Adams's backward glance at Rome and Williams's glance at a possible future. But Adams also looks forward, when he follows his claim that "Rome was actual" with "It was England; and it was going to be America" (E 91). Both Williams and Adams have future-oriented responses. But whereas Williams is concerned with constructing a new center to power, Adams adopts a perspective from which both present and future centers of power can already be seen as the monuments of failure that they will become. For Williams, London's monuments are both barriers to political progress and testaments to humanity's power to overcome such barriers. For Adams, Rome's monuments both undercut any claims that the present may make to superiority over the past and remind us that even the past's magnificence ended in failure.

43

Monuments of failure they may be, but they still generate wonder in Adams. Adams's peculiar capacity for wonder seems lacking in both sides of today's canon debate. On the one hand, those celebrating the classics retain a capacity for wonder, but only by turning what Adams admits to be failures into monuments of success. On the other hand, those attacking the classics have lost the capacity to wonder at what they, along with Adams, insist are monuments of failure. In doing so they risk hastening their own failure by falling prey to the naive belief that somehow a secure foundation on which to build a new world order will be uncovered either by razing the accepted monuments of the past or by nostalgically raising works from oblivion and transforming them into new monuments of success.

In this climate Adams's capacity for wonder might seem to suggest a third position, the liberal one that it is more important *how* we teach students to read than *what* we teach them. After all, as Henry Steele Commager noted as long ago as 1937, the success of Adams's rhetoric of failure results from his willingness "to ask questions which he couldn't answer."[13] This "literary technique" encourages a Socratic mode of inquiry that would seem to generate in *The Education*'s readers the capacity to question its own limitations and failings.

I admit my attraction to this position, but feel compelled to point out the contradiction that it produces, since it is a specific technique and a specific text that helps to generate that critical mode of thought. Indeed, as I have argued, *The Education* itself challenges the liberal emphasis on method at the expense of content. Questions remain unanswered, *The Education* suggests, because of a *Pteraspis*-like materiality that resists efforts formally to translate it into terms that we can understand. Questions do not arise in a vacuum but in response to the pressure of specific material situations. In other words, the questions that we face at a particular time and place in history are not negotiable. The importance of *The Education* is not merely its capacity to raise questions but its challenge to face specific questions that we – like Adams before us – have inherited from the past. In this regard, its comprehensiveness is one of its most important qualities, but not because that comprehensiveness leads to successful comprehension. Instead, precisely the failure of its comprehensiveness to answer the questions that it raises suggests various questions that our generation has inherited from Adams's.

As canonbusters are quick to point out, that failure results in ideological as well as formal flaws, as evidenced by Adams's attitudes on race, class, and gender.[14] We should no more ignore such flaws because *The Education* is a complex work of literary genius than we should ignore the complexity of *The Education* because it produced them. But we should pay attention to *The Education* not because, as White would have it, its flaws allow us to transform *The Education* into an example of "self-conscious and self-celebrating creativity" (CF 212). Instead, we can recognize them as resulting in part from Adams's own failure to keep true to his rhetoric of failure and seeking to posit answers to the riddle that *Pteraspis* poses to him. Indeed, Adams attributes *Pteraspis*-like qualities to both race and sex. Speaking of "race-inertia" (E 441), Adams implies that race resists evolution. Sex does also, even more powerfully.

Of all movements of inertia, maternity and reproduction are the most typical, and women's property of moving in a constant line forever is ultimate, uniting history in its only unbroken and unbreakable sequence. Whatever else stops, the woman must go on reproducing, as she did in the Silura of *Pteraspis;* sex is a vital condition, and race is only a local one. If the laws of inertia are to be sought anywhere with certainty, it is in the feminine mind. (E 441)

Race and sex become for Adams metaphors that promise to answer questions that he cannot account for. While we may object to Adams granting those metaphors a naturalistic base – in the passage just quoted, for instance, creativity becomes a feminine force – the concern that the present generation of critics continues to have with both race and sex suggests the persistence of questions that Adams could not satisfactorily answer. Unless we want to adopt the position that we now possess the truth that can answer those questions, we would be wise to continue to wrestle with his text. And not merely because those who forget the past are condemned to repeat it, but also because, as Adams's image of Rome suggests, there is no foundation on which to build a future other than one that includes an interaction with monuments of past failure. The nature of such interaction is implied by the one moment of success that Adams reports about his education at Harvard.

Though a recognized outsider, Adams was surprised to learn that he was "chosen the representative of his class – the Class Orator" (E 66). Puzzling over why he was chosen to speak for his class, he decides "They saw in him a representative – the kind of representative they wanted – and he saw in them the most formidable array of judges that he could ever meet, like so many mirrors of himself, an infinite reflection of his own shortcomings" (E 67–8). If *The Education* retains the representative status that a classic must possess, it is because it still has the capacity to enter into a relation with its present audience that generates a dynamic mirroring of one another's failings. Of course, if the present chooses, like Charles Eliot, not to respond to *The Education,* such a dynamic interaction will not take place. But that refusal might well be a sign of the present's unwillingness to see a reflection of its own failings. The success of *The Education*'s rhetoric of failure is in part its willingness to do just that.

NOTES

1 "The Great Books Reading and Discussion Program: Fifth Series." The Great Books Foundation was founded in 1947.

2 Ernest Samuels, *Henry Adams: The Major Phase* (Cambridge, Mass.: Belknap Press of Harvard U.P., 1964), p. 334. Designated (HA) in the text. Other works to be cited are: Henry Adams, *The Education of Henry Adams,* ed. Ernest Samuels (Boston: Houghton Mifflin Co., 1973) (E); Charles W. Eliot, "The Editor's Introduction," *The Harvard Classics,* v. 50 (New York: P. F. Collier & Son Co., 1910) (HC); T. S. Eliot, "What Is a Classic?," in *Selected Prose of T. S. Eliot,* ed. Frank Kermode (London: Faber and Faber, 1975) (WC); Howard Mumford Jones, *O Strange New World* (New York: Viking Press, 1964) (NW); Frank Kermode, *The Classic* (New York: The Viking Press, 1975) (C); Ezra Pound, *ABC of Reading* (New York: New Directions, 1934, rpt. 1960) (ABC); and Hayden White, "The Context Is the Text: Method and Ideology in Intellectual History," in

The Content in the Form (Baltimore: The Johns Hopkins U.P., 1987) (CF).

3   Samuel Eliot Morison, *Three Centuries of Harvard: 1636–1936* (Cambridge, Mass.: Harvard U.P., 1936), pp. 389–390.

4   See John S. Haller, Jr., *Outcasts from Evolution* (Urbana: U. of Illinois P., 1977).

5   On the eighteenth century see John Rowe's "Henry Adams," *Columbia Literary History of the United States,* ed. Emory Elliot (New York: Columbia U.P., 1988), pp. 645–667.

6   T. S. Eliot, *Complete Poems and Plays: 1909–1950* (New York: Harcourt, Brace and World, 1952), p. 141.

7   White ends "Narrative in the Representation of Reality" with the question, "Could we ever narrativize without moralizing?" (CF 25), implying that the answer is "No."

8   James N. Cox, "Learning through Ignorance: *The Education of Henry Adams,*" *Sewanee Review* 88 (1980), 198–227.

9   Robert Scholes, *Textual Power* (New Haven: Yale U.P., 1985), pp. 129–148.

10 See Charles Vandersee, "Henry Adams and the Invisible Negro," *South Atlantic Quarterly* 66 (1967), 13–30, and Richard Drinnon, "Outcast of the Islands: Henry Adams," in *Facing West* (New York: New American Library, 1980), pp. 243–254.

11 Ezra Pound, *The Cantos of Ezra Pound* (New York: New Directions, 1969), p. 522.

12 Raymond Williams, *The Country and the City* (New York: Oxford U.P., 1973), pp. 5–6.

13 Henry Steele Commager, "Henry Adams," in *The Marcus W. Jernegan Essays in American Historiography,* ed. William T. Hutchinson (Chicago: U. of Chicago P., 1937), p. 191.

14 Arthur Schlesinger, Jr., calls *The Education,* "the great document of neo-Hamiltonian frustration." *The Vital Center* (Boston: Houghton Mifflin Co., 1949), p. 19. On gender see Martha Banta's essay. On race see n. 10.

3

Being a "Begonia" in a Man's World

MARTHA BANTA

I.

IN 1870 the *North American Review* printed a free-lance piece on
the recent congressional session by Henry Adams. Senator
Timothy Howe, Republican from Wisconsin, shot back a rejoin-
der that judged Adams's worth in regard to a series of career
choices. *Adams as journalist recording the facts:* "He must fail as a
historian." *Adams as literary man:* "The author has a talent for
description and a genius for invention. He might succeed as a
novelist." *Adams as member of the Adams family,* inextricably associated with the vocation of statesmanship:

The author is proclaimed to be not only a statesman himself but to
belong to a family in which statesmanship is preserved by propagation –
something as color in the leaf of the Begonia, perpetuating resemblance
through perpetual change.[1]

Thirty-five years later, in looking back upon 1870 in the chapter from his *Education* entitled "Chaos," Adams refers to that
long-ago reference in order to make his own mocking observations.

The begonia is, or then was, a plant of such senatorial qualities as to
make the simile, in intention, most flattering. Far from charming in its
refinement, the begonia was remarkable for curious and showy foliage;
it was conspicuous; it seemed to have no useful purpose; and it insisted
on standing always in the most prominent positions. Adams would have
greatly liked to be a begonia in Washington, for this was rather his ideal
of the successful statesman. . . .[2]

In this little incident, in which Adams keeps the "begonia"

simile alive by nurturing it in the rich soil of his memory before replanting it within his autobiography, we see Adams taking note, one more time, of the labels by which he was known to others and to himself: labels that identify the individual self in relation to the value accorded to the work one does in the world. Howe's negative response to Adams's ostensible task as reporting journalist simultaneously assesses his status as historian, novelist, and statesman – with the label "statesman" complicated first by Howe's linking of statecraft to familial birthright, and second by the twist Adams gives when implying a contrast between what it once meant to be an Adamsian statesman (quietly useful dedication to principles) and what this term now means to the Washington crowd (conspicuously useless self-aggrandizement).

The Education of Henry Adams is an elaborate sequence of observations concerning the questions, What work am I to do in the world? What place am I to hold? To what use, if any, are my inborn and acquired energies to be put? To ask these things of oneself and one's contemporaries at the edge of modern times is to propose a commitment to what in the past had been a sacred contract. Long centuries ago a man waited for the divine voice to call him to perform a particular task. To hear rightly and to act diligently meant he had found his "vocation." The earthly reward? He knew his place, his worth, and the innermost truth of his being.

Henry David Thoreau had not blushed to press the point of the sacredness of meeting one's calling, but by the time Henry Adams came into his majority the analysis of any "pure" relation between sacred vocation and the world's work had been handed over to academics such as Weber and Tawney who looked at it as an historical phenomenon from times past. The necessity to work continued as part of the human condition, but rarely was work's purpose defined by the Lord God of the Puritans; now it was Karl Marx or the industrialists of the Black Districts of northern England blighted by factory smoke who did the defining. But the absence of a direct call from on high to lead a useful, influential life did not erase anxiety over what one's vocation ought to be.[3]

Henry Adams, a man overwhelmingly concerned with vocation and the success to be made of an elected calling, faced complications almost past enumerating – the consequence of factors introduced prior to any making of those choices. There were the credentials one brought into the world at birth and those acquired in the formative years. They had to do with class (defined both as social and economic entities), race, attributes of body and nerves, nation, region, family, and – very definitely – one's sex.

Whatever importance a male of Adams's generation might or might not give to matters of vocation, he could hardly skirt the matter of the "maleness" adhering to whatever he did or did not accomplish. The basic assumptions that shaped his social being seemed indelibly defined: *male* equates with "influence" (sometimes called "power," often named "force"), the ability to stamp one's presence upon society, upon politics and business (especially in those arenas), and upon the universe; *female* equates with "powerlessness" (except in the peripheral areas of Society, that is, culture). It matters to our understanding of *The Education of Henry Adams*, therefore, whether its author viewed himself as living up to his credentials as a male within the masculine society through which he moved between 1838 and 1905, the year he completed his accounting.

What was there about Adams's credentials that not only determined how well he followed the call toward the right and proper vocation, but also how well he fulfilled his society's expectations of being both an Adams and a male? Would the manikin foregrounded in the Preface – an artifact used to reveal the "fit" between the individual and the universe – measure up to being "a man of the world equipped for any emergency" even though its contemporaries perceived it as merely a shopwindow dummy flaunting a begonia in its buttonhole? (EHA, xxx).

The opening pages of *The Education* delineate the ways in which the child born "in the third house below Mount Vernon Place" on February 16, 1838, was "distinctly branded." *Social class:* aristocrat in a "republican" society, knowing that "Never in his life would he have to explain who he was," although as a Harvard man he was "neither American nor European, nor even wholly Yankee . . ." (EHA, 64, 65). *Economic ranking:* well-off but continually grumbling about lack of income, since the amount of salary an Adams was unable to command reflected adversely upon his "value" in the American economic ethos; yet with no apparent regard for the tribulations of classes beneath his own. *Race:* defiantly Anglo-Saxon; scornful of latecomers, whether "old" immigrants like the Irish "South Enders" whom he and his Latin School chums battled upon Boston Common, or "new" immigrants like the "furtive Yaccob or Ysaac still reeking of the Ghetto, snarling a weird Yiddish to the officers of the customs" (EHA, 238). *Region:* impressed upon by the New England mindset whose inborn nature exerted its demands twice over by tossing him between Quincy and Boston, yet also (as we shall see) affected by being one quarter Maryland born. *Physical and nervous system:* marked at an early age by scarlet fever, a malady that particularly "affected boys seriously"; only five-foot-three in height, his "character and processes of mind" sharing "in this fining-down process of scale," which means he was "not good in a fight, and his nerves were more delicate than boys' nerves ought to be" (EHA, 6). *Family:* the most searing brand of all since, whereas God or society determined the worth of ordinary men, Adams had to concern himself with the approbation of his "fathers."

By the time he is thirteen years of age the boy realizes he "should have been, like his grandfather, a protégé of George Washington, a statesman designed by destiny, with nothing to do but look directly ahead, follow orders, and march" (EHA, 51). Such a career as a loyal soldier does not preclude ambition. Ambition Adams-style means doing one's work well, "not on my own account, but as a family joint-stock affair" (HA, 215). If the son does not take sufficient care, he will be judged as having allowed "mediocrity" to fall "on the name of Adams"; if, for instance, he turns out to be merely a writer, lecturer, "dabbler" (HA, 28).

Adams, alas, was barred from having "nothing to do but look directly ahead." At twenty, he admits that "if I only behave like a gentleman and a man of sense," he could "take a position to a certain degree creditable and influential," yet "my ambition cannot see clearly enough to look further."[4] The imperative to uphold the name of the "fathers" was clear enough; in doubt, exactly what the son must *do* in the father's name.

Part of the uncertainty is caused by the family that is both inspiration and obstacle.[5] Part is the failure of Adams to play the man's role exacted by the fathers that preceded him. Part is the fact that *that* role had been weakened by the inability of the Adamses as a family enterprise to be fully "male" in terms recognized by the prewar and postwar America that lay beyond Boston – once, but no longer, the Hub of the Universe. By the time of Charles Francis Adams, the men of the family had slipped out of the slots accredited by either "old" or "new" Boston. No Adams had an "affinity with the pulpit," or with the "literary group led by Ticknor, Prescott, Longfellow, Motley, O. W. Holmes," or with science and medicine (EHA, 27). Father and son alike "stood alone" and exposed as being out of place (EHA, 28).

Had there not been that unending pressure to uphold the standards of the family (a pressure exacerbated for a son who has no settled notion of what to do with himself), Henry Adams would have preferred – "like every other true Bostonian" of his class – to take up the lifelong avocation of the clubman, to yield to "the ease of the Athenaeum Club in Pall Mall or the Combination Room at Trinity" (EHA, 29). But no, a son of Adams must resist the temptation *not to do*. For him, "nothing but work will do. . . . It breaks one's spirit and crushes one's hope to keep one's eyes fixed on an unattainable standard; but it's the only way for a man who is not a dunce or an ass" (Letters, I:558).

Hovering here is the unspoken assumption that concerns the fate of the male who is in part the female. A man can choose to repudiate the role of the dunce or the ass, but can a woman be anything else? Can it matter that the silly creatures have no vocation, since they never have to fuss over their work in the world – never have to answer to what is exacted of all American males, even those not fathered through the line of the Adamses?

Keep these gender issues in mind. With them we approach *The Education* with a fresh set of questions to ask of its manikin and of the man who lies outside within his letters and the biographical appraisals of others. The point is to see what we find when sizing up the costumes Adams assumed in terms of the male/female "clothes philosophy" ruling his lifetime, as well as the social and philosophical accessories he inherited from the past.

Be assured, the following interrogation does not take as its modus operandi the wish to "reclaim" Henry Adams as a closet feminist. Upon the surface, and penetrating well into the second cutaneous layer of his social consciousness, Adams's credentials as a male chauvinist are impeccable. But in reading (and "reading") Adams, it is necessary to note the *tones* of Adams's utterances (mocking, teasing, sarcastic, self-deprecatory, arrogant, playful, cutting, melancholy, ebullient). The possible meanings of his remarks are so varied, ambiguous, and ambivalent that it is unwise to flat-out declare his final stance on any issue, much less what he thinks women are "essentially" like.

Adams's letter of March 1872 to his friend Charles Milnes Gaskell announcing his engagement to Marian ("Clover") Hooper that declares that his fiancee is "open to instruction" and "*we* shall improve her" could (grudgingly) be taken as being harmless enough (Letters, II:133). The extended remarks he makes shortly thereafter to Gaskell in regard to the general nature of women's thought processes is, however, blatantly sexist, as is the linked implication that inferior minds are incapable of doing important work.

In fact it *is* rather droll to examine women's minds. They are a queer mixture of odds and ends, poorly mastered and utterly unconnected. But to a man they are perhaps all the more attractive on that account. My young female has a very active and quick mind and has run over many things, but she really knows nothing well. . . . (Letters, II:137)

True, Adams is having a good time amusing himself in describing a woman who, "certainly not beautiful," has an "intelligence and sympathy, which are what hold me" – the kind of woman he had described years earlier as meeting his deepest needs: "a good, masculine female, to make me work" (Letters, I: 501). True, he reports that Clover is participating in the sport by instructing Adams to tell Gaskell "that she would add a few lines to this letter, but unfortunately she is unable to spell." But even if we skip, with averted eyes, past letters he sent from Berlin as a callow youth of twenty years, which conclude that "all women are fools and playthings until proved the contrary" (HA, 30), Adams's letters to Gaskell throughout the 1870s – when he is old enough to know better – continue to make snide distinctions between the superior qualities of the male mind (that which contributes work) and the inferior mental capacities of the female (that which is restricted to leisure activities).

Women's strong suit is "sympathy, not science." It is "worse than useless for women to study philosophy" (Letters, II:107). Adams assails "Our men" who "Cram themselves with second-hand facts and theories till they bust," thereby creating "a new set of simple-minded, honest, harmless intellectual prigs as like to themselves as two dried peas in a bladder" (Letters, II:235), but his release of venom upon men who misuse their intelligence is a different matter from suggesting women could do no better if they tried.

A bit of foreshadowing, however. In contrast to these letters of the 1870s, Adams's later assessments of the workings of the "female" mind will alter. He will not change his position in regard to what that species of thought is like; he will alter his position on its contributions. This comes about once he realizes that even science – that most masculine of thought processes – admits the male way is inadequate to the comprehending of the "female" disconnectedness of the universe. With this shift, he moves away from the irate stance he takes at the meeting of the American Historical Association in 1883, where he dislikes most of the papers his male colleagues delivered and the presence on the program of the historian Lucy Salmon, she who has only "female story-telling" to offer (HA, 199). "Sympathy" and "story-telling," rather than science, will finally seem the best way to take on the chaos of events.

Adams's most compelling project became the study of women, the same to him as the study of the universe. His obsession was not to know what women "are" – since for Adams all females are irrevocably "the Other" – but what they "do" in the world. He would pass from (1) the study of archaic women-as-progenitors of the Family who overshadow the contributions of the Fathers, to (2) the study of the women's lives who had paralleled, and shaped, his own life, to (3) the study of the New Woman who granted him a glimpse into the future, and finally (although never fully acknowledged on his part), the study of the women's roles he himself was "called" to work at in a man's world.

II.

For a son of a family self-defined by the accomplishments of the patrilineal line, it is interesting to see that Adams traces his family heritage through the years "from his greatest grandmother's birth" (EHA, 7). Just as interesting, the first family member he singles out as having influenced the direction his life takes is his father's mother, "the Madame."

As a child Adams senses that he shares many of the Madame's qualities: delicate, decorative, reclusive, an exotic, her fate "never to be Bostonian" and thus possessed of the "vague effect of not belonging" within either the geographical region of New England or the familial nation of the Adamses. Oh, the boy is of New England all right, and an Adams, but not totally so. There is implanted in his future what his grandmother's life has been: one of going where she must; trailing after John Quincy Adams's career, "whether she was happy or not, whether she was content or not"; doing her duty but suffering as a woman does when her will has not been taken into account by family, society, or the universe (EHA, 16–17).

It is from the Madame that Adams knew himself to be "half exotic." "As a child of Quincy he was not a true Bostonian, but even as a child of Quincy he inherited a quarter taint of Maryland blood" (EHA, 19). Offspring of cultural miscegenation, Adams was a "quadroon" repelled by and drawn to the "intermixture of delicate grace and passionate depravity that marked the Maryland May." The North was abolitionist, repressed, austerely male; the South represented the immorality of slavery, but also all that was "sensual, animal, elemental . . . half Greek and half human," and very female (EHA, 268).

The "pure blood" of the patrilineal line thus "tainted," no

wonder that Adams in his guise as historian and would-be scientist was drawn to the study of "archaic women." During his Darwinist period in 1867 and 1868, while located at Wenlock Edge, he became "an American in search of a father," pleased to find that he was descended from *Pteraspis* (EHA, 229). But once he was back in Washington, D.C., assessing the possibilities of a political life in 1869–1870, he acknowledged that " 'the vast maternity' of nature showed charms more voluptuous than the vast paternity of the United States Senate" (EHA, 282).[6]

It is one thing for Adams to admit privately that he is like unto the female in certain crucial respects; it is quite another thing to do this in public. He needed to distance himself from the intriguing object of his intellectual inquiries. When he decides to join Harvard's faculty as a professor of history in 1873, he appears to realize he can have it both ways. By assuming the acknowledged male role as historian dedicated to the field of ancient and medieval law, he can go with impunity deep into the analysis of the "organization of the Family," the basis of "all the nearer subjects of historical study" (Letters, II:155).

Lewis Henry Morgan's *Ancient Society*, with its "careful scientific inquiry" into the place of women and marriage customs among the Indians, impressed Adams. In short order, he examined the Pocahontas story and delivered his 1876 Lowell Lecture on "The Primitive Rights of Women" the evening prior to Susan B. Anthony's suffrage address to another Boston audience (HA, 11, 113).[7] By 1890 he was absorbed in an ethnological scrutiny of the "old gold" matriarchs of Samoa (Letters, III:287 ff). By 1903 he had decided that if he were starting anew, "I should drop the man, except as an accessory, and study the woman of the future. The American man is a very simple and cheap mechanism. The American woman I find a complicated and expensive one. . . . She is still a study. She is all that is left to art" (Letters, V:497).

Before looking further at the twists and turns involved when an Adams takes the Woman as his primary "subject" in his effort to live up to the male imperative to pursue the right vocation, let us review the list of Adams's women to determine whether their influence (mark of the life that is *not* begonia-like) upon Adams is equal to the influence he wished to gain within the male world. But prior to this little review, hear what Adams says about the creation of man-made images that suggests he was aware of the topic that greatly concerns many today: the social construction of "objects" that comes about when women (by becoming one's "subject") are scrutinized as "the Other": "Images are not arguments, rarely even lead to proof, but the mind craves them, and, of late more than ever, the keenest experimenters find twenty images better than one, especially contradictory; since the human mind has already learned to deal in contradictions" (EHA, 489).

This is Adams speaking in 1904 of the images the mind "craves" for "a new centre, or preponderating mass" by which he is released to speculate about "the law of acceleration." But throughout *The Education* images of the woman provide Adams with successive new centers and masses whose trajectory the scientific historian must track – "fetish forces" whose study gives him the vocation that best "suits" his own manikin construction.

Adams realizes the relation of men to women by imaging the Woman.

> The study of history is useful to the historian by teaching him his ignorance of women; and the mass of this ignorance crushes one who is familiar enough with what are called historical sources to realize how few women have ever been known. The woman who is known only through a man is known wrong, and excepting one or two like Mme. de Sevigne, no woman has pictured herself. The American woman of the nineteenth century will live only as the man saw her. . . . (EHA, 353)

Partially in error, of course, are the views held by this white, elitist, New England male chauvinist equipped with set notions about all such "primitive peoples" (American women; South Sea Islanders) whom he considers incapable of representing themselves in ways recognized by Western males. Other women have indeed pictured themselves; the nineteenth-century American woman is, thank you, living not only as the man once saw her. But Adams's perception of the basics does not lag behind

Pamela L. Caughie's statement that "the features we either valorize or lament in women's art (for example, inconclusiveness,
contradictions, ambivalence) are not the *property* of women writers; rather, they are the *effects* of a different way of conceiving
art. . . . "[8]

Seeing Adams see women as other men see them discloses
that "the features we either valorize or lament" in Adams's own
art (ambivalence, inconclusiveness, contradiction) are not entirely the property of the female sex; they are partially "the
effects" of the way the manikin (dressed now as a man, now as a
woman) was educated to conceive of his self-adornments.

First in the strong line in Adams's "long and varied experience
of bright women" was his eldest sister Louisa. If what the Adams
family did best was talk about literature and politics, it was
Louisa who led the table talk (EHA, 35).

She was the first young woman he was ever intimate with – quick,
sensitive, willful, or full of will, energetic, sympathetic and intelligent
enough to supply a score of men with ideas – and he was delighted to
give her the reins – to let her drive him where she would. It was his first
experiment in giving the reins to a woman, and he was so much pleased
with the results that he never wanted to take them back. In after life he
made a general law of experience – no woman had ever driven him
wrong; no man had ever driven him right. (EHA, 85)

Tell-tale signs of chauvinism are apparent here. Louisa is one
of many muses (always designated as female) praised for the
inspiration by which they supply "a score of men with ideas."
And although Louisa later provided Adams with his initial image
for woman's fate as one who suffers and accepts, we note that
her courage when dying of tetanus is likened to that of a military
man, facing death, "as women mostly do, bravely and even gaily,
racked slowly to unconsciousness, but yielding only to violence,
as a soldier sabred in battle." Even so, Louisa as muse and cadet
embodied one of the most profound "ideas" that ever came to
her brother concerning the eternal adversary. "The last lesson –
the sum and term of education" – comes to Adams regarding the
suddenness, the unpredictability, the cruelty of death; even

more, the fact that it is Nature, the primal She, who "enjoyed [death], played with it, the horror added to her charm. . . ." (EHA, 287–288).

In happier days Adams flourished in the midst of his women, especially the married ones. What a pity that old Boston feared their importance. The females that male children encountered at home, at school, or in ordinary society "counted for little as models." An alert boy "might not even catch the idea that women had more to give" (EHA, 48).[9]

After Clover Adams's death, Adams slid his women acquaintances comfortably into the categories of "married" or "nieces." These untouchable females protected him from the terrors of remarriage. They amused and tranquilized him, surrounding him as buffers against more suffering, more loss, more guilt over failure.[10] But while Clover lived, he benefited greatly from the ambitions she had for him. She was able to "man" him whenever he found himself sliding into feminine inconsequence; she prodded him onward by the strength of her will; she was eager to take on the role of a wife within the Adams family. "My fiancee, like most women, is desperately ambitious and wants to be daughter-in-law to a President more than I want to be a President's son" (Letters, II:135).

With Clover, Adams experienced equivalence between the sexes, bonded by "mutual attraction."[11] On occasion he detected the attributes of the female found in the shape of the masculine form, costumed – as manikins may be – in male attire: First with Rooney Lee, later with Algernon Swinburne. Lee, Harvard classmate and epitome of the prewar Southerner, was charming, ignorant, childlike, an animal with no mind but endowed social instinct and the habit of command – a fine figure of the feminized male who was first cousin to Adams by nature of the "quadroon" strain this offspring of Quincy inherited from his Maryland grandmother (EHA, 57–58). Swinburne was yet another feminized male, but one who met success, not the failure that was Rooney's fate. Swinburne gave the awestruck Adams a lesson in "real genius" in the form of "a tropical bird crested, long-beaked, quick-moving, with rapid utterance and screams of humor" (EHA, 141).

With such role models as Louisa, Clover (women who died tragically, but vividly), and Rooney and Swinburne (men who "died" tragically, but vividly), could an Adams ever agree to don the clothes of "the typical American male"?

III.

Always sensitive to time and habitat, Adams pegged "the national character" (male, mainstream) to the postwar surge in business activities centered in New York and Chicago by 1870. In defining this phenomenon as the "restless, pushing, energetic, ingenious person, always awake and trying to get ahead of his neighbors," Adams excludes his kind from the equation. But there are similarities between "the national character" and the Adams persona: work "to excess"; work as "a form of vice"; less interest in "money or power" than "the amusement of the pursuit."[12]

How was it that Adams came close to matching the qualities of this type but with a miss that is as good as a mile? Not because the American male "was ashamed to be amused" or "could not face a new thought" – hardly the Adams type. Not from the fact that, whereas "Work, whiskey, and cards were life" to the man of action, Adams "never played cards" and "loathed whiskey." The essential difference lay instead, and paradoxically, in what linked Adams with the prototypical American: their shared conviction that work is life, but with this crucial distinction. An Adams is incapable of achieving work according to the rules laid down by "the national character."

The American male "other" took "All his immense strength, his intense nervous energy, his keen analytic perceptions" and "oriented [them] in one direction" (EHA, 297–298). In contrast, Adams's mind and will operates in terms of the "female" disconnectedness he decried but which he discerned as an essential of his nature. Placed against the male of the 1870s, Adams could only expose his lack of force.

But wait. By the time Adams gets to 1903 and lets his description of "the modern American man" surface in a letter written to his muse, Elizabeth Cameron, female qualities are in ascendance;

61

qualities, take note, seldom evidenced by the women Adams knows, but rather by the males, as in the case of Theodore Roosevelt, the public incarnation of so-called American masculinity.

> He likes to be ruled. He is a peaceful, domestic animal, fond of baby-talk . . . helpless and sympathetic; afraid of himself, of his women, of his children; yearning for love and dough-nuts; shocked at automobiles and Trusts; proud and puffed-up at riding a horse or shooting a bear. (Letters, V:497)

In the universe of uncertainty created by the bisexual imagination that authors *The Education of Henry Adams* one thing is certain: Adams was never "the Cameron type" (EHA, 333–334). The man who was unfortunately (or fortunately for a man like Adams who wishes to avoid remarriage even with the woman he idolizes) the husband of Elizabeth Cameron, Senator Don of Pennsylvania represents "simplicity," the "primitive strain," what is "not complex," the one who can be counted on to be "the safest" when it comes to "practical matters."

Up to this point, the description given to the Cameron type is not unlike that for the "old-gold type" Adams finds in the matriarchal culture of the South Seas. Patriarchal maleness obnoxiously comes to the fore once we see that the Senator is a cog in the Pennsylvania political machine which runs upon the force of a narrow national chauvinism that is unable to detect differences between non-Caucasian races, that is untroubled by "scrupulous purity or sparkling professions," and that works "by coarse means on coarse interests."

Men of the Cameron type, using their "machine" maleness, achieve "practical success." This gives them the illusion of being *in it;* no begonias they, or so they think.[13] Men like Adams who are half-in and half-out of realms of power are begonias before their world: hardly useful, but at least visible, able to contribute a bit of decorative flair to the social scene.

Adams almost made a profession of feeling "shut out" and "in exile," ever existing "somewhere else" than where he happens to be. Feminists and historians of women's lives rightly disdain this self-serving, self-pitying guise. As Clover Hooper's biographer observes, men "were at least permitted to fail in an active sense," whereas women too often suffer the ignominy of being society's true wallflowers, so peripheral no one notices them or asks them for a dance; of no earthly use even as ornamentive objects.[14] On the other hand, men who fail, however actively, will be chastised for having subverted the male standards of a male-run society. They will be publicly accused of being "something *operatic*; a kind of rosepink, artificial bedizement."[15]

Adams names his most heinous crimes. Through his complicity in being both "butterfly" and "dilettante," he fails twice over: at the work-ethic instilled by his membership in the Adams male line; at the expectations for worldly success exacted by his nation's men of action. Butterflies are not wallflowers at the ball; their guilt arises from their being all too successful at trivial pursuits. 1870 was the high point of Adams's questionable talents at leading "a brilliant sort of butterfly existence" and in being known as "one of the three best dancers" in the nation's capital (Letters, II:60, 94). Prior to that, in the mid-1860s, he had been enticed into the "English garden of innate disorder" of "taste" and "dilettantism." The fact that brilliant men led the way did not justify an Adams following their example. They were, after all, *English*men besides being landed and/or titled aristocrats – persons abhorrent to the self-made American, the only kind worthy of the name of male.

Adams might have kept going up this primrose path (plucking begonias and rosepinks along the way), remaining forever in the Bower of Bliss, succumbing to its "summer-like repose," its "self-contained, irresponsible, devil-may-care indifference to the future," its "feeling that one's bed is made, and one can rest on it till it becomes necessary to go to bed for ever," its "editio principes quality . . . which only a Duke, or a very rich Earl of ancient foundation, could feel at twenty-five" (Letters, II:448). Indeed, Adams departed Harvard willing to become "a social butterfly" out of his "contemptible weakness for women's society" (Letters, II:130), but this was a young man's folly. Within the next decade he was drawn into, but escaped from, the English version of the dilettante's existence. Even so, he continues to bemoan the betrayal he had made to his American roots. Because of "my bourgeois ease and uniformity," there is "not in this wide continent of respectable mediocrity a greasier citizen, or one more contented in his oily ooze, than myself" (Letters, II:344).

No lack of trying to become the accepted American male led to this bad, sad state of affairs. It happens as the consequence of the lacks endemic to each of the series of professions to which Adams puts his hand between 1859 and 1905. According to the gendered demands placed upon any such professional experiments, the ability to make money was the sign of one's membership in society (read as "having power"; read as being "a man"). But how easily attainment of this status could be thwarted, even if a man did not start with the flaws riddling Adams's nature, weaknesses represented by begonias, butterflies, and wallflowers (showiness, weightlessness, or invisibility: read as "having no influence" on the world: read as taking "the woman's position").

"The national character" cared more for the process of gaining money than in having it, but Adams knew what money meant in defining American manhood. "Unless one makes money in some way, one has no place in our world." He comments, "This is what ails our women, and makes them so restless" (Letters, V:115). He could have added that this is what made him restless from first to last.

The Education as an ongoing narrative (at least through Chapter 20) is structured upon movements from one experiment to another in the hope of attaining "worth" – signaled by the number of dollars a man commands in salary. Adams's personal financial situation was such that he did not have to make money in order to live, but he knew he was not living properly unless the world saw him as meriting money in the marketplace.[16] Presence or absence of the monetary worth was of paramount importance, yet Adams could still be labeled as "one of that butterfly party" – as one of the "females" of his generation – if he pursued careers viewed as being less than masculine.[17]

Adams is tossed to and fro. In 1859, the law seems the answer; not because it was "best" for him but because it offers "more" than the demeaning status accorded the literary life by which he would "lose [his] whole life and gain nothing" (Letters, I:15). Interest in the law quickly fades and the Civil War begins, opening up one of the traditional (although not cost-efficient) ways to manhood. But Adams declares that joining the army would be "ridiculous" for him (Letters, I:371). But if he stays out, as he does in becoming part of his father's entourage at the American legation in London, he is fated to pass four intensely womanized years far from the battlefields back home.[18]

The war over, Adams hopes those four years at the legation meant that "his hands [were] actually touching the lever of power," furnishing him an apprenticeship he can parlay into a real man's position back in the States; but "between the President and the Senate, service of any sort became a delusion" (EHA, 210). What was there for Adams to do now, unable as he was to command that symbolic five-dollar salary that coded the terms for contemporary success?

Journalism comes next. Adams acknowledges it "gives me money to buy gloves with, and a certain power to make myself felt," but he soon gives it up as an unworthy "butterfly existence" (Letters, II:60). Then Adams, who "knew nothing about history, and much less about teaching," goes to Harvard in 1873 as professor in medieval history and editor of the *North American Review:* positions a man could assume without shame for he cannot be accused of not giving himself over to work; "good, hard, work," Adams called it; a life without women's company, "gray, monotoned, calm as a monk" (Letters, II:94, 101). But a man's life as "a school-teacher" was thin, with editorship "thinner still" (EHA, 307). He might as well be a woman for all the influence he had in the public world.

Two more experiments lie ahead once Adams commits himself to the most risky of all male enterprises: (1) *the writer* who is (a) the "dabbler" – the man of letters, or (b) the "novelist" – the historian; (2) *the husband* who experiences (a) the success of married life and (b) the failure of becoming a suicide's widower. In seeking, first, the significance of Adams's election of the vocation of writing, and of the writing of history at that, one thing is certain: this choice would not have gained him representation upon the Virgin Portal Tympanum of the west facade at the Cathedral of Chartres.

IV.

The cathedral and its century formed "the point of history when man held the highest idea of himself as a unit in a unified universe." *Mont-Saint-Michel and Chartres: A Study of Thirteenth-Century Unity* enabled Adams "to fix a position for himself" by which "he could label" *The Education of Henry Adams* as *a Study of Twentieth-Century Multiplicity*.[19] It was also the position by which its author could measure the worth of authoring in that century (the nineteenth) whose standards of measure are dictated by the sexless Dynamo overseen by mechanized masculinity, not by the eternal feminine of the Virgin before whom all men once bent their knee.

The Virgin Portal Tympanum centers upon the Seven Liberal Arts for which the Virgin is the patroness. High upon the archivolt, female figures depict the arts in the abstract; below them are representations of the mortal males who became famous through their contributions to Dialectic (Aristotle), Rhetoric (Cicero), Geometry (Euclid), Arithmetic (Boethius), Astronomy (Ptolemy), Grammar (Donatus), and Music Theory (Pythagoras).[20] It is noteworthy that the Arts, viewed by the Church as "weapons against the heretics," are visualized as anonymous female figures. In their role as muses who inspire others to use these "weapons" in sacred combat, they are recognizable solely by means of traditional "attributes" (the physical props they carry, details of outward appearance), whereas the male personages inspired by the muses are named, their earthly accomplishments thereby given an identifiable place in history.

Of supreme importance is the sacred calling each male follows. Led by Philosophy, the "mother" of them all (represented as a majestic older woman with sceptre, crown, and books), these men have devoted their lives to "the knowledge of things through their highest causes."[21] This, indeed, is what a male once aspired to (inspired by his female muse) through his confidence that he "held the highest idea of himself as a unit in a unified universe." This, indeed, is not what Henry Adams could ever hope to become.

Avid student of the Middle Ages, Adams realized the distinctions made during those earlier centuries between "worthy" and "useful" endeavors. He who had to struggle against being labeled as *not useful* (as dabbler, dilettante, and begonia) had to face up to the vocational (and gendered) consequences of the Fall from Unity into Multiplicity. The ancient Greeks had provided the Middle Ages with the "aristocratic spirit" that "distinguished between activities suitable for 'liberal' or free-born citizens and manual occupations fit only for foreigners and serfs." By the time this spirit was rigidified within medieval Christian theology, divisions were made between enterprises "vulgar" (*artes vulgares* and *artes sordidae*) and "liberal" (*artes liberales*) – the latter "embracing all that was necessary to an educated man" by carefully excluding "salaried labour" from "activities of the mind."[22]

By Adams's era matters had loosened up a bit, complicating even further the value placed upon art as *tecne* or as *ars*, practical or theoretical,[23] especially in a country like the United States where things had to get done, not just get thought about. This meant that Adams was caught between what was expected of him by the Family and by success as it was viewed by the general run of Americans, underscored by the continuing distinctions made between *"praiseworthy* and *honourable* pursuits." Aquinas's commentary on Aristotle's *De Anima* left no doubts about the choices presented to the "unified man" of that century of unity:

Every science is good and not only good but honourable. Yet in this regard one science excels over another. . . . Among good things some are praiseworthy, namely those which are useful for an end; others are honourable, namely those which are useful in themselves. . . . The speculate sciences are good and honourable; the practical sciences are only praiseworthy.

Centuries later, in the age of multiplicity, Adams must choose between "praiseworthy" activities (what "Americans" do and what Adamses once did) and "honourable" deeds (what Americans tend to dismiss and what this Adams would like to put his hand to, notwithstanding his inadequacies for the task).

Adams has the writings of the younger Seneca to answer to, as well as Aquinas's and Aristotle's, for the separations between the arts that amuse (*ludicrae*) and those that instruct (*pueriles*).[24]

He is left with a series of insidious choices that (once more) brings up the gender divisions governing the anxious question of what constitutes work that is moral, because praiseworthy and honorable, and what is inconsequential (thereby immoral).

Even in the age of the Virgin and of the queens of high fame honored in Adams's *Mont-Saint-Michel and Chartres*, the west facade of the Cathedral of Chartres speaks to the fact that the female forms which serve to inspire right-minded men to act with greater or lesser degrees of "honor" in the world remain anonymous; they are muses, not makers.[25] By Adams's day, men who give themselves to the arts that *amuse* are obviously "women" operating outside the realms of male authority. As for the arts that *instruct*, why, that is what Bostonians do best, and by doing so are judged as sexless, female, or emasculate by the masculinized cities of Chicago and New York.[26]

It is the muse Clio whom Adams finally follows. History was not inconsequential, not to the Greeks. One of the daughters of Mnemosyne and servant to the god Apollo, the virgin Clio was "she who extols."[27] To the Middle Ages, she was a winged female in a white robe who writes in a book supported by the back of Father Time, her foot firmly placed upon a solid cube.[28] Well into the Renaissance, champions of the less established arts initiated power plays in order to approach the rank still held by History, as seen in the argument launched by Philip Sidney in *Defence of Poesie*. In order to raise poetry (literature) to a level only less than that accorded the Scriptures, Sidney makes poetry the child of the blessed union between History and Philosophy. By the nineteenth century, however – at least in the jaded view of Adams when appraising his own final vocational choice – history has sunk low. It is endangered on two sides: as anecdote, it merely amuses (by telling "female stories" as Lucy Salmon threatened to do at the American Historical Association meeting); as antiquarianism tied to useless facts and more useless ideals of "social virtue," it had nothing of interest for men of modern times (EHA, 300–303).

History's main flaw is that it is not science. No matter that science as practiced in the nineteenth century might not have made it to the Virgin Portal Tympanum at Chartres. Although science still utilizes geometry, astronomy, and arithmetic (three of the liberal arts), it has severed itself from history (evolution, in contemporary terms), from virtue, and from philosophy that wastes its time "suggesting unintelligible answers to insoluble problems" (EHA, 306, 377). Under such conditions, no wonder Adams took the occasion of his (absentee) leadership of the American Historical Association to urge his fellows to stop being historians and start becoming scientists, else they lose even the rank of begonias to become wallflowers: females all.[29]

But something happened to science once scientists recognized that the object of their study, Nature, refused to submit to the domination of the masculine standards of order, unity, logic, and the efficient use of energy. Nature was chaos, multiplicity, unreason, prodigal waste; it was the female writ as large as the universe. Madame Curie, herself an aberration as a woman practicing in a male's discipline, threw upon the scientist's desk "that metaphysical bomb she called radium"; a true anarchist, she overturned whatever faith men had had in science as the rule of order and reason (EHA, 452).[30] By 1900 science had to capitulate to enterprises (psychology, physiology, and history) it previously viewed as beneath contempt. Whereas it took this long for professionals in the scientific realm to admit to the defeat of masculine control, Adams the scientist manqué was learning this lesson as early as 1870 and 1885. Contributing to his prescience were the absurd, unreasonable, useless deaths of two of the women who meant the most to his education: Louisa Adams Kuhn and Marian Hooper Adams.

The more Adams examined Nature (in her guises as the physical world, the supersensual universe, or the divine force of the Virgin), the more he recognized that the traditional notion that the males set the controlling norms is the grand illusion. Nature is like Bluebeard's wives, full of curiosity, eager to open doors forbidden them by their lords and masters, whatever the risk (EHA, 232). But in the end, Bluebeard's power is lost. The male once centered the universe around himself; now it is revealed that the male is superfluous, while the female is "essential." The

69

spider eats her mate and the queen-bee rules from her throne.[31] Sooner or later, "You must come to a conclusion . . . whether the universe is masculine or feminine" (HA, 360).

V.

It is fascinating to recognize how many female roles Adams assumed in both private and public life. It is not just that Adams is "feminized" because, as an historian, he fails at being the scientist that would have assured him an "honourable" life; it is not merely that the conception of a universe regulated by the rationality of masculine thought shifted to a perception of irrational female forces finally bringing Adams's position-as-woman into the center of affairs.[32] What strikes us most is that, throughout his lifetime, Adams shared many of the traits and activities directly associated with women's lives: Adams with high-strung nerves like his grandmother and hypochondria and melancholia like his mother; Adams experiencing the same midlife crises undergone by Elizabeth Cameron and other women of his circle[33]; Adams as the family nanny (EHA, 117; Letters, III:95); Adams the waltzer in the 1860s and the novice cyclist who takes up the sport of the Gibson Girl in 1892 (EHA, 256–257, 330); Adams experiencing what it feels like to be pregnant, "though to endure it all, and have no baby, seems to take the fun out of life" (Letters, III:287); Adams self-isolated from the collective, mechanized modes of the American male; above all, Adams knowing – like Clover – what it means to be rootless, eccentric, not representative of the times.

Because Adams was genetically a male, with a male's rights in society, he subsumed his wife to some extent, but – as *The Education of Mrs. Henry Adams* suggests – Adams also "was" Clover in many respects. Fascinating (also rather frightening) is the fact that Adams "became Clover" even more after her death. Clover-dead is the hole punched into the center of *The Education;* the black hole that swallows twenty years to efface the fact that Adams ever married, thereby negating the fact that he lost what he had once had.[34]

There has been much discussion of this absence so present to our minds as readers, this silence that resounds in our ears. In order to draw tighter the connections between the book text that we know as *The Education* and the gender issues that shadow both what is and is not included within its covers, let us take up (and conclude with) three specifically feminist arguments: (1) the nature of mourning, (2) the question of heroic action, (3) the dream of a common language. For convenience's sake, we can dip into an essay by Lynda K. Bundtzen that addresses all three issues in her analysis of how Adrienne Rich has made her own moves to gain power through the poetic vocation.[35]

In the course of her essay, Bundtzen cites Hélène Cixous concerning the difference in manner by which men and women deal with personal loss. According to Cixous's feminist theory, males fall back upon the strategy of "masculine incorporation."[36]

Man cannot live without resigning himself to loss. He has to mourn. It's his way of withstanding castration. . . . When you've lost something and the loss is a dangerous one, you refuse to admit that something of your self might be lost in the lost object. So you "mourn," you make haste to recover the investment made in the lost object. (52)

In contrast, there is "feminine expenditure," a "not withholding." The woman

takes up the challenge of loss in order to go on living; she lives it, gives it life, is capable of unsparing loss. . . . This makes her writing a body that overflows . . . as opposed to masculine incorporation. (52–53)

We put aside the reasonable argument that Clover Hooper Adams committed suicide because she was unable to "resign herself to loss" (i.e., the death of her father) in order to concentrate upon Henry Adams, since this essay is primarily about him. His letters give evidence that he did his best to "recover the investment made in the lost object" of his now-dead wife.

Four days after Clover's suicide, Adams writes Elizabeth Cameron that he has to live "on what I can save from the wreck of her life . . ." (Letters, II:641). Six years later (also to Mrs. Cameron), he remarks upon "the *me* of 1870" which was "a strangely different being from the *me* of 1890" (Kaledin, 6). Clover's biographer describes the results of his investment recovered through "the absorption of the qualities of his dead wife." By means of "internalization" and "appropriation" of the kind that suggest the tribal ritual of cannibalism (ingesting the powers of the body of "the Other"), Adams shifts his vocational emphasis: he is "no longer a scientific historian but . . . a passionate social critic" (6–7).

Adams's friend Henry James notices a similar alteration: "he became a different, more passionate man. . . . In an effort to immortalize her spirit, he wrote the story of his own life – as if he were telling it with her values, from her point of view" (Kaledin, 13–14).

In her essay "Castration or Decapitation?" Hélène Cixous describes what happens through "feminine sublimation." Through "not withholding," the woman who writes challenges loss. Loss disappears into "the oblivion of acceptance. . . . And in the end, she will write this not-withholding, this not-writing, she writes of not-writing, not-happening" (53).

This looks very much like what Adams did in *The Education*, filling the charged gap between Chapters 20 and 21 by not-writing, not-happening. Having followed through "masculine incorporation," the man who was already half-female prior to his wife's death is transformed into something very similar to her full being through his "feminine sublimation" of her loss.

In Adams's case the results do not give us a woman's text. Cixous says true "feminine" writing results in the woman who "crosses limits: she is neither outside nor in, whereas the masculine would try to 'bring the outside in,' if possible" (Cixous, 53). In his letters Adams absorbs Clover, bringing her *inside*, trying to save *his* investment out of "the wreck of her life." No question that prior to Clover's death, Adams tried to have it both ways – to live as both male and female; but thereafter he gave himself up to those acts of "leaping" which, in Cixous's view, characterizes the woman's reaction to loss.

VI.

Can Adams's reaction to the losses he experienced be considered "heroic"? A legitimate question since men have to deal with the disgusted charge, "Why don't you act like a man?" That is, be brave, be heroic, be unlike a woman.

"You are beaten back everywhere before you are twenty-four," a young Union lieutenant threw into Adams's face in 1862, "and finally writing philosophical letters you grumble at the strange madness of the times and haven't even faith in God and the spirit of your age. What do you mean by thinking, much less writing such stuff? 'No longer any chance left of settled lives and Christian careers!' " (HA, 53)

Adams had constantly to answer to what we can call "the Carlyle Factor" or else stand accused of not giving himself over to the aggressive masculinity defined by the terms laid down in *On Heroes, Hero-Worship, and the Heroic in History*. Holly A. Laird writes of the fine feminist achievement made by Elizabeth Barrett Browning's *Aurora Leigh* in 1857, inspired by the English poet's faith in Carlyle's admonition that one – male or female – "could achieve modern heroism only through the pen."[37] On the other hand, Lynda K. Bundtzen shows that Adrienne Rich has expressed "an absolutely negative judgment" of the kind of heroism that strident males like Carlyle stridently call for.[38]

For every man chastised for not rising to "extraordinary" heights at the time of "uncommon" events through "exemplary" action, as true men must, a woman faces the pressure to gain power, fame, achievement defined in masculine terms that serve to uphold the patriarchal status quo. Rich argues that women should deny male traditions of heroism; they should refigure "the heroic in a 'common' and feminine form" by being the woman-poet-as-hero" – an "essentially heretical voice" which is, in Rich's words, "disloyal to civilization."

Once again, we find Henry Adams caught in the cleft stick of the expectations heaped upon him as an Adams, an American, and a male. There is a touch of masochism in his choice to write Carlyle's admonitions in regard to modern heroism into *The Education*. Not only the chapter titled "Teufelsdrock," but much of the text is filled with Carlyle's voice and Adams's responses to the Carlylean imperative to be a hero, whether as prophet, as poet, as man of letters, or as king.[39]

Years before writing *The Education*, Adams dismissed "the great man" theory when writing his biographies of Randolph and Gallatin and his histories of the administrations of Jefferson and Madison. He was no opponent to Adrienne Rich on that score. *The Education* itself demystifies the notables of his time, from Palmerston to Grant, albeit more because of his belief in the accidental nature of events over which no mortal has control, rather than through loss of his conviction that men (particularly an Adams) *ought to do* "extraordinary" things.[40]

Rich would first take exception to any lingering wish on Adams's part to exceed (male-inscribed) norms by becoming "the uncommon man." On the other hand, she would just as vehemently object to Adams's agreement with Carlyle that any one can be heroic, although leading "modest lives" simply by *doing one's duty to society* (EHA, 315). Such an apparent impulse to support the male-made status quo denies Rich's challenge to women to provide "the heretical voice" "disloyal to civilization."

Matters are further complicated, first, by the masculine tonality of Carlyle's admonitions and, second, by Adams's own ambivalence toward these demands. Together with Carlyle, Rich would detest "Dilettantism, Skepticism, Triviality" and the "Inanity and Theatricality" that taints the "poor conscious ambitious schemer" limited to "a kind of amateur-search for Truth," although she could not accept the dismissive phrase descriptive of such "female" behavior as "toying and coquetting with Truth" (TC, 46, 73, 85). She would certainly wish her woman heroes to possess "a deep, great, genuine sincerity" (45). She would concur on the need for her women "heretics" to approach life with all "intensity" in order "To *kindle* the world" (46, 92).

We would like to know where exactly Adams stands on these crucial issues. But how can we know when faced by the ambiguous public poses of the manikin in *The Education* and masked poses Adams takes in his letters? How much does Adams condemn the "amateur-search for Truth"? Notwithstanding the times he reviles himself as a "humbug," isn't there a taste for "Triviality"? Begonias are known for their "Inanity and Theatricality," but does Adams ever stop being the "poor conscious ambitious schemer" in pursuit of "sight-recognition"?

Adams meets Carlyle (and Rich) on other scores: (1) on the

necessity for "Intensity" – especially after Clover's death that introduced the "passionate" spirit into his writings; (2) on the importance of the prophetic voice emitted by the "teacher" who defines duty to society as the act of shaking it to its foundations: "A parent gives life, but as parent, give no more. A murderer takes life, but his deed stops there. A teacher affects eternity; he can never tell where his influence stops" (EHA, 300).

To be able to affect eternity is clearly a Carlylean task; it might also be Rich's. But where Adams and hero-makers part irrevocably lies elsewhere. First, the admonition *Thou Shalt Not Have Doubt* is the commandment Adams breaks every day. Second, the conviction *Life Must Be Real* increasingly becomes an impossibility. Carlyle's hero must be the manly "Serpent-queller" who slays the "black monster, Falsehood, our one enemy" (TC, 126). Adams *is* touched by the stern command never to flee "The great Fact of Existence . . . the awful presence of this Reality" (45), precisely because fleeing is what he does all too often.[41]

What Adams cannot finally agree upon is whether there *is* truth.[42] On the one hand, his skepticism about the reality of truth rises from his struggle against solipsism, his distrust of the trap of the mind, his fear he might be "drowned" in the "reflection of its own thought." Yet there remains the historian's conviction that he must be "driven back on thought as one continuous Force, without Race, Sex, School, Country, or Church" (EHA, 432, 434). If proven true, this force would erase racism, sexism, nationalism, sectarianism. However, it might not be Truth of the kind Carlyle or Rich would admire or admit.

Adams has another problem with serpent-quelling, whether it participates in the manly male tradition of heroic action preached by Carlyle or the feminist antipatriarchal heroism advocated by Rich. It is that *Truth might not amuse*. Not that Adams is not as slippery on this matter as on almost everything. Adams as a young Darwinist in "a kind of amateur-search for Truth" gives himself over to "toying and coquetting with Truth," since he is a Darwinist "for fun" (EHA, 232). Adams as the aged Teacher (speaking "posthumously," the little joke he insists upon) opens Chapter 21 of *The Education*, breaking his twenty years' silence by stating in distinctively Carlylean tones: "Once more! this is a story of education, not of adventure! It is meant to help young men . . . but it is not meant to amuse them" (EHA, 314).

This is a case of *Do as I say*, not *Do as I do*. But Adams's *Education* finally denies Carlylean hero-theory, denies feminist theories of heroic action, denies all the man-made expectations of manly behavior because – lacking the sense of humor – they could not amuse. Talk about being made master of by Triviality, Inanity, and Theatricality! *Not being bored* becomes Adams's primary aim. The figure of the Traditional Male does not inspire him. Nor does the (to Adams) detestably mannish and mechanized figure of the New Woman. What will amuse is the loosely gendered manikin showing off, brilliantly.

VII.

Once Adams strips Carlyle's "clothes philosophy" of its authoritative Latin title, *Sartor Resartus*, and replaces the humorless, larger-than-life-size presences of Mohammed, Dante, Shakespeare, Cromwell, and Napoleon with the diminutive, tacky tailor's manikin, the matter of heroic action as validated by centuries of masculine greatness is opened up to parody, mockery, inventiveness, *amusement.*

It is heartening to know that Clover Hooper Adams once wrote a parody of an elegant social gathering in which she plays at being the magnificent hostess attended by the obligatory "great man."

The guests were received by Mrs. Henry Adams of Boston, married to the scion of a once-honored race. Mrs. Adams has a most queenly presence. . . . She was magnificently attired in ruby velvet. . . . Jewels flashed from her raven tresses and she had a winning Beacon-Street welcome for all. By her side stood her husband, a man of superb physical proportions, two well-set eyes surmounted by a brow of great height and lustre. . . .[43]

There was no way Adams was ever bored while Clover was alive. With her in his life, not just as his muse, but as her own creator, there was no way he would take over-seriously the conventions that chided them both for not being what was expected of their sex or their class. After her death he had to fight back alone. *The Education* was his way of documenting the ironies of gendered social identities with which he, together with the women of his generation, had to contend.

We have to go outside *The Education* to Adams's letters in order to witness the particular worth women gain when they take amusement and fight boredom. *The Education of Henry Adams* remains highly conventional in regard to the limits it places around women as the mothers of the race, the bearers of reproductive force, and the domesticators of the universe. Adams's letters are also conventional when he fulminates against the "odious" suffragist and the "machine-made collectivist females" who replace the "humanist" women he adores, mainly because the New Woman is "a pretentious bore" (Letters, V:531). Yet there is a sudden flash of something freer in his later response to the newest representatives of womankind.

I have seen in my lifetime nothing half so revolutionary as the silent revolt of American women against being bored in America. The men grumble and swear, but they are stupid and their sex is naturally obtuse. Unless they kill them they can't control them, and the American woman would rather be killed than bored. (Letters, VI:10)

The woman who merely revolts against being bored by Society risks being trivial and inane. It is more estimable if she revolts against the boredom of a society and a universe that misuses her altogether. In those moments when Adams realizes this, he can only offer her his own motto for action: "After all, I've preached and practised and set an example all my life, and led the women on to revolt. . . . I'll have a seal-ring cut, with the motto: – I HATE!" (Letters, V:717).

No woman wants, or needs, a man to set an example or to loan her his motto; but the two sexes might take common cause. To resist is to hate things as they are; to hate and to resist is also to be amused and avoid boredom – potentially a major revolutionary act in which they could participate together.

A common cause needs a language held in common, but also common motives. The matter of motives is what complicates the relation between the needs of women and the fact of Adams's

77

perpetual search for a universal language – one that would re-place the useless Greek and Latin given him by Harvard. He declares he should have been taught French, German, and Span-ish, but especially Mathematics, the "necessary" alphabet by which science proudly dominates the universe of thought (EHA, 38, 60, 403).

Adrienne Rich's "Dream of a Common Language" (upon which Lynda Bundtzen focuses her essay) holds forth her hope that women will attain such a language for use as an instrument of power in the world. Feminists rightly distrust imperial visions voiced by males like Adams who are given to stating that they have "everything in the world, except what I want; and with nothing to complain of, except the universe" (HA, 219).

Whenever Adams expresses his wants, he seems unwilling to share the universe in common. He sounds suspiciously like a person in possession of a special code that shapes the universe to one's private liking. But less than a year before his death, Adams jots down a dream – not his, but his to record – about the perfect woman who perfectly runs the universe by the force of her language skills.

Elizabeth Cameron had long been Adams's muse. Here in a dream that came to Aileen Tone, Adams's secretary-companion, Mrs. Cameron figures as more than the muse. She is the ruler of all.

– I thought we were in your petitsalon – Square du Bois – and you were there in a lovely pink negligee . . . – and Uncle Henry sat down and began dictating letters to you in every known language, and you knew them all – and took his dictation so fast. . . . And telephones rang – and refugees came in – and crowds of people – And you seemed to be running the universe – quite calmly and easily – in your en-chanting pink negligee. (Letters, VI:759)

In the end, it is a woman in full command of all languages and the universe itself, showing off beautifully, who steals the scene from Uncle Henry. He may never have been more than a begonia, but he has the good fortune to glimpse what it takes to run the world.

Through our own glimpses of the gendered roles Adams continually played, and the gendered readings he gave to Society, society, and the cosmos, we learn what it meant to be a male (of his class, his race, his region) who had to deal with being "known" according to the norms set by other men. Through Adams we see what it was to be a woman "known" by men; but, even more vividly, "known" as well by a man who carried within himself much of what it signifies to be a woman.

The "history" Henry Adams wrote down in 1906, because his final choice of a vocation committed him to this task, is not unlike that called for by Gerda Lerner in 1977: "What is needed is a new universal history, a holistic history which will be a synthesis of traditional history and women's history."

To fulfill Lerner's demand entails, as the editors of the collection of essays on "Constructions of Masculinity in Victorian America" maintain, the effort to compare "the historical experiences of men to those of women, and encompass the interactions of the sexes."[44] For all its quirks and its petty chauvinisms, *The Education of Henry Adams* is an excellent way to commence writing such a "universal history" – particularly in foretelling the time when one can run the universe while wearing an "enchanting pink negligee."

NOTES

1 Ernest Samuels, *Henry Adams* (Cambridge, Mass.: 1989), 89. Hereafter Samuels's one-volume biography will be cited as HA, and pagination will be given within parentheses.

2 *The Education of Henry Adams,* 292. Pagination for future quotations will be given within parentheses, cited as EHA.

3 In his recent study, *William James. Public Philosopher* (Baltimore: Johns Hopkins Univ. Press, 1990), George Cotkin speaks of the pressing need felt by the generation that included James, James Russell Lowell, the Adams brothers, and John LaFarge, to ask "What shall I be?" and "How shall I be useful?" (22).

4 Letter of November 3, 1858, to Charles Francis Adams, Jr., *The Letters of Henry Adams,* ed. J. C. Levenson et al. (Cambridge, Mass.: 1982), vol. I:5. Subsequent references, with pagination and volume given within parentheses, will be noted as Letters.

5   In 1875 there was talk of setting up a third political party led by Charles Francis Adams – a party, Henry Adams joked, that should consist entirely of Adamses. But "in no case can I come in for any part of the plunder in case of success. My father and brothers block my path fatally, for all three stand far before me in the order of promotion" (Letters, II:226). There was no way this soldier of the king could work up from private to general, much less to kingship.

6   Adams knew his man's work was held back as long as his life was "tied to that of the Chief," his father (Letters, I:325). He seemed to have solved this problem in 1868 when, showing "no very filial tenderness," he set about "abruptly breaking the tie that had lasted so long" between himself and both father and mother. What he fails to admit is that he remained "tied" to his mother until her death in 1889, tied as he never was to Charles Francis Adams both by inheritance of her disposition of chronic discontent and by service to "the queen-bee of the hive" (Letters, III:182; EHA, 37).

7   Eugenia Kaledin, *The Education of Mrs. Henry Adams* (Philadelphia: Temple Univ. Press, 1981), has assumed the unenviable task of being fair to both Clover Adams's story and the part played in it by her husband. An example of her tact comes when she describes Adams's interest in Pocahontas as submerging his conventionally masculine ("scientific") suspicion of female "intuitive" powers within his recognition that the scientific historian must not ignore the "anthropological dimension" of "primitive forces." Kaledin also commends Adams's "The Primitive Rights of Women." This lecture highlighted "the silent suffering" upon women imposed by the Church and the "protective influence" of contemporary institutions concerned as much to save "the modern family" and "property law." In addition, "Strong women emerged in Adams's imagination, as they never could politically in his own family, to dominate the institutions that restrained their vitality" (138–139, 141).

8   Caughie, " 'I must not settle into a figure': The Woman Artist in Virginia Woolf's Writings." in *The Woman Artist. Essays on Poetics, Politics, and Portraiture*, ed. Suzanne W. Jones (Philadelphia: Univ. of Pennsylvania Press, 1991), 373. Subsequent references to this edition will be given as WA.

9   Today we lament the fact that the most that women in Adams's day and class had to offer were lessons in "manners" (when they were not giving lessons in "death"), whereas Adams lamented that women were too seldom given the opportunity even to do that. But manners were something about which he, as the male histo-

rian, hoped to become an expert. Speaking of his ambitions for posterity as only a self-absorbed twenty-two-year-old can do, Adams wrote that he liked "to think that a century or two hence when everything else about us is forgotten, my letters might still be read and quoted as a memorial of manners and habits at the time of the great secession of 1860" (HA, 40). Records of manners are part of the historians' vocation, a worthy accomplishment.

10 See Letters, III:231; HA, 203.

11 Just prior to Clover's suicide, during the months she stayed by her dying father's bedside, Adams wrote one of the few letters he had occasion to send his wife (since they had never been apart until that time). He spoke to her of his great good luck: "How did I ever hit on the only woman in the world who fits my cravings and never sounds hollow anywhere?" His answer to this self-query: "Social chemistry – the mutual attraction of equivalent human molecules . . ." (Letters, II:608).

Did Clover Adams receive from Adams as much as she gave him? Eugenia Kaledin thinks so. She has carefully recorded all the right and proper things Adams did *not* do for his wife. He did not, for example, give her "official recognition for her contribution to his historical work" based on the fact "that she collated every one of Jefferson's letters with him, and . . . read over the letters in French from Voltaire to Gallatin's grandmother – fifty-three in all . . ." (145). Adams was irate when it was suggested that his wife had written *Democracy*. "My wife never wrote for publication in her life and could not write if she tried" (169). As was all too typical of the fate of women of her generation and class, "Clover's talents became entirely subsidiary or complementary to her husband's. There was nothing more for her to do when he sat down to write" (225). Gaining skill in the arts of photography was her substitute for the male choice of a worthy vocation, but it did not suffice. Kaledin continually emphasizes that Clover's life partook of attributes of the sad "New England tragedy" of highly intelligent women given nothing of great moment to think about or to do. Nonetheless, she resists placing full blame on Adams in her belief that Clover "had profited in many ways from everything that was stimulating in her environment. There can be little doubt that she enjoyed her life with Henry, and, in many dimensions, her life was always admirable, and satisfying, and surprisingly fulfilled" (228–229).

12 The American male might consider himself aggressive and self-

81

serving – a condition "correct for New York or Chicago," but when placed in other climes he is quite different. In Washington: "quiet, peaceful, shy," "somewhat sad, somewhat pathetic" (like Lincoln) or "inarticulate, uncertain, distrustful of himself, still more distrustful of others" (like Grant). In Europe: "bored, patient, helpless; pathetically dependent on his wife and daughters . . . mostly a modest, decent, excellent, valuable citizen" (EHA, 297).

13   Adams's portrayal of the Cameron type falls within the chapter of *The Education* that surveys the events of 1893. By 1902 this type no longer has the ability to retain "practical power" through control of the political machine. Once "mechanical power" takes the lead, the government controls the handful of men in charge of that power; the latter are but "forces as dumb as their dynamos" (EHA, 421).

14   Kaledin, 231.

15   This is Thomas Carlyle's characterization of Jean-Jacques Rousseau as failed hero. *Heroes and Hero-Worship,* Vol. 5, *The Works of Thomas Carlyle in Thirty Volumes* (Centenary Edition. London: Chapman and Hall, 1897), 187. (Further references to Carlyle's text will be given within parentheses as TC.) In this regard it is interesting that Rousseau is one of the "models" mentioned in the Preface to *The Education* as being unavailable to Adams's era. Would Adams, suffering from the begonia reputation, really wish to emulate the showy failure of the "rosepink"?

16   Thoreau, that other out-of-it Harvard graduate, took the opposite tack in the pre–Civil War years. To make money was to disprove one's "worth" and to fail at living. But then, Thoreau did all he could to deny the world of capitalism and, thereby, to deny the gendering of contemporary society; which is one reason he was not viewed as a man by many of his neighbors. Adams never felt free enough from his society's demands to make as blatant a protest. In 1864 Adams realized he was "without the power of earning five dollars in any occupation." By 1868 men like his father and Motley "could scarcely have earned five dollars a day in any modern industry." His own Harvard degree gave him only the "capital" of his position in Society. In the 1870s his students (a different breed from himself), believed they could convert their degrees into money in the material society of Chicago (EHA, 64, 194, 238, 305). Clarence King proved Adams's point best: "education without capital" leads to failure. King had everything a *man* should have, but "for want of money" (the proof one *is* a man), he fails. Even

science, the traditional "male" area of intellectual endeavor, had become helpless "in practice" by the late 1890s, emasculated by the demands of late-nineteenth-century capitalism (EHA, 346–347).

17   Consider Adams's derogatory assessments of the current worth accorded to the three professions one might have thought an Adams could pursue with honor. (1) *Literature:* The big-name literary men have fled to Germany, idealists in flight from American capitalism. America ignores writers since they have little instruction to offer postwar society; Britain finds its authors unfashionable, unable to amuse. Besides, literature as a manly liberal art has been defeated by the fact that "Our magazines are wholly feminine" (EHA, 61, 134; Letters, V:496). (2) *Politics:* It is the bastard child of Statecraft (the legacy of "serious" work, both "praiseworthy" and "honourable," that the child once believed he would inherit from his fathers); amusing only for "satirists and comedians," it is no longer the fount of instruction since it has been thrown "into confusion, cross-purposes, and ill-temper that would have been scandalous in a boarding-school of girls" (EHA, 272). (3) *Journalism:* With its long work hours, slight financial recompense, and inability to gain a man influence in the halls of power, it is mere "dabbling," an "inferior pulpit" (EHA, 213, 234).

18   Adams said he brought to his duties as son and secretary a character similar to a young bride who has the status of those "servants of a rather low order, whose business is to serve sources of power." He attempts to be of use: as escort, as footman, as clerk, or as "a companion for the younger children" (EHA, 103, 1117), but he fails to be of direct aid to his father – an act that would have had something in it of the male. Instead, he becomes "a sort of nurse" to the family and a "dry nurse" to his ailing mother (HA, 67, 72).

19   From the Editor's Preface by Henry Cabot Lodge (EHA, xxvii).

20   This description is provided by William Fleming, *Arts and Ideas* (3rd edition. New York: Holt, Rinehart and Winston, n.d.), 193–194. Other scholars quibble over the precise identification of Euclid and Boethius.

21   James Hall, *Dictionary of Subjects and Symbols in Art* (New York: Icon Edition, Harper & Row, 1974), 245–246, 278–279.

22   From *The Oxford Companion to Art*, ed. Harold Osborne (Oxford, at the Clarendon Press, 1986), 658. The following quotation: 658–659.

23 The term "art" had begun to loosen by the Italian Renaissance as the consequence of Leonardo's efforts to merge formerly isolated areas of painting and technology; the Baroque period continued to open up the meaning of "art" and the "arts."

24 Ibid., 658.

25 Throughout *Mont-Saint-Michel and Chartres* Adams tries to work his way through the question of whether the Virgin's admitted force is that of the muse who inspires or that of the creator who makes. Current feminist positions would find it hard to credit Adams as viewing that Woman as anything other than another "muse" – fixing her into a "begonia" role without true authority or autonomy. As Mary K. DeShazer puts it in her essay (one of a battery that assails the tradition of the woman as muse), "the concept of the muse has been a luxury of race and gender privilege, a metaphor of colonization." However, "women poets today are reimagining the muse in nonhierarchical ways, rejecting the passive, objectified version of men poets and revisioning her instead as an active source of inspiration, a force born of their own artistic energy and will." See " 'Sisters in Arms': The Warrior Construct in Writings by Contemporary U.S. Women of Color" (WA, 278).

26 Bostonians are "sexless" (not adequately male); capable only of "breeding" (the function of female bodies); and eager to "instruct" (part of the feminized schoolmarm tradition belittled elsewhere in the nation). See Letters, II;275; IV:37.

27 Oscar Seyffert, *Dictionary of Classical Antiquities;* revised, ed. Henry Nettleship and J. E. Sandys (New York: Meridian Books, 1958).

28 Hall, *Dictionary of Subjects and Symbols of Art,* 154.

29 See "The Tendency of History" (1894) and "A Letter to American Teachers of History" (1910); in *The Degradation of the Democratic Dogma,* ed. Brooks Adams (New York: Macmillan, 1919).

30 Adams credited Karl Pearson, Jules Henri Poincaré, and other late-century scientists for admitting that Nature's law of disorder gives the "lie" to science and that it renders "fantastic" what the male dominion of science had once considered "real" (EHA, 451, 454).

31 See Adams on Maurice Maeterlinck's *The Life of the Bee* (HA, 360). Also see EHA, 474, for Adams's likening (for "convenience as an image") of his "dynamic theory" to man as the spider-mind waiting to pounce upon his prey. Charlotte Perkins Gilman found it just as convenient to image the male as the female spider's meat (*Women and Economics,* 135).

32 Clover Adams's biographer, Eugenia Kaledin, refers to an unpub-

lished dissertation written by Sister M. Aquinas Healy, "A Study of Non-Rational Elements in the Work of Henry Adams as Centralized in His Attitude toward Women" (Univ. of Wisconsin, 1956). Kaledin also cites George Santayana's observation about Adams's "longing to be primitive" – which, in the gender terms of the times, meant "longing to be female" (Kaledin, 171).

33 See Letters, IV:304, for Adams's letter of sympathy to Elizabeth Cameron concerning her state of crisis so like his own for which doctors propose "complete rest and quiet amusement," however useless such remedies are – cures linked in infamy to Gilman's "The Yellow Wallpaper."

34 Adams cuts Clover Adams's presence out of *The Education*; he did not, however, excise her from his life, which is what Theodore Roosevelt did to his first wife almost from the moment of her death. Roosevelt, the man of "pure act" and Adams's bête noir, completely effaced the image, the name, the fact of the existence of Alice Hathaway Lee. See Edmund Morris, *The Rise of Theodore Roosevelt* (New York: Ballantine Books, 1980), 244.

35 Bundtzen, "Power and Poetic Vocation in Adrienne Rich's *The Dream of a Common Language*" (WA, 43–59).

36 Bundtzen's quotations are taken from Cixous's "Castration or Decapitation?" trans. Annette Kuhn, *Signs* 7 (1981). Subsequent pagination given within parenthesis is keyed to Bundtzen's essay.

37 Laird, "Aurora Leigh: An Epical Ars Poetica," WA, 355–356.

38 See Bundtzen, 46–48, for this and the following quotations.

39 Note that point in *The Education* where Adams states that he sees Carlyle crash as a fallen idol. It is the point where Carlyle's (racist) foamings against the idea of democracy offended Adams as the young patriot working at his father's side during the Civil War. Unfortunately, Adams later found Carlyle's bigotry not so offensive.

40 Adams's concern with making history scientific throws a side light upon his touchiness over the value of exceptional individuals. In his descriptions of Sumner and Macaulay (EHA, 32, 221, 258), he points out that their uniqueness makes them impossible to imitate. Adams as scientist manqué, of course, wished to hit upon the basic laws of the universe; such laws do not permit "sports" or anomalies – the one-time event that cannot be duplicated through experimentation. The hero which by definition cannot be verified through repetition is of little scientific value.

41 As a youth Adams had fled the terrible truths of northern England's

industrial Black District (EHA, 73). Upon Clover's death he acknowledged that his only chance for survival depended upon going "straight ahead without looking behind," adding that he felt "like a volunteer in his first battle. If I don't run ahead at full speed, I shall run away." Found wanting like Stephen Crane's Henry Fleming, Adams observes, "If I could but keep in violent action all the time, I could manage to master myself," but – like Fleming – his "mind gives me no let up" (Letters, II:643).

42 Adams, struggling to be the scientific historian, argued that he must avoid "truth" in order not to "falsify his facts," even though he was notoriously indifferent to "facts" per se (EHA, 457).

43 Letter of January 18, 1882, from Clover Adams to her father. *The Letters of Mrs. Henry Adams,* ed. Ward Thoron (Boston: Little, Brown, 1936), 329.

44 The quotations from Lerner's "The Challenge of Women's History" are from the introduction to *Meanings for Manhood,* ed. Mark C. Carnes and Clyde Griffen (Chicago: Univ. of Chicago Press, 1990).

4

Henry Adams's *Education* in the Age of Imperialism

JOHN CARLOS ROWE

He had nothing to do with Hay's politics at home or abroad.
    – *The Education of Henry Adams*, ch. 24, p. 366.

With Hay's politics, at home or abroad, Adams had nothing whatever to do.
    – *The Education of Henry Adams*, ch. 24, p. 373.

I HAVE always been baffled by the final one hundred fifty pages of Henry Adams's *Education*, from chapter 24, "Indian Summer," to chapter 35, "Nunc Age." The world history Adams recounts from the Spanish-American War in 1898 to the Russo-Japanese War of 1904–1905 is, of course, enormously complicated. With his penchant for finding chaos everywhere and ignorance in everyone, not least in himself, Adams wants to confuse the reader further. In a more generous vein, I might suggest that these chapters rhetorically simulate the kind of confusion experienced by a knowledgeable political observer faced with world events at the turn of the century. Confusing as those world events were, Adams makes them even more incomprehensible by digressing at crucial moments into philosophical speculations, tirades against the "New Woman," and sardonic judgments of the personalities of such major political figures as Teddy Roosevelt, Lord Pauncefote, Cassini, John Hay, and the Kaiser. Scholars and critics have labored over these pages in efforts to do justice to the coherence of Adams's prose, often developing elaborate connections among "The Dynamo and the Virgin," "A Dynamic Theory of History," and the international politics described.[1]

Few critics, however, have been willing to read these pages in terms of their essentially digressive, discontinuous, and incoherent qualities, perhaps because there seems little profit in such work other than the conclusion that Henry Adams had lapsed already into his final nihilism. Instead, his world-weary pose in the last third of *The Education* is most often used to support the view of Henry Adams as radical skeptic and ironist, who has assumed a canonical place in American *literature* by displaying that contempt for politics so characteristic of the literary moderns.[2]

Like so many of these moderns, Henry Adams has been protected by his "literariness" from critiques of his political attitudes. In Henry Adams's case, there are practical reasons why such criticism might prove embarrassing. In his letters from 1890 to 1905, the year in which he wrote much of *The Education* and the Russo-Japanese War was settled by the Treaty of Portsmouth, Henry Adams repeatedly endorses the conservative political economy of his brother, Brooks Adams.[3] For both, U.S. economic expansion into new markets in the Far East, the Caribbean and Central America, and Africa is crucial to U.S. political stability as the powerful European colonial powers were either realigning their interests or losing their control of territories. Brooks favored the expansion of the domestic economy in accord with the development of new international trade routes and geopolitical commerce.

The historian Timothy Paul Donovan acknowledges that "Henry Adams agreed to some extent with his brother's concern," but concludes that Henry "could never become quite as exercised. This was because Henry had resigned himself, at least intellectually, if not emotionally, to the fact of eventual degradation. Brooks's proposals would only delay the process; they would not avoid it."[4] Yet, Donovan's distinction of Henry's view from Brooks's depends primarily on Henry's "literary" writings, not on his correspondence in this period. The pose of world-weary, baffled, belated eighteenth-century observer of twentieth-century chaos is, as most literary critics have insisted, a highly stylized pose or narrative device. In his correspondence, Adams advises the most powerful leaders of his age to pursue policies that would consolidate the twentieth-century economic authority of the United States in international trade and serve as the bases for that special brand of U.S. neocolonialism understood in the era of the Vietnam War in the phrase "establishing spheres of influence."

Henry Adams's own contrived literary myth of the "manikin" on which the "education" of modern history would have to be draped has encouraged literary critics and even historians to forget the active role he played in U.S. foreign policy in the years of John Hay's service as Secretary of State. Despite his insistence that he was simply an "eighteenth-century observer" of the monstrous birth of the twentieth-century world, Adams was an active participant in the crucial diplomatic negotiations that established the United States as the leading economic and political power from the end of the Spanish-American War and the annexation of the Philippines to the Russo-Japanese War of 1904–1905. These seven years, under the administrations of McKinley and Teddy Roosevelt, constitute the critical moment in which a U.S. "empire" was developed. The most important figure in that period was Henry Adams's lifelong friend and neighbor, John Hay, Secretary of State under both presidents until his death in office in 1905.

Hay was Ambassador to England when McKinley invited him to become Secretary of State in place of William R. Day, who was to head the peace commission in Paris at the close of the Spanish-American War. In fact, Adams was with the Hays in Egypt when Hay's private secretary, "Spencer Eddy brought them a telegram to announce the sinking of the Maine in Havana Harbor" (*EHA*, 360) and in England with the Hays at Surrenden Dering when "the order [came] summoning Hay to the State Department" (*EHA*, 364). When Adams returned to Washington at the end of 1898, "he bumped into Hay at his 'very doorstep,' " who immediately appealed to him for help.[5] Samuels recounts how the political patronage system made it impossible for Hay to offer Adams what Hay so needed: his friend as Assistant Secretary of State or something comparable. Adams himself had hoped to succeed Hay as Ambassador to the Court of St. James (England), thus continuing the legacy of his father, in whose legation Adams served in London through the Civil War.[6] Although Adams expressed great "relief" at having so alienated the McKinley administration that formal appointment was impossible, he understood clearly that he was to play the role of personal advisor to Hay: "The two friends fell into the habit of taking a walk at four o'clock each day 'through a triangle of back streets' reviewing the day's work and, as Hay put it, 'discoursing of the finances of the world, and the insolent prosperity of the United States' " (*Major Phase*, 193).

In *Authority and Alliance in the Letters of Henry Adams*, Joanne Jacobson describes Adams's keen interest in "offering counsel on political events" to Hay soon after Hay assumed "the ambassadorship to England."[7] Jacobson interprets Adams's correspondence as generally divided between the demands of the public sphere and his desire to maintain a private world restricted to a small circle of intimates. What is striking about his letters between 1898 and 1905, however, is their directness in treating foreign policy issues and the clear sense that Adams was acting as informal counsel to Hay. Jacobson also points out that as close friends and next-door neighbors in Washington, Hay and Adams discussed U.S. foreign policy in even greater detail in conversation, making Adams's letter writing thereby serve as "an instrument of worldview – and of an alliance – within which private loyalty could viably compete with public power."[8]

Of course, Jacobson makes a good case for the *literary* qualities of Adams's epistolary mode – he was unquestionably one of the great letter writers in modern English, so her general thesis tends to stress the resemblances between the literary control of *The Education* and those of his correspondence.[9] Useful as her approach may be generally to the form and function of Adams's letters, it is still part of an aestheticizing of Adams to which he surely contributed and has distracted us from political views quite forthrightly and consistently expressed in his correspondence with and about Hay between 1898 and 1905. It is the difference separating the irony, equivocation, and rhetorical ambiguity in *The Education* from the conviction and decisiveness of his correspondence that strikes me as curious and still largely ignored by both historians and literary critics.

In the midst of the many ambitious, self-serving, greedy, and jingoistic statesmen of this period, John Hay and Henry Adams appeared to uphold principles of rational diplomacy and to balance conflicting international interests in ways that would prevent world war. The popular reputation of Hay as a selfless statesman forced to compromise rational principles of diplomacy to the imperialist zeal of Teddy Roosevelt persists in Gore Vidal's historical novel, *Empire,* and it is obviously the sort of paradoxical position that is compatible with Adams's own views on the "degradation of the democratic dogma."[10] One of the last political survivors of the Lincoln administration, Hay suited well Adams's own self-image of the eighteenth-century rationalist struggling to cope with the madness of twentieth-century politics.

John Hay was, however, far more modern than Adams or even Vidal suggests. More than anyone else in the period 1898–1905, Hay helped popularize the United States' foreign policy, in part by skillfully manipulating the public image of the Secretary of State. He was the Henry Kissinger of his own age, and he helped promote the myth that American expansion in the Caribbean, the Pacific, and the Far East expressed the commercial interests and general will of the American people. Hay initiated the custom of regular press conferences, and he had remarkably strong support from the press in an otherwise turbulent period. In his speech, "American Diplomacy," delivered at the New York Chamber of Commerce on November 19, 1901, shortly after McKinley died, Hay represents the United States as the world's peace-keeper, intent on preserving economic opportunities and the political autonomy of all nations: "We have striven, on the lines laid down by Washington, to cultivate friendly relations with all powers, but not to take part in the formation of groups or combinations among them. A position of complete independence is not incompatible with relations involving not friendship alone, but concurrent action as well in important emergencies."[11]

Certainly such a public position accords well with Hay's efforts to negotiate a new agreement to build the Panama Canal. In his early diplomatic efforts to supersede the Clayton-Bulwer Treaty of 1850, which had prevented the United States from building a canal alone, Hay was intent on a Nicaraguan canal that would be politically neutral, like the Suez Canal, as its governance had been defined in the Convention of Constantinople (1888). The new canal would have to be kept open in times of war and peace to ships of all nations without discrimination, it could not be fortified, the territory around the canal could not be colonized, and other powers were invited to subscribe to these international guarantees. That treaty was signed with Lord Pauncefote on February 5, 1900, but Congress insisted on three amendments: specific abrogation of the Clayton-Bulwer Treaty of 1850, removal of the prohibition of fortification of the Canal, and deletion of the clause requiring the concurrence of other powers. Teddy Roosevelt had argued vigorously that the original treaty created a canal that made the United States militarily vulnerable, rather than providing the sort of defense that Roosevelt insisted was necessary in the wake of the Spanish-American War. Although Hay resigned his position in response to these congressional amendments, President McKinley convinced him to try again and the amended Hay-Pauncefote Treaty was signed on November 18, 1901, the day before Hay's speech, "American Diplomacy."[12]

Whereas McKinley and Theodore Roosevelt still conceived of foreign policy in terms primarily of domestic defense, Hay viewed foreign policy in terms of the commercial interests he was convinced would replace military conquest as the focus of twentieth-century international politics. In "American Diplomacy," he equates our "peace-loving" character with "our normal activities . . . in the direction of trade and commerce; . . . the vast development of our industries imperatively demands that we shall not only retain and confirm our hold on our present markets, but seek constantly, by all honorable means, to extend our commercial interests in every practicable direction" (122). Hay's negotiations with Great Britain for a Central American canal were quite explicitly related to Hay's "Open Door Policy" in the Far East. His notes for the Open Door policy date from 1899–1900, and they are explicitly motivated by his desire to keep China and the Far East open to U.S. commercial interests: "In the same spirit we have sought, successfully, to induce all the great powers to unite in a recognition of the general principle of equality of commercial access and opportunity in the markets of the Orient. We believe that 'a fair field and no favor' is all we require; and with less than that we can not be satisfied. If we accept the assurances we have received as honest and genuine, as I certainly do, that equality will not be denied us; and the result may be safely left to American genius and energy."[13]

Self-evidently capable as the American commercial "genius and energy" might be of succeeding in "open competition" with the other commercial interests of the world, Hay was also working hard to guarantee such success. Having emerged from the Boxer Rebellion of 1900 both as a popular hero and as confirmed in the correctness of the "Open Door" policies, Hay negotiated the Canal Treaty with Great Britain in order to get Britain's assurances that it would withdraw from the Caribbean. In the press, Hay was simply defending the Monroe Doctrine, but in private negotiations Hay was trading the guarantee of U.S. dominance in the Caribbean and Central America for U.S. support of Britain's position in the Far East.

The Hay–Pauncefote Treaty involved a number of other treaties with Colombia (Hay–Herrán Treaty of 1903) and with the new Republic of Panama. In the latter case, the Hay–Bunau–Varilla Treaty of November 18, 1903, granted the United States the Canal Zone in order to realize the Senate amendments requiring U.S. fortification and defense of the Panama Canal. Thus Hay's negotiations with Great Britain regarding the Canal virtually guaranteed the United States' economic and political dominance in Central America, Colombia, and the Caribbean for the rest of the twentieth century. Hay considered these negotiations to be the beginning of a new coalition between the United States and Great Britain as the superpowers of the twentieth century. Hay was an enthusiastic Anglophile; his seventeen months as Ambassador to Great Britain had been the happiest of his life.

In *The Education* and his correspondence from the 1890s to the end of his life, Henry Adams characterized himself as a dedicated Anglophobe. In *The Education*, he revels in what he takes to be the collapse of the British Empire, although he interprets the decline of British influence to be the sign of Russia's growing dominance in international affairs in the twentieth century. Indeed, Adams's "prediction" that Russia would become the new "riddle" of historical forces for the historian to comprehend is often cited in support of his own ironic claims that "a dynamic theory of history" could be used to "predict" future events. Fear of Russia's "unpredictability" in global politics caused many of Adams's contemporaries, including vigorous anti-imperialists like Mark Twain and William Dean Howells, to advocate grudgingly alliances between the United States and Great Britain to "block" expansion by Russia and Germany, especially in Asia.[14]

In the years 1898–1905, one hardly needed the title of "scientific historian" to be able to predict the growing power of Russia and the Far East in international affairs or to anticipate the decline of the British imperium. Although he claimed not to share Hay's personal fondness for the British, Adams endorsed most of Hay's foreign policy decisions, most often on their shared understanding that the "new age" would depend upon commercial, rather than political, balances of power. In a letter to Brooks Adams of November 3, 1901, two weeks before the Hay–Pauncefote Treaty was signed and eight months after the U.S. annexation of the Philippines, Adams writes:

All our interests are for political peace to enable us to wage economical war. Therefore I hold our Philippine excursion to be a false start in the wrong direction, and one that is more likely to blunt our energies than to guide them. It is a mere repetition of the errors of Spain and England. I wish we could have avoided it, or could escape it, and return to concentrating our efforts on the North Pacific. . . . Our true road leads to the support of Russia in the north – in both cases meaning our foothold in Asia. . . .[15]

I am arguing that it makes more historical sense to understand Henry Adams as agreeing basically with John Hay's imperialist policies than as an anti-imperialist struggling to prevent Hay from pushing the United States to the center of the new global politics. Adams's reputation as historian and man of letters is built upon the scholarly account of his great powers of political prophecy: predicting in *The Education*, as well as other writings, the new balance-of-power politics, the central role played by the United States in such politics, the emergence of the United States and Russia as "superpowers," and even the horrors of European fascism.[16] Part of this myth is that Adams foresaw also the terrible costs of the new foreign policies being adopted by the United States, including our mistakes in Southeast Asia and generally in the so-called Cold War. Yet, most of what Adams "predicts" in *The Education* is the rise of the United States to global dominance, a future established rather clearly by the diplomatic work of his close and powerful friend, John Hay.[17]

My claim that Hay and Adams basically favored U.S. expansionism by way of developing commercial trade routes, opening foreign markets favorable to the United States, and controlling regions by way of "spheres of influence" is based on a rejection of the conventional accounts of both McKinley and Hay as "reluctant" advocates of imperialism, "forced" by historical events in the Spanish-American War to "pick up" that "white-man's burden" of which Kipling speaks in his odious little poem.[18] By the same token, I do not wish to portray either Adams or Hay as a cynical manipulator of mass opinion while working to consolidate the secret power of U.S. global dominance. A more nuanced historical account is needed of both figures, each of whom was a product of his historical moment and the good fortune that had positioned both men in relative situations of political power and social authority.

Hay's and Adams's responses to the Spanish-American War and the Philippine-American War are crucial elements in my thesis, not only because Hay and Adams ostensibly differed over the future of U.S. involvement in the Philippines but also because of the curious part "the Spanish War" plays in Adams's *Education*. "Indian Summer" (1898–1899) initiates the final movement of Adams's great work by invoking the complex historical questions raised by the Spanish-American and Philippine-American wars, only to sidestep the questions raised and both defer to Hay as political leader and yet separate Adams from Hay's politics. The Index to *The Education* lists one page number for "Philippines," p. 363, the second page of this chapter, and it is the invocation of the Philippines as a political issue and its repression in this chapter that renders Adams's political views so strange in this work.

The title for chapter 24, "Indian Summer," has rarely been taken to mean anything other than the idiom for "the final years of a person's life, regarded as being serene, tranquil, reminiscent, etc."[19] But Adams's reference to the "summer of the Spanish War" that "began the Indian summer of life" suggests another, ironic connotation typical of his style. The irony of Henry Adams's "Indian summer" on reaching "sixty years of age" being one hardly tranquil when viewed in terms of international politics seems typical also of the general play between public chaos and private stoicism so characteristic of *The Education*. Yet, the other connotation of "Indian" Summer is the suggestion that U.S. Manifest Destiny is finding a new project.

Adams could have easily put this irony to an anti-imperialist purpose, but he leaves it strangely undeveloped. Chapter 23 concludes with news of the sinking of the *Maine*, Hay's recall to the United States, and the Spanish-American War as the next proper topic of Adams's discussion. Instead, it is repressed or, perhaps more accurately, dismissed easily by Adams in the second and third paragraphs of chapter 24 (*EHA*, 363–364). Given Adams's strong views favoring Cuban independence from Spain, his apparent opposition to U.S. annexation of the Philippines, and his brother, Charles Francis Adams's, leadership role in the anti-imperialist movement, Adams's "silences" here are more worthy of interpretation than what he does say.[20]

These silences speak volumes about Adams's tacit endorsement of Hay's foreign policy of U.S. expansionism in the Philippines, and they set the tone for the rest of *The Education*'s criticism of imperialism as primarily the work of European powers or Russia. In effect, the United States is exempted from such criticism, John Hay serving as its personification and thus legitimation. Instead, Adams criticizes the English and the Germans in the Boer War and China, and the Russians in Mongolia and eastern Europe. What Adams does write about the Spanish-American War suggests that his reservations about U.S. involvement in the Philippines have less to do with his criticism of imperialism and more to do with his endorsement of the white-man's "burden" of colonial responsibilities:

He knew that Porto Rico [sic] must be taken, but he would have been glad to escape the Philippines. Apart from too intimate an acquaintance with the value of islands in the South Seas, he knew the West Indies well enough to be assured that, whatever the American people might think or say about it, they would sooner or later have to police those islands, not against Europe, but for Europe, and America too. (*EHA*, 363–364)

In the only other reference he makes to the Philippines in this chapter and in *The Education* as a whole, Adams understands it as a way of realizing finally the Adamses' ambitions "of bringing England into an American system" (*EHA*, 362). What Samuels glosses in this context as Adams's "characteristic overstatement of the family policy" is in effect Henry's endorsement, despite his Anglophobia, of Hay's alliance with Great Britain (*EHA*, 644, n5). In fact, what the Philippines finally mean for Adams is just this Anglo-American alliance in the new balance-of-power politics necessitated by the decline of British imperial hegemony and the rise of multiple colonial powers: "As he sat at Hay's table, listening to any member of the British Cabinet, for all were alike now, discuss the Philippines as a question of balance of power in the East, he could see that the family work of a hundred and fifty years fell at once into the grand perspective of true empire-building, which Hay's work set off with artistic skill" (*EHA*, 363).

It is perhaps just the uncanny connection between Hay's "empire-building" and his "artistic skill" that prompts Adams to digress so obviously in the remainder of this chapter from the major issue on the minds of most Americans in 1898–1899: the future role of the United States in the Caribbean (Cuba, Puerto Rico, and Central America) and the Philippines. The evidence that some sort of repression is at work in the rest of this chapter is coded between the lines, in graceful rhetorical connections left undeveloped and too subtle for any but the professional reader.

He is at Surrenden Dering with the Camerons and Hays when the "July 4, 1898" telegram arrives "announcing the destruction of the Spanish Armada, as it might have come to Queen Elizabeth in 1588; and there, later in the season, came the order summoning Hay to the State Department" (*EHA*, 364).

Of course, John Hay is Henry Adams's *Doppelgänger* in these later chapters of *The Education*, with all the psychic ambivalences built into Rank's term.[21] On the one hand, Hay is the proper heir to the political ambitions of the Adamses for the United States, a legacy Henry had failed to carry on. On the other hand, Henry insists that he "had nothing to do with Hay's politics at home or abroad," and repeats this claim in a rhetorical chiasmus that I have reproduced in the epigraphs to this essay and that forms the psychic "knot" of Adams's chapter 23. Having connected Hay with his family legacy by way of Hay's new foreign policy, Adams overtly rejects Hay's politics only to reclaim them covertly. Admiral Dewey's destruction of the Spanish fleet in Manila Bay is the equivalent of Sir Francis Drake's destruction of the Spanish Armada in the Bay of Cadiz in 1587.

Adams dances away from the real issues for Americans in 1898–1899 by substituting discussions of his visit to Italy with the Lodges, recalling his study of medieval law at Harvard, and chatting about John La Farge's stained glass windows for Trinity Church in Boston. Amid these diversions, however, the Adams who "had nothing whatever to do" with "Hay's politics, at home or abroad," continues to justify Hay's policies. Whereas Twain and Howells, among other anti-imperialists, vilified President McKinley for his expansionist policies, Adams treats the President and his Secretary of State as efficient managers. If there is irony in Adams's characterization of both with terms borrowed from the corporations, there is also Adams's admiration of the modernity of these two leaders: "Mr. McKinley . . . undertook to pool interests in a general trust into which every interest should be taken, more or less at its own valuation, and whose mass should, under his management, create efficiency. He achieved very remarkable results. . . . Himself a marvellous manager of men, McKinley found several manipulators to help him, almost as remarkable as himself, one of whom was Hay" (*EHA*, 373–374).

Adams offers the Hay–Pauncefote Treaty as strong evidence supporting his thesis that McKinley and Hay were "efficient" managers and "manipulators." Once again, the imperialist issues associated with the Philippines are sidestepped, but in a way that subtly justifies U.S. foreign policy in the South Pacific. Alliance with Great Britain is the United States' great destiny, Adams argues, and the British diplomats argue for us, as Kipling would in "The White-Man's Burden," that "the Philippines [is] a question of balance of power in the East." Working together, Anglo-American powers defeat Spain not only in military battle but also in treaties like the Hay–Pauncefote, with its consequences for U.S. hegemony in the Caribbean and British access to Asia.

Little wonder, then, that the great theorist of twentieth-century multiplicity should conclude chapter 23 by insisting upon unity: "History has no use for multiplicity; it needed unity; it could study only motion, direction, attraction, relation. Everything must be made to move together; one must seek new worlds to measure; and so, like Rasselas, Adams set out once more, and found himself on May 12 settled in rooms at the very door of the Trocadero" (*EHA*, 377–378). This sentence is curious enough in its own grammatical right – clumsily periodic, as if imitating the very multiplicity of the times that the sentence itself argues "history has no use" for, it struggles to make something out of Adams's chronic tourism and dilettantism.

Adams's apparently casual reference to his locale in Paris has considerable significance for the careful reader. Whereas the "door of the Trocadero" refers overtly to his residence on the Place du Trocadero, which was laid out in 1878, the entire site is a historical tableau of European colonialism. Originally, the area was termed "the Trocadero," the name given to the area "in 1827 after a military tournament on the site had re-enacted the French capture four years previously of Fort Trocadero."[22] Indeed, the entire area is one devoted to imperial and military display, as well as national monuments. Beyond the Place du Trocadero is the Palais de Chaillot, built on the Chaillot Hill and commanding a view across the Seine of the Champ-de-Mars, which includes in the contemporary foreground the Tour d'Eiffel and at the end of the prospect, L'École militaire (today flanked by UNESCO).

The military tournament in 1827 reenacted the successful reinstallation of King Ferdinand VII (1784–1833) on the throne of Spain with the aid of the French army. King Louis XVIII had reaffirmed French support for the Spanish King that went back to Napoleon's reestablishment of Ferdinand as King of Spain in 1813. Fort Trocadero was the site, just outside of the Spanish city of Cadiz, of the military defeat of the Spanish troops resisting the French army in the Bourbon King's bid to reinstall the Spanish monarch. "Trocadero" refers, then, to the decline of Spanish authority in Europe and to the rise of French imperial power, both in the name of Napoleon and the Bourbon monarchy that sought to expand its early nineteenth-century European power by various military, political, and marital alliances. For this reason, the battle was reenacted in this significant site in Paris. It is also, of course, a significant event in Spanish history, in large part because King Ferdinand reigned during the decline of Spain as a European and world power. It was during his reign that the Spanish colonies in South America rebelled against Spain.[23]

In a chapter that promises to tell us something of the Spanish-American War, Adams evades the central political issues and ends up in Paris, gossiping about the sights. Yet, in this case, the site of the Place du Trocadero reminds the reader of an earlier shift in the European balance of imperial powers that is now being worked out again between the United States and Spain. In fact, what was reenacted in 1827 in Paris at the Trocadero is reenacted a third time in Adams's 1907 *Education*, but now with the United States as the monumentalized power.

In the Parisian prospect Adams opens for the knowledgeable reader, there is much more than just this coded reference to "Trocadero" as the transfer of power from Spain to France and then from France to the United States in the seventy-four years separating the Battle of Fort Trocadero from the Spanish-American War. What Adams encompasses in his own cosmopolitan vista is also the Trocadero Palace built for the 1878 Paris

Exposition and the Tour d'Eiffel, recently completed in 1889. Adams's next chapter in *The Education* is "The Dynamo and the Virgin (1900)," and it opens with a reference to the Paris Exposition of 1900, the "Great Exposition" Adams claims to have "haunted, aching to absorb knowledge, and helpless to find it" (*EHA*, 379). I contend that Adams had already found the "knowledge" he needed, but had no intention of sharing with the general reader. "The Dynamo and the Virgin" is Adams's own literary version of the great Paris *expositions universelles*, along with the other "fairs" and "expositions" in St. Louis, Chicago, and elsewhere that Adams views with loving skepticism in *The Education*. In short, Adams's global and cosmic speculations in *The Education* are his versions of the spectacle of new cultural authority staged in these early modern expositions and fairs.

The Trocadero Palace is an excellent example of what Zeynep Çelik and Leila Kinney have called the "mechanisms of cultural production" that helped organize a new "global hierarchy of nations and races."[24] Built on the site of today's Palais de Chaillot, an uninspired but grand marble monument built in the early twentieth century, the Trocadero Palace was built in an eclectic style that "referred to the Islamic architecture of the [French] colonies, but its siting, size, and form as a whole created an image of France as a protective father/master with his arms encircling the colonial village."[25] The exoticism and exaggerated grandeur of the Trocadero Palace would not have been lost on Adams, who understood well the ideological purposes of such spectacular architecture.

Yet, this spectacle remains for Adams a token of an older imperial order committed to the occupation of territories and the material transformation of their cultures. The neoimperialist policies represented by John Hay's foreign policies and, I would argue, Henry Adams's grand historical theories and syntheses depended not on territorial or even spatial domination; they depended upon the command of "representational" power either in commercial markets or their equivalents in cultural productions. By chapter 25, Adams has digressed from the Spanish-American War in chapters 23–24 and the Paris Exposition of 1878 at the end of chapter 24 to the Chicago Exposition of 1893.

101

What he discovers there is not so much the secret of the new technologies by which the United States would make good on its bid to become the new imperial power of the twentieth century, but his uncanny ability to harness the representational power of these new technologies.

Admitting his ignorance of the technicalities regarding "electricity or force of any kind," Adams interprets the dynamo as "a symbol of infinity" and "began to feel the forty-foot dynamos as a moral force, much as the early Christians felt the Cross" (*EHA*, 380). This is a grand moment of rhetorical sublimity, often discussed by students of Henry Adams, but it is also typical of a certain rhetorical bombast, as grandiloquently empty as the Moorish architecture of the Trocadero Palace and as potentially dangerous. For Adams's rhetoric also organizes and hierarchizes the newly reordered "nations and races" soon to come under the sway of American authority. We have often enough understood this power to be based on American wealth or advanced technology, both of which other "nations and races" have needed with sufficient desperation to "pledge" themselves as shamelessly as King Ferdinand VII gave his allegiance to Napoleon and the French.

In a less complex manner, John Hay's "public policy" of respecting and even defending vigorously the rights of self-rule in what we now call the Third World often was merely rhetorical. Hay favored a naval coaling station in the Philippines, rather than colonial rule, and this set him at apparent odds with the enthusiastic imperialist policies of the McKinley and Roosevelt administrations. But the fact of the matter remains that Hay supported vigorously the "inevitable" colonial rule of the United States in the Philippines following the Spanish-American War. As early as November 19, 1898, shortly after he had accepted his position as Secretary of State, he wrote Whitelaw Reid about the anti-imperialist factions:

There is a wild and frantic attack now going on in the press against the whole Philippine transaction. Andrew Carnegie really seems to be off his head. . . . He says henceforth the entire labor vote of America will be cast against us. . . . He says the Administration will fall into irretrievable ruin the moment it shoots down one insurgent Filipino. . . . But all this confusion of tongues will go its way. The country will applaud the resolution that has been reached.[26]

The Philippine people did not, of course, "applaud" the Republican resolution that instituted the United States' rule of the country, and insurgents attacked Manila and declared war on the United States on February 4, 1899. Several months after Aguinaldo, the primary leader of the insurgents, was captured in March 1901, but the terms of peace between the United States and the Philippines were still to be worked out, Adams wrote Hay from Paris (November 2, 1901): "But I wish we were out of the Philippines. That is a false start in the wrong direction. . . . It leads us into a *cul de sac* in the tropics, and leads us away from our true line due west. Of course we are making mistake on mistake there, and drifting straight at the heels of England. The north Pacific is my line, not the south; our own race, and not the niggers, my instruments" (*Letters*, V, 304).

Adams had expressed similar sentiments in his correspondence from his travels with John La Farge in Polynesia, Ceylon, and the Middle East in 1890–1892. Often praised for the anticolonialism of *Tahiti* (1893) and those letters, Adams is hardly as "disinterested" in his criticism of the British and French in Polynesia as his studied role as dilettantish "tourist" leads us to believe. Behind his scathing indictment of the British and French for the disease, corruption, and social chaos they brought to the South Seas, there is Adams's own profound fear of miscegenation and the dilution of the Anglo-Saxon race.

His fears are quite specific, insofar as he discriminates easily between native Polynesians and West Indies' blacks: "Then comes the French Governor who is a Martinique negro. I am gratified to learn that some governments are stupider than our own. The French actually send here a full corps of West India negroes to govern a people almost as high-blooded as Greeks" (*Letters*, III, 403). The lineage of Tati Salmon is traceable to "a deceased London Jew named Salmon, who married the Teva heiress and created a princely house of Salmon" and to "Brander, a Scotchman of good family," and Adams finds the heirs "decidedly Polynesian, rather handsome" (*Letters*, III, 403). The five Brander sons, educated in England and accustomed to European habits and royal privileges, suffered financially when their mother took half of the estate and divided the rest among the nine children. The result is predictable: "The boys who were educated on the scale of a million apiece, were reduced practically to nothing, or just enough for a modest bachelor's establishment in Papeete" (*Letters*, III, 404). Had she read her Anthony Trollope, of course, Mrs. Brander (Adams is careful to name the Polynesian women by their European names) would have known the value of primogeniture, but this seems Adams's only complaint against intermarriage between these royal Polynesians and the European merchants, Salmon and Brander. On the other hand, Adams complains repeatedly of "the pervasive half-castitude that permeates everything; a sickly white-brown, or dirty-white complexion that suggests weakness, disease, and a combination of the least respectable qualities, both white and red" (*Letters*, III, 417).

Even as he condemns European imperialism in the South Seas, he endorses the values of European culture *and* the European family as "civilizing" influences. *Tahiti* is full of analogies between the genealogical line of Tahitian royalty and European ruling classes from the Greeks and Romans to modern times.[27] What the European powers ironically have accomplished is the fracturing of a coherent class structure that might have endured as long as the islands themselves. Adams's "solution" is simply to dismiss the South Pacific as a political and intellectual "failure," turning instead to the more insidiously racist clichés of the "March of the Anglo-Saxon" so prevalent in late nineteenth-century America and Europe:

I am satisfied that America has no future in the Pacific. She can turn south, indeed, but after all, the west coast of South America offers very little field. Her best chance is Siberia. Russia will probably go to pieces; she is rotten and decrepit to the core, and must pass through bankruptcy, political and moral. If it can be delayed another twenty-five years, we could Americanise Siberia, and this is the only possible work that I can see still open on a scale equal to American means.

These "means" are apparently commercial, since a few lines above in this letter to Henry Cabot Lodge (August 4, 1891), Adams had dismissed the Pacific islands as "financial investments" hardly "worth touching. They are not worth the West Indies, if you lumped them all together" (*Letters*, III, 519).

By working to establish a powerful international coalition with Great Britain that guaranteed U.S. domination in Central America and the Caribbean and underwrote Great Britain's interests in the Far East, Hay helped accelerate Russia's own territorial claims in Manchuria and Korea. Adams might cheer perversely that U.S. diplomatic agreements had provoked Russia into the confrontation with Japan that resulted in the Russo-Japanese War (1904–1905), whose treaty was mediated by the Roosevelt administration at the peace conference in Portsmouth, New Hampshire. The settlement of the Russo-Japanese War to the advantage of U.S. interests in Asia would have been John Hay's last great triumph, but he did not survive the negotiations. As Samuels describes it: "The task of diplomacy . . . would have to be to deprive Japan of the more dangerous spoils of victory, control of the Asiatic mainland," while Japan was given sufficient power in Asia to be "an effective counterpoise" to Russia (*Major Phase*, 322, 321).

Although scandalized as always by the "methods" of Theodore Roosevelt, Adams essentially acknowledged the great power the Portsmouth Treaty virtually granted to the United States as international "peace-keeper." But behind this noble purpose, there was the "mission" Adams shared with Hay to defuse military conflict for the sake of U.S. commerce. To his brother Brooks, in 1901, Adams wrote: "We all agree that the old, uneconomical races, Boers, Chinese, Irish, Russians, Turks, and negroes, must somehow be brought to work into our system. The whole question is how to do it. Europe has always said: Buy or Fight! So the Irish, the Boers, and the Chinese are likely to remain unassimilated. We Americans ought to invent a new method" (*Letters*, V, 306). Such a new method seems clearly enough articulated in Adams's correspondence of this period to be dramatically at odds with the speculative, relativist, bombastic rhetoric of the *Education*. The "new method" appears to be just as determin-

105

istic as the history sketched by Brooks Adams in his *New Empire:*

The road of a true policy is always that of least resistance, but it is sometimes that of no resistance at all. In other words, every country held and administered by force is a danger, and therefore uneconomical. If it leads somewhere, the waste of energy may be necessary, but in itself it is a waste. It is resources – coal, iron, copper, wheat – that force markets, and will force them over all the navies and artilleries of the world. (*Letters*, V, 306)

What Adams could conclude from all this in the *Education*, beyond the familiar "lesson" that "a student nurtured in ideas of the eighteenth century had nothing to do" with this new "system," was that "this capitalistic scheme of combining governments, like railways or furnaces, was in effect precisely the socialist scheme of Jaurès and Bebel. That John Hay, of all men, should adopt a socialist policy seemed an idea more absurd than conservative Christian anarchy, but paradox had become the only orthodoxy. . . . Thus Bebel and Jaurès, McKinley and Hay, were partners" (*EHA*, 424–5). Often praised for his grudging acknowledgment of the inevitability of "state socialism," Adams actually embraced a much more conservative and, in our own age, utterly conventional notion: that the conflicts between capitalism and socialism were part of a larger narrative that would tell the ultimate story of the international corporation.

The CEO for such commercial internationalism would hardly resemble the grasping Goulds or Fisks of the Gilded Age, the brash and aggressive political leader, like Theodore Roosevelt; he would be a diplomat in the manner of John Hay:

In his eight years of office he had solved nearly every old problem of American statesmanship, and had left little or nothing to annoy his successor. He had brought the great Atlantic powers into a working system, and even Russia seemed about to be dragged into a combine of intelligent equilibrium based on an intelligent allotment of activities. For the first time in fifteen hundred years a true Roman *pax* was in sight, and would, if it succeeded, owe its virtues to him. Except for making peace in Manchuria, he could do no more; and if the worst should happen, setting continent against continent in arms – the only apparent alternative to his scheme – he need not repine at missing the catastrophe. (*EHA*, 503)

Those who admire Adams's predictive powers ought to be reminded that this "prediction" has all the certainty of Jim's reading of the "Hair-Ball Oracle" in *Huckleberry Finn*. Peace or war, a new imperium would hold sway over the twentieth century. At its center would rule not simply the United States, but its best "representative man," the international diplomat capable of negotiating balances of power certain to be in the best interests of American genius and energy. Hay ended his speech, "American Diplomacy," with a quotation from Scripture, "which Franklin – the first and greatest of our diplomats – tells us passed through his mind when he was presented at the Court of Versailles. It was a text his father used to quote to him in the old candle shop in Boston, when he was a boy: 'Seest thou a man diligent in his business, he shall stand before kings.' "[28]

Adams's digressions at the end of *The Education* from the great and pressing historical issues of his day – that day in which the United States emerged as a new imperial power – are explained in part by his fin-de-siècle diffidence, his modernist ennui and skepticism. As each new international crisis "stumps" him, Adams turns apparently "away" to personal relations, philosophical speculations, nostalgic medievalism, "scientific" theorizing and prediction. Most of these "topics" have been used by previous critics to develop Adams's "symbolic" and "literary" response to modern politics; that is, they have been read as the predicates of his *literary* modernism.

In another sense, they may be discursive efforts to legitimate international negotiations conducted by Hay (and the McKinley and Roosevelt administrations), the details of which Adams knew quite intimately. His "confusion" and "ignorance" over such matters of foreign policy are literary poses to cover what he knew well were decisions made in the interests of a specific foreign policy intent on establishing a U.S. imperium – not in lands, peoples, or even raw materials, but in the control of nations and, of course, their markets. At the end of 1913, Adams answered a letter from William Roscoe Thayer, who was writing

107

the *Life and Letters of John Hay* that would be published in 1915 in two volumes: "The difficulties are chiefly political. You cannot possibly publish his private expressions about Russia, or Germany or Colombia, or the Senate, or perhaps others nearer to him – we'll say myself, to be cautious – yet without it, you can give no complete picture. I published all I dared" (*Letters*, VI, 629). Adams seems here to refer to the final chapters of *The Education*, in which his literary and philosophical digressions now appear means of protecting the "private" side of John Hay's work of foreign policy – an achievement unparalleled by any Secretary of State in U.S. history. Adams clearly mythologizes Hay in *The Education*, and yet he leaves his story deliberately unwritten, as if his life – the public and private man altogether – were some classified document. "Hay wrote little," Adams remarked, "He intentionally conducted his affairs by word of mouth" (*Letters*, VI, 630).

The argument that the latter third of Adams's *Education* is a deliberate effort to distract readers from the new political power elite of men like Adams and Hay borders on a reductive, conspiratorial, even *paranoid* approach to literature's ideological function. My critics would be justified in pointing out that *The Education* was privately printed, circulated among friends, and not distributed beyond that inner circle until after Adams's death. A vulgar conspiracy thesis in this regard would depend, after all, on the widest possible readership for *The Education*. Adams devotes far too much effort to his theoretical speculations and his "dynamic theory of history," even if we grant that it remains a profoundly "antihistorical" theory of history, for us to interpret these pages as written simply to distract us from the historical facts.

Henry Adams's reputation as a "major modern author" depends in large part on his recognition of the fictional foundations of every mode of human action, and this knowledge accounts well for his fatalism and skepticism. Yet, even as Adams trivializes the human subject, he celebrates the new power of the modern author. Adams's modern recognition that every form of knowledge – mythic, political, historical, scientific – lacks any substantial foundation beyond its own rhetorical design effectively transforms the compositional method of modern artists into the hermeneutic foundation for every mode of knowing. Left only with the fragments of previous systems of interpretation and thus government wrecked by History, the modern author could sign his name by way of the technical virtuosity by which he recomposed these fragments and gave his temporary illusion the formal appearance of truth.

When such a theory of the "compositional method" is applied to Henry Adams, the author of *The Education*, the conclusions are quite predictably literary and allow Adams to join those other moderns who dismantled the illusion of the philosophical subject for the sake of those personae who only partially "patch together" the authors of *The Cantos, The Waste Land, Ulysses*, and *Absalom, Absalom!* What Eliot's Tiresias and Hieronymo, Pound's Odysseus and Confucius lack, of course, is supplemented by the formal properties of the works in which they appear with new, modern significances. When applied to John Hay's foreign policies, however, the "aesthetic" of the "compositional method" helps legitimate the authority of the new statesman. John Hay was called back into the center of international diplomacy for politically expedient reasons. Hay represented the solidity, integrity, and moderate politics the McKinley Administration needed at the close of the Spanish-American War. He skillfully worked with international diplomatic instabilities produced by the European colonialism so essential to capitalist expansion. For all his great accomplishments, he "originated" nothing, merely playing with the historical fragments he inherited. The authors of the recent past – Great Britain, France, Spain, Germany, China, and Russia – became his personae. In the balance-of-power politics that he played, Hay composed a new authority for the United States that bears comparison with that of the modern literary author's.

For the modern artist, the entropic drift of the West could be reversed by way of unexpected combinations, new compositions of old elements, intellectual and disciplinary transgressions that would open the "closed system" required for the heat-death that is the end of thermodynamic entropy. For Adams, a "dynamic theory of history" depends on the assumption "that the rise of [man's] faculties from a lower power to a higher, or from a narrower to a wider field, may be due to the function of assimilating and storing outside force or forces" (*EHA*, 487). Throughout the final chapters of *The Education*, Adams stresses 1900 as the threshold of a new era characterized by the rapid acceleration of historical forces that could only appear to the citizen of the old order as confirmation of his own end. It is John Hay, however, who represents the transfer of historical energy from one epoch – 1200–1900 – to the next – 1900–2000 – in the final pages of *The Education*. The chapters, "A Dynamic Theory of History" and "A Law of Acceleration," lead directly to Adams's extended elegy for Hay in the final chapter, "Nunc Age." Nowhere is Adams's irony better illustrated than in this portrait of the dying man, John Hay, exhausted by his diplomatic efforts, and his superhuman accomplishment: "One had seen scores of emperors and heroes fade into cheap obscurity even when alive; and now, at least, one had not that to fear for one's friend" (*EHA*, 504). Adams's historical theorizing at the end of *The Education* accomplishes a marvelous prosopopeia, in which the dead John Hay speaks. Literally, of course, Hay speaks only of his own end, as Adams has him answer those who insisted he live long enough to complete the negotiations of the Portsmouth Treaty: "I've not time!" Literarily, Adams's theories have given credibility to Hay's diplomatic methods of "balancing" other world-powers for the sake of an ultimate global authority for the United States.

Adams's *Education*, then, like his pseudoscientific writings, is not just some literary diversion intended to distract us from the secret diplomatic negotiations that were consolidating a new power-elite. Adams's theorizing is performed in all good faith as the intellectual complement to the imaginative work of the new foreign policy represented by Hay. There is, then, a different sense in which we may understand Carolyn Porter's conclusion that "The narrative strategy of *The Education* . . . is designed primarily to deny what the act of writing it demonstrates – that Adams was a participant in the social process he presumed merely to observe."[29] The "contradiction" of observation and participation still belongs to a system of values in which thought and action, word and thing, are considered discrete categories. In the postindustrial era of the West that Hay and Adams helped define, such distinctions no longer have much relevance. Admittedly, both Adams and Hay still understand U.S. spheres of influence in terms of commercial markets, even raw materials; neither anticipated the economy in which no action can be distinguished from its mode of conceptual production, no thing escapes its discursive circulation.

Writing from Tahiti to Elizabeth Sherman Cameron in 1891, Adams notes: "La Farge has settled down to painting, varied by his usual mania for collecting photographs. I call it a mania because with me it has become a phobia; and he is almost afraid of telling me about his photographs because I detest them so much. Not that I blame him; for in my own line of manuscripts [in *The History of the United States*] I did the same thing, and had to collect ten times what I could ever make useful; but I hate photographs abstractly, because they have given me more ideas perversely and immoveably wrong, than I ever should get by imagination. They are almost as bad as an ordinary book of travels" (*Letters*, III, 408). Marian committed suicide by eating chemicals used in her favorite work, photography, so Adams's "phobia" about photographs is understandable, but his hatred of them is clearly more than personal here. Is the "imagination" a better representational tool in the global narrative underway as early as 1891: the rewriting of world power in terms of U.S. interests? Would the "photograph" simply reveal what Twain insisted the Kodak did for King Leopold's Belgian Congo: expose the facts behind the story of ideology? In our own time, the Kodak is, alas, obsolete; the portrait of ideology much more difficult to print. From positivist historian to literary modernist, Adams has often been celebrated for his searching critique of realisms and naturalisms of all sorts. But in light of his association with the new imperium of the United States, Adams's "hatred" of "facts" might anticipate the more ideological tasks that lay ahead for his beloved "imagination."

NOTES

1   Ernest Samuels's interpretation of *The Education* in Chapter 9 ("Twentieth Century Multiplicity") of *Henry Adams: The Major Phase*

(Cambridge, Mass.: Harvard University Press, 1964) remains one of the most comprehensive and historically specific readings of Adams's *Education*. Yet, even Samuels is distracted from the historical issues in the second part of *The Education* by Adams's complex scientific and philosophical speculations. Samuels even finds an implicit "division" in the book: "To a large degree the first – and longer – part of *The Education*, divided from the second part by the hiatus of "Twenty Years After," is shown as the drama of the potential participator whereas that of the second part is more markedly the drama of the detached observer" (382). It is a distinction that subsequent scholars and critics have generally reaffirmed, including Samuels's identification of the point of narrative division: "The succession of chapters beginning with 'Indian Summer' dramatizes the overthrow of the certainties of scientific theory and the abandonment of the assumption of the unity of the sciences" (384). The "relativism" of the last half of *The Education* thus appears to give warrant to all sorts of wild theories and half-baked speculations, even as this happens to be the period of history in which the most demonstrable and often determinate "events" were occurring.

2   It is just a step, then, from Samuels's division of *The Education* (see the preceding note) into Adams as potential participant in and as mere observer of history to the construction of Henry Adams as the "manikin" of literary modernism. With his detachment, irony, skepticism regarding history and technology, and his commitment to radical relativism, he provided an excellent complement to the values and aesthetics of the high moderns – Yeats, Pound, Eliot, Stevens, Joyce – who would begin to influence culture in the second decade of the twentieth century. To be sure, this was my argument in *Henry Adams and Henry James: The Emergence of a Modern Consciousness* (Ithaca, N.Y.: Cornell University Press, 1976).

3   David R. Contosta, "Henry Adams and the American Century," in *Henry Adams and His World*, Transactions of the American Philosophical Society, vol. 83, part iv, eds. Contosta and Robert Muccigrosso (Philadelphia: American Philosophical Society, 1993), pp. 40–41, qualify this by arguing: "Henry did not accept every detail of Brooks's theory. . . . According to Henry's version of [Brooks's] law, 'All Civilization is Centralization. All Centralization is Economy. Therefore all Civilization is the survival of the most economical (cheapest).' "

4   Timothy Paul Donovan, *Henry Adams and Brooks Adams: The Educa-*

tion of Two American Historians (Norman: University of Oklahoma Press, 1961), p. 154.

5   Samuels, *The Major Phase*, p. 192. Further references in the text as *Major Phase*.

6   Joanne Jacobson, *Authority and Alliance in the Letters of Henry Adams* (Madison: University of Wisconsin Press, 1992), p. 66.

7   Jacobson, p. 64.

8   Jacobson, p. 67.

9   Jacobson writes of the "interpenetration between Adams's letters and his imaginative works" to the degree that "a convincing case might be made for calling all these [imaginative] works 'letters,' both because they so aggressively privatized their original audiences and because they built so much mutuality into the process of reading" (p. 113).

10 Gore Vidal, *Empire: A Novel* (New York: Random House, 1987).

11 John Hay, "American Diplomacy," *Addresses of John Hay* (New York: Century, 1907), pp. 121–122.

12 William Roscoe Thayer, *The Life of John Hay*, 2 vols. (Boston: Houghton Mifflin, 1915), II, pp. 260–261.

13 Hay, "American Diplomacy," *Addresses*, pp. 122–123.

14 See my "How the Boss Played the Game: Neo-Imperialism in Twain's *Connecticut Yankee*," in *A Guide to Mark Twain*, ed. Forrest G. Robinson (Cambridge: Cambridge University Press, 1995).

15 *The Letters of Henry Adams*, eds. J. C. Levenson, Ernest Samuels, Charles Vandersee, and Viola Hopkins Winner, 6 vols. (Cambridge, Mass.: Harvard University Press, 1982–1988), V, p. 306. Further references in the text as *Letters*.

16 See, for example, Contosta, "Henry Adams and the American Century," who concludes his essay: "Despite exaggerations and downright mistakes in judgment, Adams anticipated nearly every major shift in the international balance of power during the twentieth century, including those that transpired long after his death" (p. 47).

17 The other part of this myth is that such prophecy is possible only by virtue of the poetic imagination, some vatic power that Joanne Jacobson (in *Authority and Alliance*) attributes to Adams's "speculative worldview." This is where the literary Henry Adams and the political figure might be more closely related. "Genius" may well be (and not only in this case) another name for being well connected or having some access to the powers shaping the future.

18 Both McKinley and Hay were represented in the press as "reluctant" or "inadvertent" imperialists, who had the "burden" of "liberating" Cuba and the Philippines from Spain. But anti-imperialists, like Mark Twain and William Dean Howells, were not deceived by these liberal rationalizations of imperialism. In "To the Person Sitting in Darkness," which appeared in the *North American Review* in February 1901, Twain identifies McKinley's policies in the Spanish-American War as learned from the other European "masters" of the new imperialist expansion going on all over the globe: "The Person Sitting in Darkness is almost sure to say: 'There is something curious about this – curious and unaccountable. There must be two Americas: one that sets the captive free, and one that takes the once-captive's new freedom away from him, and picks a quarrel with him with nothing to found it on; then kills him to get his land.'" Twain, "To the Person Sitting in Darkness," in *Selected Shorter Writings of Mark Twain*, ed. Walter Blair (Boston: Houghton Mifflin, 1962), p. 299.

19 *Webster's New World Dictionary.*

20 See Samuels, *The Major Phase*, pp. 185–186.

21 For the classic account of how Rank's "doppelgänger" became the modern psychological and literary concept, see Freud, "The 'Uncanny'" (1919), in *On Creativity and the Unconscious: Papers on the Psychology of Art, Literature, Love, Religion*, ed. Benjamin Nelson, trans. under the supervision of Joan Riviere (New York: Harper and Row Publishers, 1958), p. 129 ff.

22 *Michelin Guide to Paris* (Summer 1972), p. 44.

23 I am indebted to my friend and colleague, Lillian Manzor-Coats, for much of the historical information about Fort Trocadero.

24 Zeynep Çelik and Leila Kinney, "Ethnography and Exhibitionism at the Expositions Universelles," *Assemblage* (December 1990), 35, 37. I am grateful to my friend Susan Jeffords (University of Washington), for calling my attention to this essay.

25 Çelik and Kinney, 37.

26 Thayer, *The Life of John Hay*, II, p. 199.

27 See my "Henry Adams," *Columbia Literary History of the United States*, ed. Emory Elliott (New York: Columbia University Press, 1988).

28 Hay, *Addresses of John Hay*, p. 125.

29 Carolyn Porter, *Seeing and Being: The Plight of the Participant Observer in Emerson, James, Adams, and Faulkner* (Middletown, Conn.: Wesleyan University Press, 1981), pp. 209–210.

5

The *Education* and the Salvation of History

HOWARD HORWITZ

Historians undertake to arrange sequences, – called stories, or histories – assuming in silence a relation of cause and effect.[1]
  –Henry Adams, *The Education of Henry Adams*

1. Stories, or Histories

THROUGHOUT *The Education of Henry Adams,* Henry Adams's incessant search for education is intertwined with a
search for history. From the time Adams's first article is accepted
in 1867 by the *North American Review* (222), and especially after
he is appointed to the history faculty at Harvard, he frequently
meditates on the nature of history and on the office of the
historian. These meditations increasingly overlap his preoccupation with acquiring education, and as the book proceeds sometimes history seems the precondition for acquiring education,
sometimes education seems the precondition for having an account of history, and sometimes the two endeavors appear virtually indistinguishable. One might justifiably object that education
and history need not be so conjoined, but for Adams both under-
takings involve the momentous problems *The Education* so fa-
mously engages: whether or not the universe and human affairs
exhibit unity; whether humans can apprehend that unity (or its
antithesis, chaos).

The enterprises of education and history raise an issue yet
broader than whether a particular pattern – unity – exists and is
apprehensible. Finally, both involve the phenomenon of narrative. Do nature, past events, and human experience exhibit any
pattern – which Adams calls sequence – and can humans discern

pattern? This question obviously pertains to the field of history, but education, too, as Adams defines it, requires establishing narrative. Adams urges that education must "fit [one] for life" (97) or "for [one's] own time" (32). Such fit is achieved only if the student can extrapolate future trends from past patterns. "Education must fit the complex conditions of a new society . . . and its fitness could be known only from success" in foresight and adaptation (347).

Often in *The Education*, Henry Adams's experiences lead him to doubt that his correlative enterprises can issue in narrative. His supposed failure as a history teacher is typical: he "could never tell a story, chiefly because he always forgot it"; but his poor memory is, finally, an ontological inevitability, for life seems "a succession of violent breaks or waves" (312) rather than a linear narrative. Therefore, Adams's "education spread over chaos" (339): each episode of education clashes with its predecessors; no wisdom accumulates, no succession occurs, and "education always starts afresh" (367). The dubious prospect for narrative – as both phenomenon and recounting – is epitomized when Henry Adams confronts the dynamo at the 1900 Paris Exposition, which prompts this chapter's epigraph concerning the office of historians. The quiet ambiguity of "arrange sequences" raises the question of whether sequences preexist historians or are invented by them. Adams's parenthetical elision of "stories, or histories" further implies that "history" may be simply one story among many, with no greater validity and authority than fiction or legend or myth. History's truth, rigor, and utility, then – and hence its legitimacy as a formal discipline – is suspect. Certainly, historians, he continues, with their "unconscious and childlike assumptions," "had never supposed themselves required to know what they were talking about" (382).

Adams's sarcasm about the relation between history and stories encapsulates a preoccupation of many historians at the turn of the century: is history literature or a special, authoritative narrative based on scientific principles? In the lead essay of the inaugural issue of the *American Historical Review*, for example, William M. Sloane, chair of Columbia University's history department and an editor of the new journal, concedes that history has hitherto been "the highest department of prose literature"; but "the doctrine of the unity of history" adapted from science and philosophy has elevated history to a science.[2] By pairing "stories, or histories," Adams contests methodological distinctions like Sloane's; and more generally, just as it impugns idealizations of education, *The Education* routinely debunks what Adams calls "the religion of history" (91) and the naiveté of historians (342, 412), who (so says my epigraph) assume in silence cause-and-effect relations among phenomena. Adams's barbed self-deprecation when Charles William Eliot, new President of Harvard, invites him in 1870 to teach medieval history establishes this disdain for the pretensions of historians. Neither academically trained as a historian nor, he alleges, particularly familiar with premodern history, Adams is puzzled by the offer. "He knew no history; he knew only a few historians," he remarks (293). Adams's ambiguous "few" historians – he knows few and only few so-called historians merit the title – sets the pattern for *The Education*.

In the course of the book, ever fewer historians seem to qualify for the job. Historical explanations seem arbitrary and fanciful because "no one saw the same unit of measure," and so Adams's faith in the possibility of sequence seems to grow weaker, until he finds himself "with his historical neck broken" (382). Here, both the phenomenon and the discipline of history are scarcely possible. This point resonates metonymically in *The Education*, as all conclusions from experience appear merely convenient, salvific fictions, and finally failures. This is the accent commentators have most noted and appreciated in *The Education*.[3] Indeed, Adams's thorough critique of the progressive, metaphysical assumptions of fin-de-siècle Euro-American culture has led some critics to embrace *The Education* as a protomodern and finally proto-poststructuralist critique of the categories of history, knowledge, the subject, and ideology. In this view, *The Education* illustrates the postmodern problematization of judgment, identity, morality, and (in some instances) the very idea of America. Joseph Riddel extended the insights of John Carlos Rowe's *Henry Adams and Henry James* to argue that *The Education* transforms the genres of autobiography and history

117

into activities of "interminable reading" rather than conclusive realizations of self and education. Education "can prepare one [only for] questioning the end toward which education would be directed." For Riddel, *The Education* incessantly displaces the purported goals of education – definitive knowledge and the coherent ideas of American literature and culture that would be its subject. If education in *The Education* undermines the paradigms governing thought, then, as Gregory Jay extends the argument, the book's Henry Adams represents the way "human realities fail, or resist, being governed by the sociopolitical and philosophical economy of the American Order." In short, Adams's skepticism becomes the possibility of freedom from national ideology.[4]

But skepticism is not Henry Adams's only posture. He elsewhere offers a profoundly teleological view of history. When discussing his friend John Hay's frankly imperialist foreign policy, for example – which Hay and Adams called the Atlantic system – Adams remarks that "For the first time in his life, he felt a sense of possible purpose working itself out in history" (363). History is possible here because a Hegelian force of necessity is fulfilling itself under one man's guidance. In this view, any story is the inevitable and necessary outgrowth of a unifying purpose, of a great figure (Hay) and of history itself. In this moment, or more precisely in the figure of Hay, education is completed: Hay is one of the few "examples of success" in education, providing for Adams "the moment of highest knowledge" (347, 424).

In *The Education*, then, history is at once scarcely possible and perpetually fulfilling itself. Adams's affection for contradictions like this one is well known; in this case the contradiction is progressive. When he discusses the necessity for contradiction in pedagogy (Chapter 20, "Failure"), Adams adapts Hegel (in a way widespread in the period) to declare that contradiction might issue in some greater perspective. This teleological view intensifies in the course of *The Education*. At first, *The Education* debunks idealistic young Henry's quest for education; later the figure of Adams migrates between affirming and denying history, not to mention education; ultimately, Adams submits his "dynamic theory of history," which is at once his critique of history and recovery of history as unity. In the dynamic theory, history comes to an end and is thereby redeemed: phenomena are chaotic, without sequence, but at the same time recycle the same impulse and pattern. Thus, the dynamic theory converts chaos into the sign of unity after all. In this way, Adams tries to salve anxieties about cultural transformation and the passing of one (his family's) mode of authority. Finally, then, *The Education's* critique of historical assumptions about knowledge and sequence leads not to their undermining or rejection, as it might if conducted by a poststructuralist, but to their deeper realization. Reclaiming the ground jeopardized by historians' naiveté, *The Education* overcomes the crisis of knowledge and authority it narrates and seemingly inaugurates.

2. Autobiography, the Manikin, and History

The peculiar form of autobiography that Adams fashions is a corollary to his educational and historical ambition. In the "Editor's Preface" written by Adams for his friend Henry Cabot Lodge's signature, Adams announces his ambition first "to complete St. Augustine's 'Confessions,' " and second to expound "his favorite theory of history" (xxvii–xxviii). *The Education,* then, is a "literary experiment," as he called it in a letter to William James, adapting the literary genre of autobiography in order to exemplify the "domain of history."[5] Dissatisfied with the results, Adams wrote "The Rule of Phase Applied to History" (1908) and later, when that essay too seemed unsuccessful, "A Letter to American Teachers of History" (1910), which he arranged to be distributed among historians.[6] Leaving aside for the moment Adams's fascination with his so-called failures, we might ask why he did not write "Rule of Phase" and the "Letter to American Teachers" first. Why did autobiography initially seem to Adams the suitable genre to convey his dynamic theory of history?

Seeking to complete Augustine's *Confessions* would seem an inauspicious aim for an autobiography. What does it mean, after all, to complete a book whose subject is effectively dead well

119

before it ends? Augustine makes very clear that the objective of his confessions is to overcome and eradicate the self; the existence of the self marks for Augustine one's sinfulness, meaning one's distance from God. The possession of will – which for Augustine signals the existence of self – exemplifies this distance. If one must will oneself to act, Augustine explains, then one is not whole but divided, indeed "torn between several different desires." "For if the will were full, it would not command itself to be full, since it would be so already." That is, having to will oneself to act – which implies that part of oneself resists this willed action – implies one's distinctness from and incomplete love of God.[7] If, in contrast, one belongs fully to God, is "wholly filled" by God's love, then will is superfluous, virtually inconceivable; in this condition, there will be "no more toil" (232), because actions are simply signs of devotion and not really acts (willed and performed by human agents). Once Augustine discovers God, self and the action engendered by self and signaling the existence of self cease (along with memory and the sensation that makes memory possible),[8] and the closing four chapters of the *Confessions* consist, appropriately, of no events but of meditations on time and, more important, timelessness. One must wonder how a later author could *complete* such a work, already so complete that it abandons narrative and entertains formlessness as an ideal of devotion.

One way Adams completes (or rather continues) Augustinian autobiography is by speaking of himself as already dead, in an after-life, especially after the suicide of his wife Marian Hooper Adams. Indeed, as he wrote to Charles Milnes Gaskell, he conceived of *The Education* "as my last Will and Testament." Even more dramatically, the book was a means of suicide: he advised Henry James to write an autobiography in order "to take your own life in the same way" Adams had taken his.[9] Two well-known features of the *Education* exemplify the Augustinian model of self: Adams's use of the third-person narrative voice and his conceit of the manikin. The third-person voice – a stylistic feature epitomized by signing Lodge's name to the "Editor's Preface – distances the audience from *The Education*'s Henry Adams. It emphasizes that "Henry Adams" – author as well as protagonist – is, although an actual person, fundamentally a figure performing roles. The particular sort of figure that "Henry Adams" is is a manikin. In his author's "Preface," Adams writes that after Rousseau's "warning against the Ego" "the Ego has steadily tended to efface itself" and "to become a manikin" on which the autobiographer drapes "the toilet of education . . . in order to show the fit or misfit of the clothes. The object of study is the garment, not the figure" (xxx). The figure of the manikin, borrowed from Carlyle's *Sartor Resartus*, suits well Adams's Augustinian model. It captures Augustine's ideal that the self not be highly individualized nor, ultimately, the agent of one's own or anyone else's destiny. Events, history, and education become for Augustine transient and inessential phenomena, and for Adams, drapery.

The logical consequence to this vision is that *The Education*'s persons/figures, unlike people in histories and autobiographies or even characters in much literature, are not actors conveying and fulfilling intentions. This idea underlies Adams's early discussion of his travel letters from Italy published in the *Boston Courier* in 1860. However rhetorically, Adams modestly confesses that "He had little to say, and said it not very well, but that mattered little. The habit of expression leads to the search for something to express" (89). This remark parodies Locke's notion of the self as a *tabula rasa*. In Locke's philosophy the sensations and experiences that fill the slate become the property and finally the substance of the self. In Adams's vision, the fabric of habits clothing the manikin never amounts to essence but remains acquired patterns of action or thought. One doesn't express onself, as the saying goes; instead, the capacity to express is a by-product of the habit of expressing. Like the book's third-person narration, this sentence's passive voice captures (perhaps a bit too formulaically) the reflex and mechanical quality of action that Adams will emphasize in his dynamic theory. Whatever its actions and responses, the self remains a figure, occupied by the accidents it encounters and habits that drape it.

If the self for Henry Adams is a figure, however, it is nevertheless not a nullity. The narrator Henry Adams routinely reports

on the knowledge, consciousness, and memory of the protagonist Henry Adams, and can even consider whether or not he can
"satisfy himself what to do" (in this case about how to teach)
(300). Much as in the psychology of Adams's friend William
James, self, here, is palpable, enduring as a habit of mind and a
function of acquired habits and propensities. The phenomena
and events that for Augustine are merely transitory accoutre-
ments of the false self are for Adams also the crucial phenomena,
since their draping the manikin wholly constitutes its identity. In
this aspect, the manikin is a genuinely substantive figure for
self – self is not just the mechanical performance of roles but the
necessary metaphor for how those habitual performances are
coordinated.[10]

Augustine, too, thought of identity as a mass of habits rather
than as a metaphysical essence; for Augustine, habits constituting
the self remove us from the metaphysical essence that is God.
The mind, he says, "is weighed down by habit" rather than
"lifted by the truth" (172). Although foregoing Augustine's
moral framework, Adams also regards the habitualness of identity as an obstacle to truth. If the self for Adams is not sinful, it is
nevertheless mistake. For example, when (at his friends' behest)
Adams accepts his post at Harvard, he wryly comments: "He
thought it a mistake; but his opinion did not prove that it was
one, since, in all probability, whatever he did would be more or
less a mistake" (294). The better to succeed, Adams periodically
modifies his quest for education and seeks what he calls "accidental education," which he sometimes calls "practical education." Under these rubrics, Henry Adams seeks not what will fit
him for life but what will fit him for immediate exigencies.
Predictably, this modified pursuit also turns out to be a failure,
as Henry Adams continually rediscovers error when he aims at
education (whether general or accidental).

In figuring the self and its development as a series of errors,
Adams is parodying the very genre of autobiography, especially
as it has taken shape in America as the great success story that is
the archetypical "American life." If Benjamin Franklin's autobiography inaugurates this model of autobiography already as parody, Ulysses S. Grant and more recently Lee Iaccoca and Donald

Trump have written autobiography unequivocally to commemorate and even ensure their success. For Adams, in contrast, the self is always mistaken, said to fail; and formally – with the book's third-person voice and its derided manikin – the ego is diminished. (The irony of this view of autobiography is signaled by Adams's surprising selection of Rousseau as the inaugurator of the ego's effacement.)

Adams renders this attenuation of the heroic autobiographical self most dramatically when he rehearses the political tensions between the British and Union governments during the Civil War. The American diplomatic contingent in London is concerned that the British government has been aiding the Confederacy and plans to recognize it as a nation. There is ample evidence that the British – led by Foreign Secretary Lord John Russell, Chancellor of the Exchequer William Gladstone, and Prime Minister Henry Palmerston – have been not only consulting with the rebels but helping to finance and build Confederate warships. Despite their formal support of the Union, did the British harbor a "fixed intention to intervene" in the conflict, at least diplomatically (128)? Typically, Adams frames the political clash as a drama of education. The success of education depends on whether one can trust anyone's "word" (132). "There could be no sense in history" and no success in education unless motive and intention can be traced to or deduced from the various participants' words (151).

The particular problem here, of course, is that politicians lie. Nevertheless, however fraudulent a politician's words, both the student and the diplomat must "know . . . the motive that lay beyond the expression" (132–33). All the evidence points to a British inclination to recognize the Confederacy as an established government; indeed, this conclusion seems "self-evident," "except that Lord Russell obstinately denied the whole charge" (149). Adams is not terribly dismayed that he may have misinterpreted Russell and the others; misreading actions and expression is a familiar failing. But finally education fails and history lacks sense because the entire category of interpretation and hence historical pattern come to seem implausible. Russell "had no objects," meaning no intentions. Similarly, Gladstone had not meant his declaration that "Jefferson Davis had made a nation"; it was neither a policy statement nor an act of hostility toward the Union, Gladstone wrote in his memoirs, but merely a mistaken statement of fact and really an act of "partisanship" toward the North. If Gladstone and Russell speak and act without meaning, or else (although these are not equivalent) can decide forty years later that they meant the opposite of what they appeared to mean, then no "single will or intention" exists (here, to break up the Union). There is no motive to interpret and therefore no motive to history, and so Adams adandons "all reason and all hope of education" (164–65).

Henry Adams's Augustinian model of autobiography, then, jeopardizes Adams's companion objective to present his theory of history. If the categories of intention and agency are voided, then history can be at best senseless and education (as Adams defines it) inconceivable. Correlatively, his Augustinian model suspends the very category of "Political Morality" – his object in reviewing British war diplomacy – because his analysis eradicates the criteria for assessing anything like morality.

Of course, Adams is wrong to declare that he has forsaken the category of intention or motive; instead, he credulously accepts the retrospective accounts of career politicians (whose avowals and disavowals probably deserve more skepticism). And the category of motive that he recognizes is accompanied by those of history, education, and morality. Henry Adams's skeptical posture is countervailed by what one can only call the grave fervor so palpable in his critique of German and American education, of historians' naiveté, and of political morality, and conversely in his admiration for the foreign policy of men like John Hay or in his directive that citizens of the twentieth century adapt to the century's increasingly accelerating mechanics. Henry Adams's disillusion during the "Political Morality" episode may well be simply the idealism of a young man not yet persuaded of life's pointlessness. But the book's older narrator retains his hopes for an explanation of the trajectory, causes, and effects of human conduct, and the dynamic theory of history is surely a devotional to those hopes. We must try, then, to understand the integral rather than self-canceling relation that Adams envisioned between his theory of history and his adaptation of the Augustinian model of autobiography.

3. The Great Man and the Unity of History

Adams's parody of the autobiographical self resonates in his parallel genre of history-writing, and it is not accidental that the Adams persona defines the self as mistake while deciding to accept the post at Harvard. Adams's persona is a clear diminution of what E. R. A. Seligman and Charles A. Beard (both of Columbia University) called "the great man theory" of history-writing,[11] which, along with a teleological idea of progress and a methodological confidence about identifying causes and their effects, was one of the three central premises of historical discourse at the time.

The great-man theory of history is familiar to us from traditional political history. In this model of historiography, as James Harvey Robinson (also of Columbia) wrote, the historian compiles "striking events of the past" and identifies them with "the achievements and fate of conspicuous persons."[12] We "string our narrative upon a line of kings," Robinson sneered.[13] The result is an annals of statesmenship, with, Seligman wrote, events "ascribed to great men" like Caesar, Napoleon, and Washington.[14] This tendency is manifest in the major histories of the period (especially textbooks), like John W. Burgess's *Reconstruction and the Constitution* (1911) George Burton Adams's *European History* (1899) or *Civilization during the Middle Ages* (1894), and Woodrow Wilson's five-volume *History of the American People* (1901–1903), and including as well Robinson's own *An Introduction to the History of Western Europe* (1903), his colleague Beard's *Contemporary American History* (1914), and Beard and Robinson's *Outlines of European History* (1916). Henry Adams's own histories of the early republic, culminating in the monumental, nine-volume *History of the United States of America during the Administrations of Jefferson and Madison* (1889–91), were focused through the activities of people like these two early Presidents and also *Albert Gallatin* (1879) and *John Randolph* (1882).[15]

Almost despite their practice, prominent historians like the authors just listed objected that the great man theory, while it may fulfill our desire for the dramatic,[16] was far too theatrical and arbitrary. As an alternative, the revisionists, who came to be known as the progressive historians, sought to "raise history to the rank of a science," as Adams wrote in "The Tendency of History" (1894), an open letter he wrote to the American Historical Association when his tenure as its president expired.[17] By scientific, these scholars meant a history that discovered laws of historical action and development that were analogous if not equivalent to natural (meaning physical) laws. Ideally, these laws would, Frederick Teggart of the University of California wrote, "express the constant relations among phenomena."[18] These constant relations amounted to the "continuity or unity of history," as Robinson phrased the principle for the Congress of Arts and Science at the 1904 St. Louis Exposition.[19] I cite Robinson's formulation among myriad others because its typical conflation of "continuity" with "unity" so nicely suggests the assumptions driving the doctrine, assumptions that *The Education* often ridicules. "Continuity" and "unity" are not, of course, synonyms. The successiveness or even progression denoted by "continuity" connotes less coordination than does "unity." Nevertheless, the terms were used interchangeably, with the phrase "the unity of history" frequently used to stand for history's continuity.

Before the nineteenth century, the human species was thought to be discontinuous with other species, a special creature unrelated to so-called lower orders, divinely made out of nothing or out of dust. This idea was one element of the prevalent account of temporal alterations among species, called catastrophism. Catastrophism held that biological changes were sudden and wholesale, with later species, like humans, having no antecedents in earlier ones. Although portions of this idea survived to contest evolutionism, Jean Lamarck, Charles Lyell, and Charles Darwin – whatever the conflicts in their understanding of the mechanism of physiological change – generally established that humans had developed *from* other species. In their view, alterations from species to species and within species were not catastrophic, as Albion W. Small put it with reference to historical change,[20] but incremental stages in the sequential modification that all species continually undergo.

The great-man theory suited the catastrophic model of historical narrative, positing that changes occur by the chance appearance of exceptional individuals. In contrast, the evolutionists, as Henry Adams called them in "Letter to American Teachers," believed that these conspicuous individuals must be understood as manifestations of particular historical conditions and confluences. For the evolutionists, the greatness of the great man was both function and emblem of historical context, which is to say of evolving historical forces. So understood, history could become an inquiry into the development of human phenomena. This reorientation led many historians to demand that their colleagues pursue "obscure" incidents, as Wilson wrote in his Chairman's Address to the Division of Historical Sciences at the Congress of Arts and Sciences convened at the 1904 St. Louis Universal Exposition.[21] This willingness to entertain the importance of apparently insignificant matters was one of the hallmarks of the so-called New Historians, whose best known figure became James Harvey Robinson after he issued a collection of his essays entitled *The New History* (1912). Robinson forcefully opposed studying "conspicuous events and striking crises" and advocated examining "the small, the common, and the obscure," the "homely elements in human life."[22]

In practice, historians did not heed this charge in any sustained way; nevertheless, the progressives' theoretical interest in the obscure detail and homely element exemplifies their evolutionary bent. Small details were the key antecedents in a progression – not merely succession – of events, with later events evolving from (not just following) series of preceding events. Hence, these historians' commitment to evolution (continuity) was also a commitment to a narrative of progression in the root sense of the word. Antecedents did not merely precede their successors but prepared the way for them.

The continuity discoverable in the phenomenon of history became unity for these historians because they assumed that the progression they observed amounted to a teleological pattern that they called progress. Like continuity and unity, the terms progression and progress are surely not synonymous, but historians conflated them: as a narrative of progression, history was also, therefore, a narrative of progress, of what Adams called "elevation," and Adams was a rare voice criticizing historians' elevation of progression into progress. Thinking of the phenomenon of history as progress and of history-writing as both the commemoration and continuation of that progress involves two related assumptions. First, it presumes the moral superiority of later to earlier forms of social organization and human conduct; second, it assumes that later stages of development are fulfilling the possibilities of earlier stages, and that some ultimate, even perfect form of social organization and human conduct is immanent in present conditions.

Students of the development of the historical discipline, like David Noble and Dorothy Ross, have noted what they call the millennialism of turn-of-the-century American historians, for whom Western civilization and especially American society were fulfilling a divine plan for the perfection of man.[23] This teleological enthusiasm suffuses everything historians wrote. A concise example of millennialism appears in the contribution of Columbia's William Sloane to the 1904 St. Louis Congress of Arts and Science. Sloane celebrates Giambattista Vico as the first "historical evolutionist. To him the story of a nation was the record of an ever complete realization in fact of certain remnants of a pre-natal revelation." This realization reveals a "law of moral progress" through which "all human faculties . . . perfect themselves."[24]

Frederick Jackson Turner extolled history in similarly exalted terms. "History [both the phenomenon and its study] has a unity and a continuity" because it is, "in truth, the self-consciousness of humanity," a self-consciousness acquired by understanding its development from the past, "the undeveloped present."[25] Because history is the "becoming" of the present in the past and of both the past and future in the present, the study of history can "enable us to behold our own time and place as a part of the stupendous progress of the ages"; it can "enable us to realize the richness of our [unconscious] inheritance, the possibility of our lives, the grandeur of the present."[26] In Turner's most famous essay, the frontier is a receding border where past – the "inherited ways" of Europe – and inchoate present – the coarse, practical, and individualistic – cross-fertilize to provide "a gate of escape from the bondage of the past."[27] At the frontier, then, the Enlightenment past is at once continued and purified, and the present is an ever more perfect realization of democratic ideals.[28]

Charles A. Beard, best known for criticizing the American Constitution as an expression of moneyed interests, is a supreme example of the progressive historians' teleological bent. In *The Industrial Revolution*, Beard bemoans the misery unleashed by industrialism, with its mechanization of individual action and subordination of the human "desire for freedom . . . to the production of marketable commodities." Having made individualism possible in the first place, industrialism then compromised it. But ultimately industrialism redeems individualism. "The hope of the future," Beard urges in an idealistic Hegelian mode, is the very "corporate society" that evolved to sustain industrialism. For Beard, the individual is reempowered by being transfigured in the highest form of corporate organization, the trust. Without denying the trusts' dislocation of and at times violence against workers, Beard – like most Americans who contemplated it, labor leaders like Eugene Debs no less than John D. Rockefeller – considered the trust the latest manifestation and intimation of progress. Progress, Beard reflects, consists of the substitution of "organization for chaos and anarchy," and "the trusts are merely pointing the way to higher forms of industrial methods in which the people, instead of a few capitalists, reap the benefits." As the frontier does for Turner, for Beard the trust represents a higher freedom than common individual freedom, creating "unity in diversity" by "increasing intercommunication of all parts of the world." Therefore, the trust induces "education from the lowest to the highest form," "training . . . the individual, so that in seeking the fullest satisfaction of his own nature he will harmoniously perform his function as a member of a corporate society." Through the trust, individualism is redeemed by being "elevated to social service," and therefore the trust is the fulfillment of both antecedent forms of organization and an innate human desire for freedom.[29]

Beard is typical in transforming the identification of continuity in development into a celebration of progress toward a teleological order consolidated in the term unity.[30] Some historians criticized their colleagues' millennial spirit. In 1916, Frederick Teggart urged historians to distinguish Darwinian evolution from their incurably teleological ideas of progress and unity. If Darwinian evolution speaks of "an orderly process" by which new forms of life emerge from old ones, nevertheless evolution manifests no intrinsic direction and seeks no goal or final shape. It effects, as David J. Hill put it, "variations" rather than linear development in human conduct and social organization.[31] In a similar spirit, Adams wryly submitted that "evolutionists might be said to consider not the descent but the ascent of man."[32] But Adams further, and uniquely, spurned the assumptions behind the Darwinian model of scientific history.

4. *Pteraspis,* Causes, and Effects

Adams's assault on historians' commitment to unity has two stages, both ironic. In the first, he derides evolutionists' faith that natural selection spawns the elevation of species; in the second, he casts doubt on the evidence for evolution. In *The Education*, Henry Adams searches in vain for signs of progress: "Perhaps growth in human nature might show itself" in politics, or, when that fails, in religion or art. But such growth is nowhere evident, especially given features of nineteenth-century life like the dramatic increase in massacres (352). Adams is unable to persuade himself that human affairs exhibit elevation.

"Letter to American Teachers of History" addresses this point in more technical terms. This essay considers whether history can become the discipline that will "impose on a University a final law of instruction" ("American Teachers," 137). To do so, history must conduct itself according to scientific principles. But the two most prominent scientific doctrines of the late century – evolution and Kelvin's second law of thermodynamics – present contradictory models of development. "As popularly disseminated," the doctrine of evolution is comforting, trumpeting that with each episode of natural selection humankind's ability to manage nature and social organization increases (157). This narrative of ascent rests on a discredited law of physics, the law of the conservation of energy, which "assumed the unity and indestructibility of Force or Energy." In contrast, the second law of thermodynamics posits "a universal tendency to the dissipation of mechanical energy." That is, when energy is generated, some force (both generated and generating) is dissipated in the form of friction or heat. Scientifically, Kelvin's second law means that eventually the earth will become, as it once was, "unfit for the habitation of man" (140–41).

"Unfit" punningly points to the conflict between the scientific historians' models of change. Their ascent model fancies increasing fitness; the other admits what Adams calls degradation, "the steady and fated enfeeblement and extinction of all nature's energies" (157). Historians and other scientists evade this contradiction only by becoming vitalists, "adherent[s] of the doctrine that Vital Energy [is] independent of mechanical law" (146). Because neither scientists nor humanists accord vital energy (something akin to soul) to the species from which humans evolved, Adams asks whence it comes. His taunting answer is that the doctrine of evolution must include a third law of energy, that evolution *adds* energy, vital energy (154). Besides being inconsistent with the laws of both conservation and thermodynamics, this postulate flagrantly disregards the obvious fact that, as the chemist Wilhelm Ostwald noted, " 'animated beings always grow old, and never young' " (154). The survival of vitalism in scientific and humanist thought confirms for Adams that science is the latest form of religion rather than its antithesis. But if vitalism renders evolutionism logically incoherent, Adams maintains, it nevertheless furnishes the mechanism of ascent in the evolutionists' narrative of elevation.

Adams's challenge to the narrative of elevation extends to the alleged continuity of history. Adams writes in "The Rule of Phase Applied to History" that historical developments may be only "changes of phase."[33] With the term "phase," Adams adapts to history the premise of physics that a substance – or more to the point, a substance's form – is not permanent but a phase subject to dissolution by solvents into other phases. Although at any phase a substance is said to be at equilibrium, this state is always "more or less unstable." The rate of instability for any substance may be calculable (283), but this calculation can predict only rates of change, not the direction of change. By this analysis, Adams undermines the progressive model of history and resurrects a catastrophic model (that is tacit in Darwin). Changes in phases of human development and thought are potentially merely mutations (277), sudden changes without necessary antecedents and resultants (300). Hence, in *The Education*, "education always starts afresh" (367).

For its part, *The Education* tends to adopt the posture of "Rule of Phase," beginning with an ironic assault on the conclusions and supposed comforts of Darwinism. Henry Adams is enthralled with Darwin's work not because he understands it – few really did, he says – but because it abetted the current fashion of annoying theologists. With Charles Lyell's 1866 *Principles of Geology*, however,

Darwinian doctrine grew in stature. Natural Selection led back to Natural Evolution, and at last to Natural Uniformity. This was a vast stride. Unbroken Evolution under uniform conditions pleased everyone – except curates and bishops; it was the very best substitute for religion. . . . (225)

Henry Adams is perplexed by the doctrine of uniformity. If natural selection concerns changes in form, often by mutation, then how can all life be uniform? Two examples favored by evolutionists are the most damaging. *Terebratula*, discussed by Lyell, "appeared to be identical from the beginning to the end of geological time." But "this was altogether too much uniformity and much too little selection." Then there is *Pteraspis*, the first vertebrate. No known "vertebrates or any other organism" preexist *Pteraspis*, and if *Pteraspis* sprang from an "eternal void," then evidence for continuity, much less uniformity, is at best elusive (228–30).

As many critics have noted, Henry Adams regularly invokes *Pteraspis* as a conceit for the vanity of evolutionism.[34] Adams's definition of education as something that should (but fails to) "fit [one] for life" (97) is a concerted pun on evolutionism. For the younger Henry Adams, once the tenet of ascent is discredited, "nothing suggested sequence" (228), for "all he could prove was change" (230). Without sequence, no history (either as phenomenon or discipline) is possible. Henry Adams's skepticism suggests why historians' idea of continuity needed to entail the co-doctrines of progress and unity. A narrative of unity helped historians present themselves as authoritative cultural arbiters. Without the teleological bearing of "unity" and "progress," "continuity" has no particular cultural or disciplinary force because it lacks a distinct shape, or more to the point, a familiar and predictable shape from which to deduce conclusions about culture.

"Predictable," here, points in two temporal directions. Development into the present must appear to have been necessary; but the unity of history must be prospective as well, providing a basis for predictions about the future and for guidance in managing it. Every historian in the period, of whatever academic or political stripe – a conservative like Adams or an avowed radical like Robinson – argued that the study of history was indispensable to understanding present conditions and therefore to guiding future conduct. Without the doctrine of unity, this most progressive of their aims – what Robinson called "promot[ing] rational progress" by studying "the technique of progress" embodied in history – would be frustrated.[35] Continuity alone cannot furnish this benefit, because its direction can vary; it cannot warrant the linear, unified development that the progressives' progressivism demanded.

The scientific historical laws that could furnish a view of unity could be established, historians agreed, only once causes and their effects have been identified. Edward Freeman of Oxford was largely credited with securing the link between causes and effects that makes scientific history possible, but his work also displays the precariousness of this link and suggests why historians generally remained, as Adams charged in my epigraph, silent about cause-and-effect relations. Freeman was dubbed "the Nestor Historian" by Johns Hopkins' Herbert Baxter Adams, and his east coast lecture tour of 1881 and 1882 was a great rage; his motto, "History is past politics and politics present history," pre-sided above the history students' library at Johns Hopkins and was selected by Hopkins' Adams as the epigraph to the series *Johns Hopkins University Studies in Historical and Political Science.*[36] For Freeman, historical pursuit seeks the "unfolding of effects according to their causes."[37] To unfold cause-and-effect rela-tions – which would in effect anchor political behavior – histori-ans must distinguish between what he called "real" or "like" causes of events and mere occasions for them, which are acci-dental or only "apparent" causes.[38] If what appear to be like causes are only "apparent" and not "real" like causes, then one cannot "predict that the same results will follow" from present causes as followed from apparently similar past causes. Concomi-tantly, one cannot then deduce laws of history nor, therefore, prescribe future conduct.[39]

Freeman sets out to establish a method for "tracing and testing of likenesses and unlikenesses," but as he proceeds he keeps expanding the conditions under which likeness among causes may turn out to be apparitional, and so he effectively sabotages his project. First, if like causes are "counterworked by other causes," then they "cease to be like causes" and do not "lead to like effects" (*Lectures* 231). This difficulty may be surmountable because the effects of the counterworking forces can perhaps be calculated. Second, and more damaging to his enterprise, "the causes which we know of may be counterworked by other causes which we do not know of, and may thereby in truth cease to be the same causes" (211). Even if the effects of such unbeknownst counterworking could be gauged, Freeman's third caveat virtu-ally makes the first two unnecessary: "In one sense it is perfectly true that history is always repeating itself; in another sense it would be equally true to say that history never repeats itself at all. No historical position can be exactly the same as any earlier historical position, if only for the reason that the earlier position has gone before it." Since identity is a function of context, no causes, however similar, are identical because they occur in dif-ferent contexts. Therefore, even real like causes can have unlike effects "if only because the earlier result itself takes its place

among the causes of later result." Consequently, Freeman continues, the exact reproduction of circumstances, characters, or
events is impossible. Later circumstances and causes may resemble earlier ones, but such imitations are not reproductions
(210).

By the end, then, as Adams might have done caustically,
Freeman effectively but unwittingly empties the set of like
causes. He has performed what we would now call a deconstruction of his premises. His scientific history depends on a distinction between a central, determinative category (real like cause)
and a marginal or parasitic category (apparent like cause), but
the first category keeps being absorbed by the second. Freeman's
distinction – which remained seminal for some time – rests on a
semantic confusion (that signals his uncritical positivism): for
Freeman, causes can count as "like" only if they are in fact
identical. Just as historians needed to transmute continuity and
progression into the more exalted categories of unity and teleological completion, Freeman finds mere likeness insufficient to
guide and constrain either interpretations of historical phenomena or future conduct; therefore, identity or equivalence becomes his criterion for likeness, even as he shows that this criterion can never be fulfilled.

As we might expect, Freeman remained undaunted, and his
faith was shared by most of his colleagues. Each time he elimi-
nates one possible condition for sustaining his governing distinction, he unhaltingly declares confidence in his method. For example, after he concludes first that history never repeats itself
because even like causes are unlike since they appear in different
contexts, and second that like causes of which we are aware may
be counterworked by causes of which we are unaware, Freeman
nevertheless concludes: "But we are perfectly safe in such a case
if we say that the same results which happened before are likely
to happen again; that is, that they will happen, if no counterworking causes come into play" (211). Note that Freeman's
expression of confidence contains the very caveat it is intended
to annul. So does his summation twenty pages later, where,
perhaps intuiting the circularity of his argument, he revisits

much of the same ground: "We may be sure that our rule will work in every case to which it applies; but it is often hard to say whether a particular case is one to which it applies or not." Therefore we can "say very little positively, but . . . we may, without rashness, say a good deal negatively." As a result, he concedes, we know that something will change but not how or in what direction.

If this remark once again seems to undermine Freeman's method for establishing causation, it doesn't impede him from announcing historical conclusions that remained cornerstones for the next generation of historians. Freeman, indeed, discovers the unity of all history. All important past causes – i.e., human agents – are identical with present ones; we can gain instruction from any political society, he avows, because man, political man, which means European man, "is essentially the same being in all times and in all places." And history is the working out of ancient (human, specifically hellenic) ideals.[40]

5. At Long Last, Unity

One should note that Freeman's conclusion compromises his evolutionism. His account stresses the universality of all cultural forms and practices, which are finally identical since whenever they occur they are manifestations of the same immanent, metaphysical power (called humanity). In Freeman's model of history, then, development can scarcely be said to take place because modification of forms is not, finally, incremental but negligible. Freeman articulates a uniformitarianism (the evolutionary alternative to catastrophism) so radical as to preclude substantive change. Adams will exploit such logical and methodological problems among the evolutionists in order to challenge both Darwinism's assumptions about progress and historians' uncritical acceptance of facts, causation, and sequence. This celebrated skepticism, however, does not rest with the modernist or even postmodern sense of discontinuity and fragmentation regularly ascribed to Adams.[41] Instead, his skepticism makes Adams work harder than most to salvage his faith in unity. He challenges the categories of knowledge, narrative, and self in

136

order to reconstitute them on different grounds, and I would submit that it is this strategy that constitutes his modernism. Finally, his faith is the more secure because founded on the very phenomena that led him to question other historians' convictions. He rediscovers unity, that is – and the authority attending it – precisely where he loses it, in chaos.

He loses a view of unity, we have seen, because he doubts the evidence and arguments for progress and unity either in the natural world or in human conduct. Moreover, his suspicions about attributing intention and agency to humans dislodges the foundation for Robinson's ideal of rational progress in human affairs. As a result, he reverses a familiar maxim about discovering order and unity in multiplicity, and concludes that the only perceivable order is chaos: "in the last synthesis, order and anarchy were one, but . . . the unity was chaos" (407). Faith in unity and unilinear development, he recognizes, requires self-evident truth; but the only self-evident truth is that no philosopher has ever been convinced of an objective basis for believing in unity (407).

With this swipe at the category of "self-evident truth," Adams is trampling on a final premise underlying scientific history, the objectivity of knowledge.[42] In fact, prominent historians like George Burton Adams, Herbert Baxter Adams, Robinson, and especially Wilson and Teggart, candidly waived the ideal of objectivity, noting that laws of historical development are more difficult to isolate from their context than physical laws. Most agreed with Carl Becker of Cornell that the historian (or any observer, for that matter) cannot achieve what Becker influentially called "detachment." Therefore, the perspective of the scholar – and hence the literary element (as historians defined it) of the enterprise – cannot be eradicated.[43]

It would seem that without their claims to objectivity historians would have had to forgo the ideal of ascertaining the unity behind disparate phenomena. Surely this is the initial force of Adams's critique. For those who engaged the question of objectivity, however, the subjective element of historical study did not diminish the discipline's claims but made it an heroic endeavor. Because historical study engaged the imagination of the historian, historians declared, historical narrative captured and exemplified ideals of progress all the more. As Becker wrote, "It is not because [the historian] is detached from his environment, but because he is preoccupied with a certain phase of it, that his history becomes 'scientific' " (26). Rather than undermining the scientific basis of history, history's subjective element confirmed for historians their scientific mission: ascertaining unity.

Adams at first deflates but finally augments his peers' elevation of history-writing by characterizing interpretation as wholly subjective.[44] He develops this account of interpretation in three stages. First, he decides that all interpretations of phenomena are mistaken: "all opinion founded on fact must be error, because the facts can never be complete, and their relations must be always infinite" (410). Later, adapting conclusions by scientists Ernst Mach and Karl Pearson, he modifies this point: it is not so much that interpretations are mistakes as that phenomena are in principle "unknowable," because all matter is motion (of imperceptible particles) and therefore not substantial in the forms we commonly perceive. For Pearson, there is only "chaos behind impressions" (453–54). Consequently, third, Adams abandons the search for truth (see 435) and declares that interpretation is projection: "One sees what one brings" (387). Adams quotes Pearson's remark that "Order and reason . . . are characteristics and conceptions . . . solely associated with the mind of man." For Adams, such a remark does not doom humans to pointless subjectivity but in fact expunges the methodological problem of history. If unity is not just an aspiration but rather the human epistemological condition – by this account, humans inevitably project coherence onto phenomena – then unity is in fact the abiding phenomenon of history. Whatever the condition of natural phenomena (chaos, likely), unity constitutes human experience; the impulse to unity *is* the phenomenon of history and must be captured in historical narrative. As a result, the dreaded literariness of history – the concern that causal relations are really just projections by observers – becomes the salvation of history as science by elevating history to epic status, a genre recounting the unity that historians' devotion to science promised.

In one sense, Adams's view imperils the commonplace conviction of historical unity: neither the phenomenon nor discipline of history can exist because history's elements are too unstable to form a developmental trajectory. From this point of view, *The Education* as parody of autobiography is the perfect forum to explode the pretensions of history. At the same time, Adams's subjectivism is also the salvation of history: "The history of the mind concerned the historian alone, and the historian had no vital concern in anything else, for he found no change to record in the body" (401). If one cannot write about objects except insofar as they are projections of the mind, one *can* write about mind; indeed, one can write *only* about mind, because "history," like any other narratively organized phenomenon, is precisely mental.[45]

Some commentators on Adams have called his position relativism, but subjectivism seems to me the more appropriate term.[46] If the two terms have often been associated, in Adams we find, I think, epistemological subjectivism without the relativism of values often associated with it. Quite the contrary. The reflexivity of the historical enterprise heartens Adams, since the writing of history now turns out to constitute and fulfill history; subjectivism supplies the principle of absolute unity otherwise lacking in history. Subjectivism rediscovers order in anarchy: "In the last synthesis" – the synthesis of mind – "order and anarchy *were* one" (407, italics added). It is precisely because "force . . . [is] a mode of thought"[47] that Adams's dynamic theory of history emerged alongside two more topical discussions – his admiration for Hay's foreign policy and his fascination with the corporate phenomenon of the trust.

The "Dynamic Theory of History" is both unusual for its time and the fulfillment of the hopes of Adams's peers. It is unusual because it dispenses with the units of measure that usually compose history, mainly human agency as commonly understood. The dynamic theory includes neither "great men" nor important developments, only functions of "force." Henry Adams comes to see "lines of force all about him, where he had always seen lines of will" (426). In the age of the dynamo, an historian or other student can no longer study substances and development but only dynamics, what Adams calls economies of force – rates of attraction and acceleration among forces and particles moved

139

by forces (379–83). Mind is but one of these entities that is simultaneously a force and a particle upon which force operates, and all emotions and aspirations, ratiocination no less than sentiment, are comprehensible as functions of force and attraction (the successors to cause and effect).

This view, of course, is simply an extension of conclusions Henry Adams has been arriving at since his youth. He makes it very clear at the outset of *The Education,* for example, that his character is largely a function of his heritage. It is a cliché of the book that this particular manikin is an eighteenth-century creation confounded by the headlong rush toward the twentieth century; his character and temperament are set by the environment in his home and adapt unevenly to new economies of force. The difference between his eighteenth-century heritage and his twentieth-century environment is that the economy of his youth circulated around great figures like his grandfather, who could, as John Quincy Adams does when Henry is disrespectful toward his mother, simply take a young man by the hand and establish firm boundaries. The twentieth century is witnessing the passing of such figures of unimpeachable authority. Yet the two periods do not exhibit a different *mode* of agency; both operate according to an economy or dynamic of force in which individuals are "channels" or "conductors" of force. The particular economies do differ. In the earlier period authority can center around the powerful (and publically powerful) male figure; in the latter, no one compels the imagination as a John Quincy Adams once did.

It is because different eras can be spoken of as different "kingdoms of force" (383) that Henry Adams can incorporate into his dynamic model of agency the twelfth and thirteenth centuries – the era of the Virgin. Like the dynamo of the contemporary world, the Virgin is the "symbol of infinity" in an earlier period (380), animating and organizing the production and distribution of energy. If the dynamo is perhaps a less "human" symbol, its symbolic function is nevertheless comparable to that of the Virgin: both furnish the principle of unity by organizing energy. The difference between the two symbols is precisely the degree of animation and humanness attaching to them, but not their unifying function.[48]

The Virgin is distinctly more human, more a symbol of human reproduction, and this feature explains at least in part why the 1905 *Mont-Saint-Michel and Chartres* feels so much more vibrant than *The Education*, which often conveys the ennui Henry Adams frequently says he feels. *Mont-Saint-Michel* credits its figures with no more agency than does *The Education* and quite explicitly declares that the magnificent structures Adams visits are not the work of people; they are the work of the organizing force of the period, the Virgin herself. Nevertheless, throughout *Mont-Saint-Michel,* people are palpably acting, creating structures to house and celebrate the faith that animates them, and Adams's descriptions regularly address and indeed recapitulate the sentiment inspiring endeavors even as he is attributing them to the Virgin. In *The Education,* in contrast, once figures like John Quincy Adams expire, few if any human figures replace them as fulcrums of animation. Often, as at Harvard or in Berlin, and even when many people are mentioned, Henry Adams's cultural landscape feels oddly unpopulated. That is, the contemporary figures, although no less agents than those who populated an earlier era, feel more like figures incapable of acting if only because the present organizing symbol is more mechanistic than earlier ones.

Under such circumstances, and concerned to revive the fulcrum of authority that his family and especially grandfather once represented, Henry Adams despairs at discovering unity, and the well-known "failure" that he continually notes is largely metonymy for the disappearance of this fulcrum. Adams's subjectivist model of interpretation salvages the search for unity, however. Because the economies of force that constitute any historical period turn out to be representations of the Will (432), unity is not only possible but indeed inevitable. Henry Adams is at first dissatisfied with Henri Poincaré's explanation: "the mind has the faculty of creating symbols" and has always imagined continuity; therefore unity exists (455). In the end, however, a spiritualized version of this explanation assuages Adams's anxiety about not readily discovering objective unity:

man's mind had behaved like a young pearl oyster, secreting its universe to suit its conditions until it had built up a shell of *nacre* that embodied all

141

its notions of the perfect. Man knew it was true because he made it, and he loved it for the same reason. He sacrificed millions of lives to acquire his unity, but he achieved it, and justly thought it a work of art. (458)

Here, unity – finally identity – is a narcissistic, aesthetic achievement worth the sacrifice of millions of lives. Humans seize and will not quit the unity that is an "Eden of [man and woman's] own invention" (459).

The "Dynamic Theory of History" is a grand narrative of this reflexive self-confirmation that constitutes human identity. The theory consists of repeated efforts by the force called will to attach objective symbols to phenomena that are reflections of the will in the first place. Early in the human epoch, "unable to define Force as a unity, man symbolized it and pursued it" (476), and this endeavor seems a sufficient condition for believing in unity.[49] "Except as reflected in himself, man has no reason for assuming unity in the universe." Although particular exercises of this "*a priori* insistence on . . . unity" (484) may be frustrated, the insistence is itself proof of the unity sought, precisely because it encompasses all human endeavor. Finally, the search for unity in the age of the dynamo exemplifies the same "process" as the search for *Civitas Dei* (485). The dynamic theory, then, is a stock narrative, imagining even more dramatically than Freeman an unchanging humankind seeking and doing the same thing throughout the human epoch. The details, too, of the dynamic theory are conventional, with episodes in the economy of force centered around standard religious modes forming the framework for industrial and mechanical inventions. Where could one *not* read a history of this sort in the period? More crucially, despite Adams's critique of the uniformitarianism that evolutionism cannot justify, his vision is the most uniformitarian of all. Every action is but another episode of the same endeavor – the striving for unity.

The dynamic theory does remain distinctive insofar as it actually completes the progressive ideal even Freeman only envisioned. The dynamic theory presents history as in effect completed from its outset. For Adams, history consists of the same event – the aspiration toward unity – perpetually repeated (albeit in different forms). This vision redeems history from the atomism it displayed to the younger Henry Adams; historical phenomena are no longer disconnected episodes in economies of force and random shifts of direction but actually the same event repeated.[50] This view of history has the virtue of rendering negligible specific differences or changes among phenomena – the very things that make palpable history possible. Instead, what gives phenomena significance is their identity as effects of the human effort toward unity. In this regard, *The Education* does after all complete Augustine's *Confessions,* as Adams fashions an aesthetic model of history that overcomes change and the motors of change – mere distractions from teleological aspiration – and therefore history itself.

Adams's enthusiasm for John Hay's imperialist foreign policy has at times been an embarrassment to Adams studies, but it is in fact a crucial corollary to and even bulwark of Adams's dynamic theory. Hay's foreign policy appeals to Henry Adams (who helped design it) because it so clearly seeks to make diplomatic relations a reflection of the will to unity. Much like Henry Kissinger's ideal of détente in the 1970s, Hay's Atlantic system sought a "general peace" (423) by establishing an equilibrium among the major European nations: they would agree on how they, smaller European nations, and non-European nations would be aligned, meaning agree which master nations would control which subject nations. Despite his suspicions of the ideal of equilibrium in thought and nature, Adams viewed these alignments as part of a physical equilibrium. In a letter to Hay, he spoke of the Atlantic system as a manifestation of "the law of mass" which would achieve "balance" and "remove . . . friction" among nations.[51] The Atlantic system and his advisory contribution to it strike Henry Adams as a splendid realization of his heritage and of the authority he attaches to his grandfather: "the family work of a hundred and fifty years fell at once into the grand perspective of true empire-building." It is because empire-building is the latest expression of humankind's innate desire for unity that the Atlantic system seems a "possible purpose working itself out in history," "the working of law in history" (363). The obstacle to this fulfillment of history is the Constitution, which accords the Senate, with its merely political rather than metaphysical motives, the prerogative to accept or reject treaties. The Constitution is therefore America's "original mistake" because it institutionalizes the very conflict that Hay's and Adams's aspirations for unity hope to transcend (374).[52]

The Atlantic system would achieve diplomatic equilibrium by realizing abroad what Adams calls "McKinleyism," "the system of combinations, consolidations, trusts, realized at home" (423). Adams's regard for the trust resembles Beard's: the trust focuses disparate wills toward a unified end no individual will alone can foresee or achieve. The Atlantic system would consolidate governments so that they work harmoniously, without discord, and finally without politics. Similarly, the Standard Oil Trust, for some years secretively, absolutely controlled the oil market by melding separate business concerns into one large combine. By eliminating volatility and conflict from the market, the Standard effectively voided the oil market. Henry Adams effectively accepts the claim by the Standard's trustees that they did not manage the combine; the market managed itself and naturally gravitated toward combination (344–45).[53] Similarly, for Adams, the Atlantic system was really an "instinct" (423), nothing Hay (or his advisor Adams) consciously conceived but a tendency in nature toward combination that Hay, like some channel, intuited.

On this view, the Atlantic system and the trust are not historical developments but manifestations of the mind's – and finally the race's – instinct to unity. Unity and the submission to the dynamic of history are racial instincts for Henry Adams, and he believes that racial instinct unites the most elemental units of history and experience, friendship and family life. "Friends are born, not made" (106; see also 311), and family environments count for him as biological necessity. Just as "Roosevelts are born and never can be taught" (419), Henry Adams believes that the environment of his upbringing fixes his character because it results from and amounts to biological inheritance. Typical of the Lamarckianism of the period, he supposes that one can inherit taste (182), inherit a family's principles – he is "anti-slavery by birth" (25) – and even inherit feuds (24). If Adams injects some irony into the latter two remarks, he nevertheless does not question this racial model of acquiring habits and beliefs. For example, when complaining late in the book, with typical irony, that the human mind is basically "inert," Adams specifies that "minds [are] unequally inert." His irony does not undo the content of the remark. "The inequalities amounted to contrasts. One class of minds responded only to habit; another only to novelty. Race classified thought. Class-lists classified mind" (441). "Race-inertia seemed to be fairly constant" among the Russians, he concludes. "Race ruled the conditions; conditions hardly affected race," he says elsewhere of the Baltic area of Europe (411). Finally, for Adams, history is inert despite its accelerations because cultural formation is a function of racial makeup.

I do not remark Adams's preoccupation with race and genealogy to castigate it as racism (justifying social hierarchies by reference to racial distinction), but to identify a crucial mechanism for relaying the unity of history. As R. P. Blackmur points out, Adams elevates what was called the race question – which included virtually every domestic issue and international venture (immigration, labor, the "Yellow Peril," etc.) – to a metaphysical principle governing historical change.[54] For Adams, history exhibits unity because its teleological patterns are manifest through race. Those with the proper inheritance, like John Hay, can intuit the acceleration of forces. By identifying important inheritors of taste and power, *The Education* secures the benefits of the great-man theory of history even as it eschews the great-man theory's simplistic account of agency. The man of proper inheritance intimates the trajectory and accelerations of force precisely by not being an agent and by being instead a "conductor" or "channel" of those ineluctable economies. As such a conductor, the historian can comprehend history, furnish a "chart of relations" to help manage the future (488), and even "teach reaction." One remarkable feature of this achievement is that, according to Adams, the historian "claimed no share of authority" and "had no responsibility for the problem" (496). This disavowal of responsibility seems inconsistent with Adams's subjective account of interpretation, but it is in fact consistent with the attenuation of agency throughout the book, bolstered by Adams's idea that those of proper inheritance are mere conductors for racial in-

145

stinct. No one acts in Adams's schema; there is neither action nor development, only the unfolding of an ineluctable dynamic intuitable by those of proper inheritance. Perhaps surprisingly, Henry Adams ascribes to this dynamic progress and equilibrium.

Under Hay's hand, for example, "even Russia [so racially inert] seemed about to be dragged into a combine of intelligent equilibrium" (503). It may seem implausible that equilibrium can issue from the violence and dislocations that for Henry Adams characterize historical transformations. But this is indeed the end-game of a parodic autobiography that is actually shaped like a sentimental novel. The young Henry Adams grows up in a secure environment, with (unlike many sentimental works) comforting patriarchal figures. He is then alienated from this source of authority by the waning of his family's power and passing of its senior male figures. His life then consists foremost of mishaps which he takes to be metaphysical failures. Ultimately, these principles of failure are transformed into the conditions of the unity that eluded the younger Henry Adams. If *The Education* early on thumbs its nose at the idea of progress, by the end progress is the epiphenomenon of the acceleration of forces. Adams's avowed pedagogical failure at Harvard was not, finally, inevitable, as Adams presents it at the time, but simply a result of looking for unity in the wrong objects – in objects, that is, rather than in economies of force. Later, however, education becomes distinctly possible, perhaps inevitable. "The teacher of 1900 . . . if intelligent, might balance"; "the forces would continue to educate, and the mind would continue to react. All the teacher could hope was to teach it reaction" (497). Progress is built into the dynamic of forces, so that the American of the year 2000 "would think in complexities unimaginable to an earlier mind" and "would deal with problems altogether beyond the range of earlier society" (497); "progress would continue as before" (501) because it is an unfolding in which the violence of the acceleration of forces is absorbed into a greater unity.

If this structure has some basis in a sentimental tradition, it more generally displays a teleological aesthetics that Adams termed "romance." Augustine's *Confessions* appeared the best example of this "literary form," Adams wrote William James, be-

146

cause it has "an end and object, not for the sake of the object, but for the form."[55] *The Education* seeks to fulfill an impulse in the Western tradition – to know the true, or God, unequivocally – of which the sentimental is one manifestation. For Adams, romance fulfills this aspiration by concentrating, as Augustine deliberately did, on its own formal realization, thereby eliminating the distance between subject and object that made knowledge precarious (for Descartes) or even sinful (potentially for Descartes and certainly for Augustine). This achievement, in effect, erases the temporality that a distinction between subject and object occasions. Hence, the form of Augustine's *Confessions*. It is therefore appropriate, if ironic, that Adams describes himself in the *Education* and in his letters as already dead. Similarly, in the dynamic theory, history as unity becomes possible only when temporality (or at least substantive historical change) ends.

Henry Adams's intellectual gymnastics in forging the salvation of history are, of course, a deep expression of the impulse that led him to contemplate the attractions of Catholicism. His teleological fervor explains why his characterization of himself as a "conservative Christian anarchist," a phrase meant to shock his readers as multiply oxymoronic, is finally entirely apt, since for him anarchy *is* unity. Adams's is one strategy available to a patrician class feeling besieged by cultural developments it could not control. His hard-earned vision redeems violence and dislocation and regains control by imagining historical change as the intimation of immanent unity. Thus, although temporality has ended, progress – greater command of environment, the dream of historians that Adams himself mocked – is inevitable: "every American who lived to the year 2000 would know how to control unlimited power" (496).

NOTES

I am grateful to the staff of the British Museum library for assistance in using its resources. I wish to thank Robert Caserio for his generous and helpful comments on a draft of this essay.

1   Henry Adams, *The Education of Henry Adams*, edited by Ernest Samuels (Boston: Houghton Mifflin, 1973), p. 382. Subsequent refer-

ences to this edition will be cited in parentheses in the body of the text.

2   William M. Sloane, "History and Democracy," *American Historical Review* 1 (October 1895), p. 2.

3   Most commentators on Adams's view of history arrive at some version of this point. See William H. Jordy, *Henry Adams: Scientific Historian* (New Haven: Yale University Press, 1952), especially his final chapter, "Failure," where he characterizes Adams as a "disillusioned Comtist" (288). In *America the Scrivenor: Deconstruction and the Subject of Literary History* (Ithaca: Cornell University Press, 1990), Gregory Jay has formulated the point concisely. Adams exhibits "the self-conscious collapse of the Hegelian model for historicism, in which History is narrated as the progressive, dialectical movement of Spirit's self-realization" (205). See also: John Patrick Diggins, " 'Who Bore the Failure of the Light': Henry Adams and the Crisis of Authority," *New England Quarterly* 59 (June 1985), pp. 165–92; and Keith B. Burich, " 'Our Power Is Always Running Ahead of Our Mind': Henry Adams's Phases of History," *New England Quarterly* 62 (June 1989), pp. 163–86.

Susan Mizruchi provides a more inflected version of this position (*The Power of Historical Knowledge: Narrating the Past in Hawthorne, James, and Dreiser* [Princeton: Princeton University Press, 1988], pp. 60–64), as does Carolyn Porter, in *Seeing and Being: The Plight of the Participant Observer in Emerson, James, Adams, and Faulkner* (Middletown: Wesleyan University Press, 1981), pp. 184–204. In his biography of Adams, Ernest Samuels presented a modified account of the failure of history. Samuels argues that finally Adams "arrived at . . . a working philosophy of history" (*Henry Adams: The Major Phase* [Cambridge, Mass.: Harvard University Press/Belknap, 1964], p. 374) – the dynamic theory – but Samuels retains the idea that Adams adopts impressionism in place of principles of sequence and coherence (373–95). I will be arguing that Adams in fact recovers ideals of progress and self-realization unburdened by the vagaries of historical change.

4   Joseph Riddel, "Reading America/American Readers," *Modern Language Notes* 99 (September 1984), pp. 921–22, 927. Jay, *America the Scrivenor*, p. 235. See Rowe's seminal *Henry Adams and Henry James: The Emergence of a Modern Consciousness* (Ithaca: Cornell University Press, 1976), especially pp. 120–29. Rowe presents Adams as "the archetype for the modern man of interpretation . . . condemned to the unreliability of his language" (129). Relation having replaced

truth as the basis for knowledge, only an incomplete history rather than a total history is possible (125, 127). Like Riddel, Wayne Lesser has argued that *The Education* disrupts notions of a positivist historical paradigm, for us as well as for Adams's contemporaries. Presenting a more positive account of freedom than either Jay or Riddel, Lesser argues that if history is made a "mode of inquiry" we can explain ourselves and finally establish a ground for moral examination of conduct. ("Criticism, Literary History, and the Paradigm: *The Education of Henry Adams,*" *PMLA* 97 [May 1982], pp. 378–80, 387, 391).

5   Letter to William James, 11 February 1908, *The Letters of Henry Adams,* Vol. 6: 1906–1918, edited by J. C. Levenson, Ernest Samuels, Charles Vandersee, Viola Hopkins Winner, with the assistance of Jayne N. Samuels and Eleanor Pearre Abbot (Cambridge, Mass.: Harvard University Press/Belknap, 1988), p. 118. Adams spoke of his use of autobiography as illustrating the domain of history in the prefatory letter accompanying copies of "The Rule of Phase Applied to History" that he sent to friends. Samuels reprints the letter, *Education,* pp. 515–18; see especially, p. 516.

6   Adams's younger brother Brooks assembled these essays posthumously in *The Degradation of Democratic Dogma* (1919).

7   St. Augustine, *Confessions,* translated and introduced by R. S. Pine-Coffin (New York: Penguin, 1961), pp. 172–73, 175. Subsequent references to this edition will be cited in parentheses in the text.

8   Augustine applies to memory the same analysis he applies to will, and appropriately speaks of memory as one form of action. Memory, without which self is incomprehensible, means one has access to the self through an image (222); because understanding the self necessarily involves memory, "I have become a problem to myself" (223). Therefore, "I must pass beyond memory to find you, my true God" (224).

9   Letter to Charles Milnes Gaskell, 10 May 1907 (*Letters,* Vol. 6, p. 63); letter to Henry James, 6 May, 1908 (*Letters,* Vol. 6, p. 136). Samuels helpfully reprints these and other letters surrounding *The Education;* see Appendix A.

10   For William James's discussion of these matters see his chapters on "Habit" (chapter 4), "The Stream of Thought" (chapter 9), and "The Consciousness of Self" (chapter 10) in Volume 1 of *The Principles of Psychology* (1890; rpt. New York: Dover, 1950). I am adjusting here the emphasis of Rowe's fine discussion of the manikin in *Henry Adams and Henry James.* For Rowe, the manikin represents "an

essentially hollow, emptied self" (30), an analysis continued by Hayden White ("Method and Ideology in Intellectual History: The Case of Henry Adams," in *Modern European History: Reappraisals and New Perspectives*, edited by Dominick LaCapra and Steven L. Kaplan [Cornell University Press, 1982], p. 295). In my reading, Adams's self is not hollow but a function of and metaphor for drapery, i.e., the habits animating and constituting the self. Lesser has aptly observed that the manikin figure "attempts to discredit our uniqueness by showing that we conform to historically determined principles of organization and change" ("Criticism, Literary History, and the Paradigm," p. 393, n. 5).

11   Edwin R. A. Seligman, *The Economic Interpretation of History* (New York: Macmillan, 1902), p. 7. Although Seligman belonged to Columbia's economics department, he is writing here on historical narrative. For Beard's discussion of this term, see *The Industrial Revolution* (London: George Allen & Unwin, 1901), p. 37.

12   James Harvey Robinson, *History* (New York: Columbia University Press, 1908), pp. 7, 6.

13   Robinson, *The New History: Essays Illustrating the Modern Historical Outlook* (New York: Macmillan, 1912), p. 14.

14   Seligman, *Economic Interpretation of History*, 97. For discussions of the great-man theory of history as indispensable to political history, see Seligman, p. 2, and Robinson, *History*, p. 13. Most historians around the turn of the century contested the great-man theory, but for a prominent exponent of the theory, see: Edward A. Freeman, *Lectures to American Audiences* (Philadelphia: Porter & Coates, 1882), p. 214.

15   Notably, Adams's book on Randolph, first published in 1882, was later reprinted in a Houghton Mifflin series called *American Statesmen*.

16   For some discussions of the dramatic effect of organizing histories around the struggles and accomplishments of heroic figures, see Wilson, "Variety and Unity of History," *Congress of Arts and Science: Universal Exposition, St. Louis, 1904*, edited by Harold J. Rogers (Boston: Houghton, Mifflin, 1906), Vol. 2, p. 4; Freeman, *Lectures to American Audiences*, p. 214; and Robinson, *New History*, p. 10.

17   "The Tendency of History," in *The Degradation of Democratic Dogma*, introduction by Brooks Adams (New York: Macmillan, 1919: pp. 125–33), p. 128. Hereafter this essay will be cited as "Tendency."

18   Teggart, *Prolegomena to History, The Relation of History to Literature, Philosophy, and Science, University of California Publications in History,*

Vol. 4, No. 3. (Berkeley: University of California Press, 1916), p. 159.

19 Robinson, "The Conception and Methods of History," *Congress of Arts and Science: Universal Exposition, St. Louis, 1904*, edited by Harold J. Rogers (Boston: Houghton, Mifflin, 1906), Vol. 2, p. 42.

20 Albion W. Small, "The Beginnings of American Nationality: The Constitutional Relations between the Continental Congress and the Colonies and States," *Johns Hopkins University Studies in Historical and Political Science*, 8th Series, nos. 1–2 (January–February 1890), p. 8.

21 Wilson, "Variety and Unity of History," p. 11.

22 Robinson, *The New History*, pp. 14, 48, 51. For a discussion of the New Historians see Peter Novick, *That Noble Dream: The "Objectivity Question" and the American Historical Profession* (New York: Cambridge University Press, 1988), pp. 89–108. For a discussion of Robinson and the New History and its relation to "the new historicism," see Brook Thomas, *The New Historicism, and Other Old-Fashioned Topics* (Princeton: Princeton University Press, 1991), pp. 89–96, 152–56.

23 David W. Noble, *Historians against History: The Frontier Thesis and the National Covenant in American Historical Writing since 1830* (Minneapolis: University of Minnesota Press, 1965); and Dorothy Ross, *The Origins of American Social Science* (New York: Cambridge University Press, 1991). Ross delineates the millennialism of practitioners of all the social sciences.

24 William M. Sloane, "The Science of History in the Nineteenth Century," *Congress of Arts and Science: Universal Exposition, St. Louis, 1904*, edited by Harold J. Rogers (Boston: Houghton, Mifflin, 1906), Vol. 2, pp. 25, 30. In the closing phrase Sloane is proudly quoting Kant.

25 Frederick Jackson Turner, "The Significance of History" (1891), in *The Early Writings of Frederick Jackson Turner* (Madison: University of Wisconsin Press, 1938), pp. 65, 53. Turner is adopting this idea from the German historian Johann Droysen. I am indebted to Steve Tatum for discussion of Turner's essay.

26 Turner, "The Significance of History," pp. 52, 58. Turner's Hegelian language was common. Seligman, among others, credited Hegel's idea that no thought is final with being a basis for the progressive thesis of history (*Economic Interpretation of History*, p. 19).

27 Turner, "The Significance of the Frontier in American History" (1893), in *The Frontier in American History* (New York: Holt, Rinehart and Winston, 1920), pp. 38, 36.

28 See especially three addresses collected in *The Frontier in American History:* "Pioneer Ideals and the State University" (1910, pp. 269–89), "The West and American Ideals" (1914, pp. 290–310), and "Social Forces in American History (1910, pp. 311–45). Turner's romanticism and millennialism have often been noted. See Richard Hofstadter, *The Progressive Historians: Turner, Beard, Parrington* (New York: Knopf, 1968), pp. 47–164, David Noble's chapter in *Historians against History,* pp. 37–55, and Noble's differently oriented discussion of Turner in his more recent *The End of American History: Democracy, Capitalism, and the Metaphor of Two Worlds in Anglo-American Historical Writing, 1880–1980* (Minneapolis: University of Minnesota Press, 1985), pp. 3–40.

29 Beard, *The Industrial Revolution,* pp. 3, 53, 83, 104–05. Beard's rhetoric was typical of debates about the trust problem; for a discussion, see: Howard Horwitz, *By the Law of Nature: Form and Value in Nineteenth-Century America* (New York: Oxford University Press, 1991), pp. 171–212.

30 Noble has observed that historians managed to imagine their office as that of chief theologian of the culture (*Historians against History,* p. 17).

31 Teggart, *Prolegomena,* pp. 245–46; Hill, "The Ethical Function of the Historian," *American Historical Review* 14 (October 1908), pp. 21, 20.

32 "Letter to American Teachers of History," in *The Degradation of Democratic Dogma* (pp. 135–265), p. 157. Hereafter this essay will be cited as "American Teachers."

33 Adams, "The Rule of Phase Applied to History," in *The Degradation of Democratic Dogma* (pp. 267–311), p. 300. Hereafter this essay will be cited as "Rule of Phase."

34 See, for example, Rowe, *Henry Adams and Henry James,* pp. 112–14, who observes that for Adams evolution "comes to stand for man's general dream of an ordered sequence and an unified history" (113–14). Jordy discusses Adams's catastrophism and critique of evolutionism extensively (*Henry Adams: Scientific Historian,* pp. 172–88), as does, more briefly, Samuels (*The Major Phase,* pp. 36–40, 278–83). See also, Lesser, "Criticism, Literary History, and the Paradigm"; Porter, *Seeing and Being,* p. 193; and T. J. Jackson Lears, *No Place of Grace: Antimodernism and the Transformation of American Culture, 1880–1920* (New York: Pantheon Books, 1981), pp. 289–90.

35 Robinson, *New History,* pp. 24, 252. Robinson is more cautious than some of his peers in espousing the virtues of studying history. He urges suspicion "that certain lessons could be derived from the

past, – precedents for the statesman and the warrior, moral guidance and consoling instances of providential interference for the commonalty" (17). Nevertheless, the study of history can, if appropriately conducted, promote rational "social betterment" (252) "not because the past would furnish precedents of conduct, but because our conduct would be based upon a perfect comprehension of existing conditions founded upon a perfect knowledge of the past" (21, author's italics excised). Historians do not yet occupy this Godlike position, Robinson clarifies, but it is the rational ideal to which they must aspire. Compare Robinson's careful approach to his progressive aspirations with that of Sloane, who more typically declares that "The science of history seeks to find in the past the means of determining both the evolution occurring under our eyes and the probabilities of the future" ("The Science of History in the Nineteenth Century," p. 23).

36 Freeman, "A Review of My Opinions," *Forum* 11 (April 1892), p. 157. Adams called Freeman "the Nestor Historian" in introducing Freeman's inaugural essay to the *Hopkins Studies* series, which he edited: Herbert B. Adams, "Mr. Freeman's Visit to Baltimore," *Johns Hopkins University Studies in Historical and Political Science* 1 (1884), p. 6.

37 Edward A. Freeman, "On the Study of History," *Fortnightly Review* 29, n.s. (March 1881), p. 320.

38 *Lectures to American Audiences* (1882), pp. 209–12, 231–32; see also "On the Study of History," pp. 334–35; and Freeman's essay opening the *Johns Hopkins University Studies in Historical and Political Science*, "An Introduction to American Institutional History," Series 1, No. 1 [1884], p. 14.

39 Freeman, *Lectures*, pp. 211–12.

40 *Lectures*, pp. 231, 232, 235. The last conclusion summarizes the force of much of Freeman's work, and is the main force of "Introduction to American Institutional History" (esp. pp. 19–24). I am grateful to Jennifer Hammett for discussions about Freeman's work.

41 Riddel ("Reading America"), Hayden White ("Method and Ideology"), and Gregory Jay *(America the Scrivenor)* present the most radical examples of this argument, whose trajectory was begun by Rowe *(Henry Adams and Henry James)*. In his entry on Adams ("Henry Adams") for the *Columbia Literary History of the United States* (General Editor, Emory Elliott [New York: Columbia University Press, 1988]), Rowe inflects his argument differently, in ways that

are closer to mine. "Adams's break with his past is greatly exaggerated," Rowe explains, and *The Education* "is Adams's effort to resolve the crisis of thought in his own period" (647, 665).

42　See Novick's discussion of this premise among early modern historians in *That Noble Dream*.

43　See Carl Becker, "Detachment and the Writing of History" (1910), in *Detachment and the Writing of History: Essays and Letters of Carl L. Becker*, edited by Phil L. Snyder (Ithaca: Cornell University Press, 1958), pp. 3–28.

44　If the nine-volume *History* of the Jefferson and Madison administrations presupposes the objectivity of the historian, Adams was by 1895 formulating a subjectivist account of interpretation in the debut issue of the *American Historical Review*. See "Count Edward de Crillon," *American Historical Review* 1 (October 1895), pp. 51–52.

45　For a similar view of *The Education* (along with *Mont-Saint-Michel*) as a "process of salvation" see: Olaf Hansen, *Aesthetic Individualism and Practical Intellect: American Allegory in Emerson, Thoreau, Adams, and James* (Princeton: Princeton University Press, 1990), p. 152. For Hansen, the salvation is achieved "by the effort of collecting empirical facts in order to prove the existence of the imagination." Hansen concludes that unity "had to be deduced from the realm of cognitive method" (152, 166).

46　Jordy makes this argument very powerfully in *Henry Adams* (pp. 230–47), and he has been followed by critics such as Mizruchi (*Power of Historical Knowledge*, pp. 62–63). See also Rowe, *Henry Adams and Henry James*, p. 128. Jordy takes his most telling evidence from Adams's letters and marginalia in his copies of works by Pearson, John Stallo, and Henri Poincaré. Yet in these remarks, while Adams does abandon absolute objectivity as an aim and method of analysis, he never uses the word "relativism," even when his scientific sources do (236–37). Adams's restraint leads me to consider it important to distinguish between subjectivism and relativism in his late work.

47　Adams wrote this remark in the margins of his copy of John Stallo's *The Concepts and Theories of Modern Physics*. Quoted in Jordy, *Henry Adams*, p. 236.

48　Most other accounts of the content and tone of Adams's discussion of the dynamo and its relation to the Virgin see the two symbols as dichotomous, with the dynamo an empty version of the Virgin's embodiment of faith, faith being no longer possible in the modern world. Some, like Lears, have argued that Adams desired – and failed – to find a "synthesis" in the "dialectic" of the dynamo and Virgin (*No Place of Grace,* p. 294). My sense is that the dynamo is a differently oriented form of the impulse to unity that the Virgin also embodies (perhaps more directly). For a related view, see R. P. Blackmur, *Henry Adams* (New York: Harcourt Brace Jovanovich, 1980). Blackmur argues that there is a "crossing" between the Virgin and the dynamo: "the force of the one is seen as a phase of the force of the other" (244).

49 Rowe presents a concise account of Adams's interest in unity: "Adams came to view the basic impulse toward unity as the force that could give coherence to the multiplicity of experience" (*Henry Adams and Henry James,* p. 9). Rowe believes, more than I do, in *The Education*'s relative failure to realize this vision formally and thematically: "the quest for unity always seems to end in multiplicity" (128).

50 Daniel Sutherland cites an 1873 letter to Henry Cabot Lodge that bespeaks the idea of history I am arguing Adams dramatizes in *The Education*. If my account is correct, then Adams's ambitions for history remained more continuous than scholars have thought and than he expressly presents it. "America or Europe, our own century or prehistoric time, are all alike to the historian if he can only find out what men are and have been driving at, consciously or unconsciously" (*Letters,* Vol. 2: 1868–1885 [1982], p. 156; cited in Sutherland, "The Viscous Thought: Henry Adams and the American Character," *biography* 12 [Summer 1989], p. 229).

51 Letter to John Hay, 3 May 1905. The point, he wrote Elizabeth Cameron later that year on August 27, was to "fortify an Atlantic system beyond an attack" (*Letters,* Vol. 5, pp. 651, 709).

52 Lesser discusses Adams's admiration for Hay in similar terms – Hay represents a "balanced" mind – but Lesser associates this ideal of equilibrium with the spirit of balance embodied in the Constitution ("Criticism, Literary History, and the Paradigm," p. 391). If Lesser's analogy may be correct, Adams does not concur with it.

53 On this claim by the Standard's trustees, see Horwitz, *By the Law of Nature,* pp. 181–86. In his letter to Elizabeth Cameron (cited in note 49), Adams applies to the Atlantic system the language of "concentration" (*Letters,* Vol. 5, p. 709).

54 See *Henry Adams,* p. 248. In "Henry Adams" (1988), Rowe also speaks of Adams's attempts to reaffirm the "genealogically transmitted rights to rule that [he] associates with an enlightened aristocracy" (661). Blackmur's discussion of Adams's view of "race

inertia" is compelling, but I disagree with his view of Adams's use of irony. For Blackmur, irony becomes in Adams a "constructed possible" that "occasionally triumphs over both ignorance and assurance" – the expressions of race inertia (158). It seems to me, however, that Adams's irony is no alternative to race inertia. Instead, irony is a trait inherited by the likes of Adams and Hay but unavailable to the likes of Russians. It is therefore one element in what Blackmur rightly calls Adams's "genealogical obsession" (244), and it forms a resolution rather than an obstacle to the problem of unity and continuity. Blackmur's view of Adams's view of race is consistent with his sense that Adams wanted "to modify necessity," of which race inertia was one form (246). My sense, in contrast, is that Adams sought harmony with necessity, from which history and international politics were diverging, and that his preoccupations with race and genealogy were ways of glimpsing that harmony.

55 Letter to William James, 17 February 1908. *Letters*, Vol. 6, pp. 119–20.

Notes on Contributors

Martha Banta is Professor of English at the University of California, Los Angeles. Her most recent books are *Imaging American Women: Idea and Ideals in Cultural History* (1987) and *Taylored Lives: Narrative Productions in the Age of Taylor, Veblen, and Ford* (1993). Her current project is "Barbaric Intercourse from Victoria to Theodore: Satiric Fantasy and the Culture of Conduct."

Howard Horwitz teaches American literature and culture at the University of Utah. He is the author of *By Law of Nature: Form and Value in Nineteenth-Century America* (1991) and numerous essays on American culture and contemporary theory. His current project is "Administrative Aesthetics: Representation and Social Engineering in America, 1890–1920."

John Carlos Rowe directs the Critical Theory Institute and teaches American literature and culture at the University of California, Irvine. He is the author of *Henry Adams and Henry James: The Emergence of a Modern Consciousness, Through the Custom-House: Nineteenth-Century American Fiction and Modern Theory,* and *The Theoretical Dimensions of Henry James.* He has co-edited with Rick Berg, *The Vietnam War and American Culture.* His current project is "Postmodern Speculations."

Brook Thomas directs the Humanities Core Course and teaches American literature and culture at the University of California, Irvine. He is the author of *James Joyce's "Ulysses": A Book of Many*

157

Happy Returns, Cross-Examinations of Law and Literature: Cooper, Hawthorne, Stowe, and Melville, and *The New Historicism and Other Old-Fashioned Topics.* He is also the editor of *"Plessy v. Ferguson": A Documentary History.* His present project is tentatively titled, "American Literary Realism and the Failed Promise of Contract."

Selected Bibliography

Ernest and Jayne Samuels's annotated edition of *The Education of Henry Adams* (Boston: Houghton Mifflin, 1973) is available in paperback in the Riverside Editions. The annotations are indispensable for the contemporary reader, and they often offer much more than mere historical information. As the Samuels point out, *The Education* was intended by Adams as a complement to his previous work, *Mont-Saint-Michel and Chartres*, published in a public edition by Houghton Mifflin for the American Institute of Architects in 1913 and available in a contemporary edition from Doubleday Anchor Books. The recent scholarly edition of *The Letters of Henry Adams*, eds. J. C. Levenson, Ernest Samuels, Charles Vandersee, and Viola Hopkins Winner, 6 volumes (Cambridge, Mass.: Harvard University Press, 1982–1988) finally makes available the full range of Adams's personal and political views from 1858 to 1918. These volumes also include some of the most extraordinary epistolary style in the English language. Gore Vidal's *Empire: A Novel* (New York: Random House, 1987) offers a wonderfully realized account of the times of Henry Adams, as well as fictional portraits of Adams and such important contemporaries as John Hay, Presidents McKinley and Theodore Roosevelt, and many other historical figures and members of the Adams family who play important parts in *The Education*.

A complete bibliography of books and articles concerning Henry Adams's life and writings would be very extensive; most of those works treat *The Education*, Adams's most celebrated work. The following works should help the reader pursue some of the issues raised by the authors of the essays included in this volume.

Banta, Martha. *Failure and Success in America: A Literary Debate.* Princeton, N.J.: Princeton University Press, 1978.
Bercovitch, Sacvan. *The American Jeremiad.* Madison: University of Wisconsin Press, 1978.

Selected Bibliography

Blackmur, R. P. *Henry Adams*, ed. Veronica Makowsky. New York: Harcourt, Brace, Jovanovich, 1980.

Commager, Henry Steele. "Henry Adams." In *The Marcus W. Jernegan Essays in American Historiography* ed. William T. Hutchinson. Chicago: University of Chicago Press, 1937.

Contosta, David R., and Muccigrosso, Robert, eds. *Henry Adams and His World. Transactions of the American Philosophical Society*, 83, part iv. Philadelphia: American Philosophical Society, 1993.

Cox, James N. "Learning through Ignorance: *The Education of Henry Adams.*" *Sewanee Review*, 88 (1980), 198–227.

Decker, William Merrill. *The Literary Vocation of Henry Adams*. Chapel Hill: University of North Carolina Press, 1990.

Donovan, Timothy Paul. *Henry Adams and Brooks Adams: The Education of Two American Historians*. Norman: University of Oklahoma Press, 1961.

Hanson, Russell L., and W. Richard Merriman. "Henry Adams and the Decline of the Republican Tradition." *American Transcendental Quarterly*, 4 (September 1990), 161–184.

Jacobson, Joanne. *Authority and Alliance in the Letters of Henry Adams*. Madison: University of Wisconsin Press, 1992.

Kaledin, Eugenia. *The Education of Mrs. Henry Adams*. Philadelphia: Temple University Press, 1981.

Levenson, J. C. *The Mind and Art of Henry Adams*. Boston: Houghton Mifflin, 1957.

Porter, Carolyn. *Seeing and Being: The Plight of the Participant Observer in Emerson, James, Adams, and Faulkner*. Middletown, Conn.: Wesleyan University Press, 1981.

Rowe, John Carlos. *Henry Adams and Henry James: The Emergence of a Modern Consciousness*. Ithaca, N.Y.: Cornell University Press, 1976.

. "Henry Adams." In *Columbia Literary History of the United States*, ed. Emory Elliott. New York: Columbia University Press, 1988, pp. 645–667.

Samuels, Ernest. *The Young Henry Adams*. Cambridge, Mass.: Harvard University Press, 1948.

. *Henry Adams: The Middle Years*. Cambridge, Mass.: Harvard University Press, 1958.

. *Henry Adams: The Major Phase*. Cambridge, Mass.: Harvard University Press, 1964.

Spiller, Robert E. "Henry Adams," *Literary History of the United States*, ed. Robert E. Spiller, et al. New York: Macmillan, 1947.

Vandersee, Charles. "Henry Adams and the Invisible Negro." *South Atlantic Quarterly,* 66 (1967), 13–30.

White, Hayden. "The Context in the Text: Method and Ideology in Intellectual History." In *The Content of the Form.* Baltimore: Johns Hopkins University Press, 1987.

Index